Everything That Floats

Pat Sullivan, Hal Banks, and the
Seamen's Unions of Canada

DATE DUE

An infamous chapter in Canadian labour history is explored in this penetrating study of the Canadian Seamen's Union and its successor, the Seafarers' International Union. At the heart of the story are the two men whose personalities shaped the organizations: Pat Sullivan, who founded the CSU with help from the Communist Party of Canada, and Hal Banks, an ex-convict who directed the SIU through a regime of violence and corruption.

William Kaplan's account charts the course of the unions from the birth of the CSU in 1935, through devastating strikes, criminal charges, political scandals, Banks's flight from the country in 1964, up to the imposition of a government legislated trusteeship over Canada's maritime unions. To write this book Kaplan delved into records only recently made available in Canada through the Access to Information Act, including material from the Department of Labour and the RCMP, and in the United States through the Freedom of Information Act, including records of the State Department and the FBI. And he interviewed countless players in the drama: ordinary seamen, politicians, lawyers, and union leaders, even Banks himself.

WILLIAM KAPLAN is a member of the Faculty of Law, University of Ottawa.

WILLIAM KAPLAN

Everything That Floats

PAT SULLIVAN,
HAL BANKS, AND
THE SEAMEN'S UNIONS
OF CANADA

UNIVERSITY OF TORONTO PRESS
Toronto Buffalo London

© University of Toronto Press 1987
Toronto Buffalo London
Printed in Canada

ISBN 0-8020-2597-8 (cloth)
ISBN 0-8020-6623-2 (paper)

Canadian Cataloguing in Publication Data

Kaplan, William, 1957-
   Everything that floats

   Bibliography: p.
   Includes index.
   ISBN 0-8020-2597-8 (bound) ISBN 0-8020-6623-2 (pbk.)

   1. Seafarers' International Union of North America.
   2. Canadian Seamen's Union.   3. Banks, Hal.
   4. Sullivan, John Alan, 1896-   .   5. Trade unions –
   Merchant seamen – Canada – History.   I. Title.

   HD6528.S42S45 1987   331.88′1138750971   C86-094887-0

Front cover photograph:

CSU sailors in a sitdown strike, 1949.
Vic Davidson, *The Gazette* (Montreal) /
Public Archives of Canada / PA 146845

Back cover photograph:

Hal Banks talks to reporters at a 1963 meeting of
the Seafarers' International Union of Canada.

Mac Juster / Public Archives of Canada / PA 146861

In honour of my father

IGOR KAPLAN

14 February 1931 to 14 November 1980

Contents

Preface

'I will soon be in the dubious position of being the top labor man in all of Canada,' Hal Chamberlain Banks wrote home in April 1949, 'but let me tell you that now I know that uneasy lies the head that wears a crown.'[1] Hal Banks, an ex-convict and representative of the Seafarers' International Union of North America, was by nature a boastful man, but there was more than a little truth to what he wrote. Financed by the shipping companies and assisted by the federal government, the Royal Canadian Mounted Police, and the Canadian National Railways Police, Banks, along with a small army of SIU strongmen imported from the United States, had, in a matter of months, waged and won a violent battle against the long-established national Canadian Seamen's Union. With only a few companies outside the SIU orbit, Banks controlled the collective bargaining rights of almost every seaman employed on the Canadian flag fleet and, with an iron fist, would do so for more than a decade. Eventually Banks's activities would be investigated by a commission of inquiry and, facing imprisonment, he would be forced to flee Canada in disgrace. In 1949 the situation was much different. Flush with the success of his incontestable victory, Banks exploited it to the hilt. How and why Banks and the SIU arrived in Canada is the first part of this story.

Acknowledgments

Professor Robert Bothwell, both as teacher and as friend, has made a substantial contribution to this book. Susan Krever read many drafts of the manuscript, and gave great encouragement at every stage. Cara Feldman, Michael Kaplan, Merle Rosenhek, Earl Cherniak, Louis A. Wiesner, Steven Barrett, and John L. Howard also read one or more versions of the manuscript and made useful suggestions. Virgil Duff of the University of Toronto Press gave support, advice, and assistance. Rosemary Shipton made an indispensable editorial contribution. Sylvia Lassam assisted with typing. Considerable help was provided by the Public Archives of Canada and, in particular, by Dan Moore, Glenn Wright, John Smart, Jim Whalen, Kathy Hayman, and Joy Houston. T.M. Eberlee, deputy minister of the Department of Labour, made available important documents and the staff of the library in that department were always very helpful, as were the staff at the Vancouver City Archives, Robarts Library at the University of Toronto, John F. Kennedy Library, Lyndon B. Johnson Library, and the Public Record Office in Great Britain. The Canadian Labour Congress made its records available to me without restriction, as did the Canadian Brotherhood of Railway Transport and General Workers union. Canada Steamship Lines allowed me to view certain important documents. The Seafarers' International Union did not permit me to consult its papers, nor did it provide me with research assistance of any kind. Captain Eric Brand Ret., the late William Dodge, the late Mr Justice Victor Dryer, Richard Greaves, George Haythorne, and the late Tom Houtman gave me access to their personal papers. Mrs Jean Crowe allowed me to consult the papers of the late Harry Crowe. Kathleen Seaver and Charles MacDonald permitted me to read their unpublished studies of the Canadian Seamen's Union. The theses of Gerald S. Swartz and Joanne Miko were useful. Many people granted me interviews, while numerous others assisted me in countless ways during the five years I spent researching and writing this book. While their names are not listed here, I am grateful for their support. The University of Toronto provided me with financial aid and the Department of Labour awarded me an important research grant. This book has been published with the help of grants from the Social Sciences Federation of Canada, using funds provided by the Social Sciences and Humanities Research Council of Canada, and from the Canada Council and the Ontario Arts Council under their block grant programs.

Interview summaries, correspondence, research materials, notes, numerous drafts, and the Victor Dryer Papers have been deposited at the archives of the University of Toronto. Most of this material is available without restriction. Readers interested in a more detailed account of this subject are welcome to consult my thesis, which is also available at the archives of the University of Toronto. Errors in fact, as well as in interpretation, are mine alone.

WK
Ottawa, June 1986

Abbreviations

ACCL	All-Canadian Congress of Labour
AFL	American Federation of Labor
AFL-CIO	American Federation of Labor–Congress of Industrial Organizations
CBRT	Canadian Brotherhood of Transport Workers (now known as the CBRT-GW, the Canadian Brotherhood of Transport and General Workers)
CCF	Co-operative Commonwealth Federation
CCL	Canadian Congress of Labour
CIO	Committee of Industrial Organizations (later the Congress of Industrial Organizations)
CMU	Canadian Maritime Union
CSU	Canadian Seamen's Union
NAME	National Association of Marine Engineers
NSA	National Seamen's Association
RCMP	Royal Canadian Mounted Police
SIU	Seafarers' International Union
SIUNA	Seafarers' International Union of North America
TLC	Trades and Labour Congress

The ss *Mohawk Park*, a typical wartime Canadian merchant ship.
PAC, PA 117254

J.A. (Pat) Sullivan, founder and president of the Canadian Seamen's Union.
PAC, PA 146859

J.L. Cohen, csu lawyer and noted civil liberties advocate. pac, pa 112763

CSU members in Montreal celebrate the end of the 1946 Great Lakes strike.
PAC, PA 115221

Captain Eric S. Brand, controller of Great Lakes shipping.
Courtesy Mrs Eric Brand

Percy Bengough, president of the TLC, feared a confrontation with the American Internationals.
PAC, C 25015

Frank Hall, leader of a railway union, encouraged Banks to come to Canada and then turned against him.
PAC, PA 93492

CSU members demonstrate in Toronto against Pat Sullivan and his new union. *Canadian Tribune*, photo by Helene Wasser

CSU picketers demand unions of their own choice. PAC, PA 93867

The 1949 deep-sea strike paralyzed shipping around the world. PAC, PA 128759

As the 1949 strike began, CSU members refused to leave their ships, Vic
Davidson / *Montreal Gazette* / PAC, PA 146845

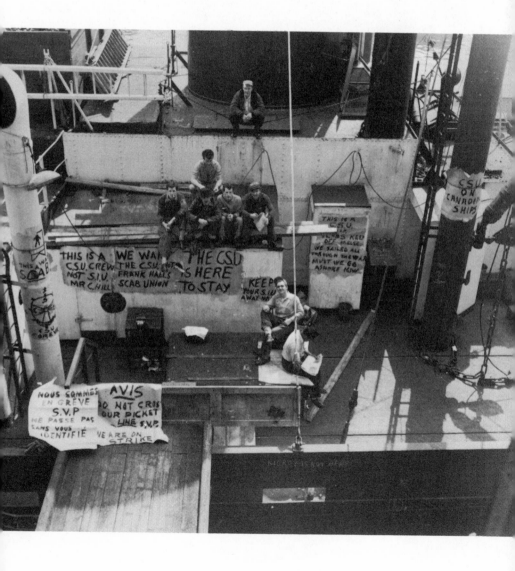

Claude Jodoin, president of the Canadian Labour Congress. An early Banks
supporter, Jodoin was forced to take measures against him and the SIU.
PAC, PA 122486

Tom Houtman and Jack Leitch of Upper Lakes Shipping. Against heavy odds,
Leitch fought Banks and the SIU. Courtesy Felicia Houtman

Marc Lalonde, junior commission counsel, Charles Dubin, commission counsel, and T.G. Norris, commissioner. Courtesy Mrs T.G. Norris

At the Norris Commission, left to right, Luc Couture, counsel for the St Lawrence Seaway Authority, J.A. Geller, counsel for Upper Lakes Shipping, Harry Crowe, research director for the CBRT, and CLC lawyer Maurice Wright. Courtesy Jack Geller

Banks testifies at the Norris Commission. Dominion Wide CP Wirephoto /
PAC, PA 146854

T.G. Norris leaves the commission hearings held at the Supreme Court of
Canada in Ottawa. Courtesy Mrs T.G. Norris

Paul Hall, president of the Seafarers' International Union of North America, with the leader of the Canadian District, Hal Banks. *Montreal Star /* PAC, PA 146699

Hal Banks accompanied by SIU lawyer Joseph Nuss. Blackham / PAC, PA 146852

SIU members discuss their grievances with freshman Montreal MP John Turner outside the House of Commons. Paul Taillefer / PAC, PA 146847

Banks speaks to reporters after the October 1963 Parliament Hill demonstration.
Mac Juster / PAC, PA 146861

Pearson and Kennedy met at Hyannisport in April 1963. Among the issues they discussed was the disruption in Canadian shipping. UPI / PAC, PA 117603

EVERYTHING THAT FLOATS

1

The Canadian Shipping Industry and the Birth of a Union

The Merchant Marine

Canadian ships and shipping are much older than the country. As early as 1606 Acadian-built bottoms were launched at Port Royal. A shipbuilding industry was established in the early eighteenth century when the French minister of marine encouraged, and more importantly subsidized, a shipyard on the banks of the St Charles River. Merchant vessels were built for delivery in France and the French West Indies, along with warships for the French navy. By the early nineteenth century shipyards had been set up in Quebec, by then a British colony, and in Nova Scotia and New Brunswick. These colonies enjoyed abundant supplies of lumber suitable for the construction of ships and for the overseas export market. The industry began to grow.[1]

Almost all of the larger ships built between 1800 and 1840 in British North America were loaded with lumber and dispatched to the United Kingdom, where both vessel and cargo were sold. The colonial shipyards first supplemented and then began actively to compete with British production of ocean-going bottoms. Colonial economic life became increasingly dependent on the rapidly emerging industry. In 1875 the industry peaked, with Canadian shipyards producing almost five hundred ships that year. During the remainder of the century Canadian shipyards turned out, on average, forty bottoms a year.[2] A small shipping industry also began to develop. Canadian-owned ships, which naturally plied the coastal trades, started to service both the British and West Indies shipping market. The industry was given a further boost by the discovery of gold in California and by the Crimean War. The fast-sailing Canadian ships were suddenly sought around the world. Just one decade after Confederation the Canadian merchant marine was the fourth largest merchant fleet in the world.

In contrast to its steady growth, the decline of the Canadian shipbuilding industry came rapidly. Towards the end of the 1800s steel ships began to supplant wood ships. The large-scale production of steel for shipbuilding in the United Kingdom during the 1880s restored Britain's historical position as the major builder of ships in the world, but spelled the end of the Canadian shipbuilding industry, one which was in any event beginning to suffer from a decline in easily accessible timber. There was no feasible means of competing with Britain in the construction of steel ships. Canada had little domestic demand for ocean-going ships, and without a sophisticated indigenous iron and steel industry (along with highly developed engineering skills), competition would have been fruitless.[3] Between 1878 and 1900 the total tonnage of Canadian registered shipping decreased by almost 50 per cent. By 1914 Canada's foreign-going merchant marine had, with the exception of the Canadian Pacific Steamship Company and a few small lines, ceased to exist.[4]

The domestic shipbuilding industry paralleled this decline and all but disappeared. Many of the shipbuilding facilities were closed or put to other use. The half-dozen surviving companies which were actually building ships turned out bottoms solely for the local market: small cargo vessels, barges, and government steamers. The few other remaining companies did repairs.[5] Activity remained sunk at this low level until 1917 when British authorities, alarmed by the heavy losses inflicted on British ships by German U-boats, sent a team of experts to Canada to investigate facilities for steel shipbuilding. Their report was not encouraging, but the need for ships was urgent and it was decided to make the best possible use of the existing facilities and to establish new ones.[6]

The Imperial Munitions Board placed contracts with ten firms to build steel ships ranging in size from 1800 to 8800 tons. Forty-one ships were built and, upon completion, were delivered to managers appointed by the British government. The Canadian government then decided to embark on a shipbuilding program of its own. Keels were laid for Canadian ships, ships which were intended solely to assist Britain in the transport of munitions and other vital war supplies. However, before any of the ships were completed, the war ended and Ottawa was faced with a difficult question: What was it to do with the almost-finished ships?[7]

In order to provide employment in the dislocated postwar economy and to ensure sufficient vessels for the carriage of its overseas trade, the government decided to continue its shipbuilding program. The Canadian

Government Merchant Marine Limited was incorporated to operate a fleet which by 1921 numbered sixty-three ships. Built by more than a dozen firms, six different types of ships were launched, ranging in capacity from 2800 to 10,500 deadweight tons.[8] In 1919 and 1920 the merchant marine established regular sailings on existing trade routes and opened new ones. The opportunity for expansion was created in part by a world-wide postwar scarcity of merchant ships, placing those available in great demand. Large revenues were earned by the government-owned fleet; the decision to proceed with its construction appeared sound. However, the prosperity of the Canadian Government Merchant Marine was both transitory and illusory. The bubble did not take long to burst.[9]

The Canadian ships were built when wartime inflationary influences and costs were at their peak. The sixty-three ships represented an expenditure of more than $70 million, considerably more than they would have cost had they been built before the war. As well, these ships were designed and built to meet an immediate need and could not compete with the faster, less expensive, and more fuel-efficient bottoms which were launched after the war. To make matters worse, in 1921 ocean freight rates dropped sharply, on some commodities by as much as 50 per cent. The merchant marine began to lose money – almost $2 million, for example, in 1921. The directors and managers of the fleet struggled to keep losses down and the ships afloat. Although some of the smaller ships were sold off, it quickly became apparent that only a massive government subsidy could save the fleet. Considering that the remaining ships were out of date, a subsidy did not make any sense. Accordingly, the government made the only decision possible in the circumstances, and by 1936 all the ships were sold. The demise of the merchant marine was not inexpensive. When the final tally was taken, it had suffered a loss of $82 million.[10]

Expensive as this venture was, it was not a complete fiasco. The ships filled a vital need in the immediate postwar period and, although ultimately abandoned by the merchant marine, new and important overseas trade routes were opened up, many of which were subsequently and profitably exploited by others. In 1925, for example, Ottawa negotiated a trade treaty with the West Indies which provided for the establishment of regular passenger and cargo shipping. The Canadian National (West Indies) Steamship Company was formed to implement the treaty and it was able to acquire, at bargain basement rates, a number of cargo ships from the merchant marine to service the new route. That route became so successful that CN Steamships was later able to commission five passenger-cargo ships to ply the lucrative West Indies trade. The most valuable

valuable benefit derived from the merchant marine was the training and experience gained by Canadian officers, sailors, and administrative personnel, put to good use during the Second World War.[11]

When that war began in September 1939 the Canadian fleet consisted of only thirty-eight ocean-going ships of 1000 gross tons or more. Of these, eleven were owned by CN Steamships and ten were tankers belonging to Imperial Oil. Much of this 'fleet' dated from the First World War. In the interwar period Canadian shipyards had been inactive. There was almost no market for their products and services. Only forty-two ships longer than 150 feet were launched between 1918 and 1939. In effect, the Canadian shipbuilding industry had not progressed since the dark days of the Great War.[12]

This time around it was clear at the outset, to both British and Canadian authorities, that victory depended in large measure on the existence of a merchant marine and that Canada's thirty-eight ships were, at best, a nucleus. Ottawa moved quickly and efficiently to build up the fleet. At first, shipbuilding was placed under the authority of the War Supply Board, established to oversee the purchase of weapons and other war material. The immediate need was military and, by February 1940, the government had commissioned sixty-four corvettes and fourteen minesweepers. Several months later the Department of Munitions and Supply was formed and shipbuilding became one of its branches. In the fall of 1940 the British government placed orders with the rapidly revitalized Canadian shipyards for twenty-six 10,000-ton merchant ships. The following April, Wartime Merchant Shipping Limited,[13] a crown corporation, was formed to supervise a vastly expanded, incredibly ambitious merchant shipbuilding program.[14]

Not all of the merchant ships built were handed over to Great Britain. In April 1942 the Park Steamship Company was formed to supervise the management of a Canadian merchant marine. Ships were constructed under contract with Ottawa, but they were immediately handed over to private Canadian companies on a management-fee basis. The government's second wartime venture in merchant shipping was, unlike the earlier experience, almost an unqualified success. The Canadian-built ships, carrying soldiers and supplies, helped win the war. Almost four hundred merchant ships were built for the allied cause at an average cost of only $10 more per deadweight ton than the ships of the Canadian Government Merchant Marine. By war's end the Park Steamship Company had turned over to the government of Canada earnings on operations of more than $80 million. Canada's merchant fleet was for the second time in less than one hundred years the fourth largest in the world.[15]

Inland and Coastal Shipping

Before the Second World War forced the revival of the merchant marine, Canadian shipping was largely centred on the coastal trades, the Great Lakes, and the St Lawrence River. The coastal trade, as its name suggests, involves the shipment of goods from one coastal port to another. The many small ships involved in the coastal trade performed a vital and indispensable service, but this part of the shipping industry, considered alone, never constituted anything more than a small portion of Canadian shipping. It was shipping on Canada's inland sea, the Great Lakes and St Lawrence River, which accounted, both before and after the First World War, for the greatest percentage of Canadian water transportation.

The shipping season on the Great Lakes and St Lawrence River is limited by winter freeze-up to, at most, eight months of the year, from April, in a very warm year, to early December. A more significant constraint on the industry, before the completion of the St Lawrence Seaway system in 1959, was the geography of the waterway and the restrictions it imposed on shipping. One system of canals connected the Great Lakes to each other, while another system enabled ships to bypass various rapids along the St Lawrence. Ships which could navigate all or part of one canal system were often unable to navigate the other. In particular, large cargo ships called 'Lakers' were confined to the upper Great Lakes. The Welland Canal, which created a shipping lane between Lake Erie and Lake Ontario, was not big enough to handle these bottoms. Before the canal system was improved, the lakers crisscrossed the upper Great Lakes. Those in the grain trade, for example, would sail to the Lakehead, pick up their cargo, and transport it to ports on Lake Huron and in Georgian Bay, where the grain would be unloaded into elevators. The grain was later either loaded into smaller ships or railed or trucked east. Other bulk cargos, including coal and iron ore, were also shipped in this manner. After the expanded Welland Canal opened in 1932, the lakers were able to sail all the way down the lakes as far as Kingston or Prescott, Ontario.

Kingston marks the official starting point of the St Lawrence River, which some thousand miles away empties into the Atlantic Ocean. The canal system on the St Lawrence before 1959 was navigable, but not by the giant lakers. Twenty-two locks between Galop and Lachine limited transit to ships less than half the size of the lakers, which were therefore required to unload their cargo into elevators for storage and ultimately transfer to smaller ships able to navigate the St Lawrence canal system.[16] These small ships, called 'Canallers,' with shallow draughts, bluff rounded bows, and smokestacks placed aft,[17] were easily able to carry cargo down the St Lawrence. Once the canallers reached the Port of Montreal or points east, cargos with an international destination were again trans-shipped to ocean-going vessels. Other ships able to ply these waters included package freight carriers, small oil tankers, small passenger vessels and excursion steamers.[18]

When the St Lawrence Seaway opened in 1959,[19] the entire character of Great Lakes shipping changed. Gone were the costly trans-shipments and time-consuming delays at the frequent bottlenecks in the fourteen-foot-deep canals. Gone also were the canallers which required a crew almost as large as the lakers, but which carried perhaps one-eighth the cargo. These ships were sold abroad or converted by being cut in half and lengthened with the addition of a new centre.[20] The twenty-two locks along the St Lawrence were reduced to seven. Most importantly, these locks were lengthened, widened, and deepened.[21] The locks now measured 859 feet by 80 feet and the Seaway could accommodate ships with a draught of twenty-six feet. Lakers, as well as most ocean-going ships, could sail the longest inland waterway in the world. The volume of shipping, which had been steadily growing for years, increased dramatically: in the first five years following the official opening of the Seaway, the amount of cargo shipped through the St Lawrence canals almost doubled.[22] Great Lakes shipping had become an extremely important industry.

The Great Lakes and St Lawrence River Shipping Industry

The Great Lakes shipping industry was not always dominated by a relatively small number of companies although it eventually turned out that way. In the 1920s approximately 350 Canadian and American companies vied for cargo on the lakes with close to two thousand ships.[23] The Depression and fierce competition in an industry generally run by private-family – operated companies drove many of the smaller, weaker lines out of business. By the 1930s only a few companies of any significance were left.

The most important of these companies was Canada Steamship Lines, which traced its history back to the mid-nineteenth century.[24] Naturally, Canada Steamship Lines had competitors and these companies were run by fiercely independent businessmen. N.M. Paterson, later summoned to the Canadian Senate, founded N.M. Paterson and Sons Limited. Scott Misener controlled a line that bore his name, and owned the Colonial and Sarnia Steamship companies. Other forces to be reckoned with were the Upper Lakes and St Lawrence Transportation Company Limited; the Reoch Line, formed by a one-time employee of Canada Steamship Lines, Norman Reoch; and the Quebec and Ontario Steamship Company.[25] Of all these shipping lines, Canada Steamship Lines and Upper Lakes will play important roles in the events which follow.

Shipping Company Organizations

Despite the intense competition that characterizes the shipping business, the shipping companies realized early in the twentieth century that there were, for one matter in particular, significant advantages to acting in concert: dealing with labour. In 1903 Montreal shore workers, unhappy with poor working conditions and low pay, engaged in work slowdowns, and ultimately went on strike. Shipping was, as intended, hampered. A number of shipping companies principally engaged in the overseas trade responded by binding together and forming the Shipping Federation of Canada. The principal motivation for the formation of the federation was the labour problem. Strikebreakers were imported from abroad to shore up the local labour force and the militia was ordered onto the Montreal wharfs to protect them. Under these circumstances, the strike failed.

Buoyed by its victory, the Shipping Federation expanded its labour relations operations beyond Montreal to most eastern Canadian ports. In addition, the federation represented its members in other areas in which there was a community of interest, such as government legislation.[26] Other than in its dealings with labour, the Shipping Federation resembled countless other industrial associations.

Perhaps coincidentally, an organization representing the inland shipping companies was also formed in 1903: the Dominion Marine Association. In contrast to members of the federation, members of the association were interested in having their association further interests other than labour relations. For example, when the proposed Georgian Bay ship canal (following the seventeenth-century fur trading route from Georgian Bay up the French River to Lake Nipissing, across the Mattawa River and thence down the Ottawa River to Montreal, cutting 300 miles off the Lake Superior–Montreal voyage) was debated during the early 1900s, the Dominion Marine Association took a strong stand against it.[27] The members of the association were committed to the lower Great Lakes–St Lawrence route and had no desire to see public funds expended on this undertaking. Similarly, when the modern St Lawrence Seaway project was formally announced, the association, along with many shipping companies,[28] was extremely critical of the proposal, fearing competition from the cheaper, less expensively operated foreign flag ships. During strikes and other labour disputes the Dominion Marine Association took a strong and vocal stand but, more than anything else, it was a lobbying organization for its members.

Mates, Engineers, and Sailors

Hierarchy and discipline are more important on board a ship than in most other industrial settings. Orders given must be readily obeyed; the safety of the crew and vessel depend on it. Under the supreme authority of the captain, a modern ship's complement is divided into three groups: the mates and deck officers who assist the captain in running the ship; the engineers who supervise the operation of the ship's engines; and, comprising the bulk of the crew, the ordinary seamen. On the lakers and canallers the mates and officers were often former ordinary seamen who had worked their way up through the ranks. On board the deep-sea ships the officers were usually British. Generally the ordinary seamen, also known as unlicensed personnel, were divided into three classifications: deck or forward crew, aft or engine-room crew, and members of the steward's department.

Members of the deck department worked under the supervision of the mates. Included in this group were seamen of unspecified rating whose responsibilities included the removing of hatches and strongbacks prior to unloading, and the replacing of strongbacks and battening down the hatches when the loading or unloading was completed. All painting, chipping, cleaning, and washing on board ship, with the exception of engine-room work, was carried out by these crew members. The most dangerous part of their duties was performed when their ship was navigating a canal.[29] The unlicensed seamen were required to throw out the ship's lines to lock guards, who pulled in the vessel with the aid of steam winches and then looped the lines over snubbing posts. Unless the lines were pulled taut, the ship would thrash violently when water was let in or out of the lock.[30] If the job was not done properly, a serious accident could, and often did, result. The least skilled of all the ship's crew, these sailors worked a shift known as the four-watch, which in practice meant four hours on duty followed by four hours off duty in a repeating cycle, often seven days a week when their ship was at sea.

A more specialized and more highly rated deck department crew member was the deck hand. A hand, on call twenty-four hours a day, was responsible for many of the deck department duties, and on many ships also worked as a coal passer, assisting the fireman. The fireman kept the ship's engines stoked with fuel. Another member of the deck department was the wheelsman, who had at least several years' experience on board ship. Two wheelsmen were on each ship, working two watches a day of six hours each. Although responsible while sailing for the maintenance of the wheelhouse, the main duty of the wheelsman was steering the ship. When in port the wheelsman regulated the mooring lines and the amount of water in the ballast tank, inspected the bilges, and generally assisted with work of a routine nature. The remaining member of the deck department was the watchman. These sailors, who worked the same watch as the wheelsman, acted as lookouts while their ship was at sea.[31]

Members of the engine-room department, responsible for everything related to the operation and maintenance of the engines propelling the ship, worked under the supervision of the chief engineer. There were two classifications within this department. One was the oiler, who, working a two-watch shift of four hours on followed by four hours off followed by four on, was required to check the water levels of the boilers, operate the ballast and sanitary pumps and the refrigeration and electrical plants, as well as grease, oil, and maintain the main and steering engines. The other classification was the fireman. Because of the intense heat generated by the ship's furnace, the fireman worked a shift of three hours on followed by six hours off, and so on. The position was the most arduous on board ship.

The steward or cook, assisted depending on the size of the ship by a second cook, began the day at 4:45 AM when breakfast was prepared for serving between 5:45 and 6:45 AM. After breakfast, lunch was made and served generally between 11:45 AM and 12:45 PM. Dinner was served at 6:00 PM and, after clean-up, the midnight lunch was made. The job was rarely finished before 8:00 PM, and the galley crew worked seven days a week.[32]

Not only were the hours for all classifications long but the pay was low. In the 1920s deckhands received approximately $30 a month or $240 a year, since few ordinary seamen were able to obtain work over the winter layover.[33] Wages did not improve during the Depression, when many sailors considered themselves lucky to find a berth. Nevertheless, some shipping companies maintained that sailing was one of the easiest jobs around. N.M. Paterson and Sons, for example, claimed that its crews had so much leisure time that they did not know what to do with it.[34] In fact, this was rarely the case. The long hours of work left little time, and inclination, for leisure even if there had been any facilities.

To work on board a ship determined for an employee where he lived, the food he ate, and the society in which he shared his existence. The 'foc's'le' was frequently crowded, unsanitary, and poorly ventilated. Food was rarely good (although some ships were better in this regard than others), and seamen went without fresh produce and dairy products for long periods while at sea. When a lake ship was in port or laid up for more than a day, all but essential crew was discharged.[35] These sailors were often left to fend for themselves, usually in ports far from home. Sometimes, depending on the captain or the company, the discharged crew was allowed to stay on board ship and put in a few hours work each day in exchange for board. Transportation money back to the point of hire was rarely paid.[36] The amenities of a civilized existence were denied seamen, as a rule, by shipping companies anxious in a marginally profitable industry to keep costs down. Labour was one of the costs and, faced with the draconian provisions of the Canada Shipping Act, there was little that sailors could do collectively to improve their lot.

Once a man signed shipping articles either for voyages at sea or on the Great Lakes, he became a member of a group apart; his rights and duties were closely circumscribed by a special code of law. In theory, the act imposed obligations on both captains and crew. In practice, the act, based almost entirely on an earlier British statute, the Merchant Shipping Act, reflected conditions of a bygone era and created a highly authoritarian, in some cases almost military, regime. Those sections of the statute dealing with discipline were relevant when voyages took many months and ships sailed far from home. Discipline problems arising on speedy ships equipped with radar and radios on voyages of relatively short duration were very different from those that arose on the sailing ships. Nowhere was this reflected in the act.

The few statutory rights and privileges enjoyed by seamen were largely illusory. Three or more members of a ship's crew were, for example, entitled to complain to the authorities if they considered the water or provisions on board ship unfit. If the complaint was not sustained the ship's owner was entitled by law to deduct up to one week's pay from each of the sailors. If the complaint was sustained the owner faced a small fine; under the 1952 act it could not exceed $100.[37] Acting as a further disincentive to a seaman making a complaint was the provision of the act which required that a ship's master prepare at the end of every voyage a written report on the sailors' conduct and character. Masters could write what they wished and there was no formal mechanism by which an unfair report could be challenged. Sailors seeking employment on board other ships were required to produce their records and were all too conscious of the effect a negative report could have on their sailing careers.

Seamen had no right to industrial self-government and even the hint of collective action was met with the heavy hand of the law. The act provided that any person who boarded a ship without permission was subject to imprisonment. If a person was found guilty of this offence, a prison sentence was mandatory. Loitering near a ship was also a punishable offence.[38] These provisions, although never intended for this purpose, were used by shipping companies to keep trade union organizers at bay. Even talk of strike action saw union organizers whisked off to prison under that section which prohibited enticement to desertion. There was certainly no legal right to strike, even if a ship's crew had been organized. All strikes were illegal as desertion,[39] and striking seamen faced prison sentences, forfeiture of their personal effects, and loss of all outstanding wages, which their employer was entitled to turn over to the receiver general of Canada.

Some of the seemingly harsh sections of the Canada Shipping Act were respected by sailors. It is a fundamental principle of the law of the sea that strikes of any kind are forbidden at sea and in foreign ports since they endanger the lives of passengers, officers, and crew and place the vessel itself in jeopardy. In forbidding this type of conduct the act appropriately gave effect to this principle. However, there is a difference between conduct which is properly restricted by law and laws which restrict proper conduct. The act did both. Sailors were among the most badly treated workers of their generation and there was little they could do about it. What ordinary seamen needed more than anything else in the mid-1930s was an organization to represent and protect them, a trade union.

Before the federal government was persuaded by organized labour during the Second World War to guarantee the right of working people to organize and bargain collectively, trade unions usually existed solely by virtue of their strength. Under the Canadian constitution, Ottawa enjoys legislative control over the labour relations of industries within its jurisdiction. Shipping is one of those industries, and the applicable statute was the Industrial Disputes Investigation Act.

Based in large part on the ideas of William Lyon Mackenzie King, the Industrial Disputes Investigation Act was intended to balance the competing interests of labour and management. Although initially welcomed by organized labour, it quickly became apparent that, in practice, the act favoured management. Employers were not compelled to recognize democratically elected unions, and property rights were generally given precedence over personal and group rights. The legislation imposed a cumbersome and time-consuming system of official investigation and compulsory conciliation in industrial disputes as a legal precondition to a

lawful strike or lockout. The delay caused by investigation and conciliation favoured the employer, particularly since many of the early disputes
were over union recognition. The employer was entitled during the
period of compulsory conciliation to arrange for strikebreakers, relocate
production, and establish management-oriented and -directed employees'
committees. None of this conduct was forbidden by law and, by the time
a union was finally in a position to exercise a legal right to strike, there
was usually no point.[40]

The legislation also failed to distinguish between types of industrial
conflict. Disputes over wages and working conditions are generally amenable to mediation and conciliation. But disputes over recognition, where
an employer denies the legitimate right of a union to exist, are amenable
to neither. By imposing conciliation in these circumstances the statutory
scheme served no useful industrial relations purpose and, more importantly, invariably benefited the employer to the detriment of the union.[41]
Under this legislation scheme, workers faced formidable obstacles in exercising their limited rights to organize. Sailors, however, were particularly
disadvantaged.

A ship, unlike an industrial plant, is not stationary. In the event that a
union succeeded, notwithstanding the provisions of the Canada Shipping
Act, in organizing the sailors on board a particular ship, the operator
could always tie up that ship, wait out any strike, and continue with its
other operations vitually unhampered. Furthermore, as important as it
was to the running of a ship, the work of an ordinary seaman was relatively unskilled. Any ship carrying a full complement of mates and
engineers could sail manned with a crew of newly recruited employees
who had never been to sea. The strategy of the shipowners (who were
uniformly opposed to unions) in an industrial dispute of any significant
dimension was obvious: hire strikebreakers. Only through preventing the
strikebreakers from boarding ship could a seamen's strike hope to succeed.
That hope was usually forlorn. Strikebreaking was and is lawful and the
police generally ensure that this legal right is not denied. In these circumstances, most early attempts to organize seamen failed.[42]

The one notable exception was the creation in the early 1930s of
the National Seamen's Association. Founded by a former employee
of Canada Steamship Lines, Captain Hubert Newbold McMaster, the
National Seamen's Association was little more than a crimping agency, an
organization that procures seamen for shipping companies in return for
money. McMaster and his association (which he ran as a family affair,
placing a son and daughter on the payroll) had it both ways. Not only was
the National Seamen's Association intimately connected with certain ship-

ping companies but it also managed to collect dues from its members. 'Right thinking' seamen were urged to join this self-proclaimed company-oriented outfit, which promised its members many things but delivered few.[43]

As bad as it was, the National Seamen's Association was the only organization around and McMaster naturally made every effort to conceal his relationship with the shipping companies. Many sailors were shanghaied into the organization by McMaster's backdoor deals with the shipping companies, but others, not aware of the association's true character, joined with only honourable intentions. This was certainly the case when, in the mid-1930s, a small group of cooks and stewards led by John Allan Patrick (Pat) Sullivan approached McMaster about membership in the National Seamen's Association. In due course, Sullivan was put on McMaster's payroll.[44]

Very little is known about Sullivan's early years, and the few facts available have been largely subsumed by stories and legends, some of which are, to say the least, inspired.[45] The story Sullivan encouraged was the one which made him an IRA partriot on the run after a fatal ruckus.[46] The only part of this story which is undeniably true is that Sullivan came to Canada from Ireland. Born on 19 June 1893 in Carrick-on-Shannon, Ireland,[47] Sullivan married in 1916 and, with his wife and son, immigrated to Canada in 1923. Apparently, both Sullivan and his wife began working as cooks on lake ships. Sullivan's early sailing career was unremarkable. However, he possessed a way with words which, along with his boundless energy, inspired confidence in his leadership. He worked briefly for McMaster. When Sullivan realized that the National Seamen's Association was not a seamen's association at all, he decided to start a new union. The problem was how. Organized labour was by the mid-1930s in chaos. The cause of this disarray was an event which had taken place many years earlier.

At the turn of the century, both indigenous national craft unions and American international unions represented Canadian workers.[48] Many of these unions were affiliated with a central organization, the Trades and Labour Congress of Canada. The TLC, which was the oldest and largest central body at this time, was associated with an equivalent body in the United States, the American Federation of Labor. The membership of the TLC included most, if not all, of the unions affiliated to the AFL which were also operating in Canada. These unions, known as Internationals, constituted a large part of the membership of the TLC. Founded several years before the AFL, the TLC operated as an autonomous body until the early 1900s.

At the turn of the century Samuel Gompers, the president of the AFL, detected in the leadership of the TLC certain nationalist and socialist tendencies as well as a willingness to accept industrial unionism. At the 1902 TLC Convention the AFL international unions affiliated to the TLC, on Gomper's orders, brought the TLC back into line.[49] As a result, thousands of unskilled workers who, in the economic expansion of the 1920s, clamoured for union organization were ignored. In 1927 Aaron Mosher, the head of the Canadian Brotherhood of Railway Employees, founded a rival national labour body, the All-Canadian Congress of Labour. The All-Canadian Congress of Labour was everything the TLC was not. Young and nationally oriented, it welcomed into affiliation unions which represented both skilled and unskilled workers.

In late 1935 or early 1936 when Sullivan formed his union, the All-Canadian Congress of Labour was the only central labour congress which would consider chartering a national seamen's union. Following discussions with Sullivan, a charter was issued in the name of the National Seamen's Union. After renting an office in Montreal, Sullivan started to work.[50] It was tough going organizing a seamen's union from scratch. The rival National Seamen's Association had most of the Great Lakes companies under contract, and those which were not organized had no intention of assisting Sullivan in his enterprise. However, Captain McMaster, acting quite out of character, indirectly gave Sullivan and the slowly growing membership of the National Seamen's Union the break they were waiting for.

Sometime in 1935 McMaster circulated among seamen a letter which he claimed had been sent to companies under contract with the National Seamen's Association. The letter was a militant call to arms, threatening shipping operators with a strike unless wages were raised and conditions improved.[51] Wages did not rise and conditions did not improve. At the appointed time, National Seamen's Association members at ports along the St Lawrence and on the Great Lakes walked off their ships and turned to McMaster for support. Captain McMaster made an appearance in Cornwall, Ontario, a centre of strike activity, but cowardly refused in the presence of the police to take any responsibility for the illegal strike.[52] The strike would surely have failed had it not been for the intervention of Joe Salsberg, a leading member of the Communist Party of Canada with specific responsibility for the union movement.[53]

The Communist party, which was then a force to be reckoned with, hoped that by boring from within it could replace the nascent union movement's 'reactionary' leadership with revolutionary leadership and use organized labour as an instrument for the overthrow of the capitalist system.[54] The party pursued this policy throughout the 1920s, but by 1930 the leadership of the TLC and the All-Canadian Congress of Labour became cognizant of the party's goals. Accordingly, party members were made unwelcome in these labour movements and the Communist Party of Canada, on orders from the Moscow-directed Red International of Labor Unions (which in turn was controlled by the Comintern, the Soviet organization charged with promoting the cause of worldwide Communist revolution), formed its own labour centre, the Workers' Unity League. The league was an aggressive militant organization which enjoyed remarkable success in organizing industrial workers and the unemployed. By 1935 Joe Salsberg, as head of the league, led more than 40,000 members, most of whom were not members of the Communist party.[55] When Salsberg learned that the striking sailors had been abandoned by McMaster, he stepped in to fill the gap.

Guided by Salsberg, who was acting behind the scenes, two rank-and-file leaders, Dewar Ferguson and Joe Turnbull, emerged and negotiated a settlement of the strike with Canada Steamship Lines, the company most affected by the dispute.[56] Canada Steamship Lines agreed to take back all the striking seamen except Ferguson and Turnbull. Again guided by Salsberg, the displaced leaders decided to form a union of their own, the Maritime Workers' Union of the Great Lakes.[57] Ferguson was quickly and secretly recruited into the Communist party. When Sullivan learned about this new seamen's union, he warned sailors to stay away because it was controlled by Communists.[58] But by the summer of 1936 Sullivan was a Communist party recruit himself, converted by Fred Rose, the leader of the Quebec branch of the Communist Party of Canada.[59]

Both the Maritime Workers' Union and the National Seamen's Union were now firmly within the Communist party sphere of influence, and party functionaries decided that the two unions should merge.[60] The proposed merger was not discussed in advance with the membership of either union, nor were any of the members given a subsequent opportunity to ratify it. Had the National Seamen's Union, as the merged union was known, been formed even one year earlier there is no doubt that it would have been immediately affiliated with the Communist party's Workers' Unity League. However, in 1935 Moscow's labour strategy changed. To meet the rising threat of fascism in Europe, the Red International of Labor Unions (on orders from the Comintern) decided that a common front of workers was necessary. In North America, Communist party leaders were instructed to pursue a policy of continental labour organization. Accordingly, the Workers' Unity League was disbanded and its leaders and members ordered, if possible, to find their way back into the internationally oriented TLC.[61] For the same reasons, the continued affiliation of the National Seamen's Union to the nationalist All-Canadian Congress of Labour was unthinkable.[62] The feeling, by the fall of 1936, was mutual.

Following the Maritime Workers' Union-National Seamen's Union merger, the All-Canadian Congress, concerned about the influence that non-member Communists were wielding in the National Seamen's Union, decided to place it under trusteeship. When the officers of the National Seamen's Union learned of this plan they decided to withdraw their union from affiliation.[63] Sullivan called a membership meeting and, charging, rather ironically, that the All-Canadian Congress was interfering with seamen's democratic rights, engineered a membership resolution disaffiliating the union from the congress.[64] Another membership resolution empowered Sullivan to seek a new affiliation.[65] There was not very much choice. In line with Communist party policy, Sullivan had to end up with his union affiliated to the internationally oriented TLC. The easiest way of doing that was by becoming an affiliate of the International Seamen's Union, an American union which was an affiliate of the AFL. In this way the National Seamen's Union would virtually be guaranteed affiliation to the associated TLC. The International Seamen's Union was, by the mid-1930s, well past its prime and Sullivan's offer of new members and money was accepted with alacrity. He was given a charter for all of Canada and the decision was made to call the affiliate the Canadian Seamen's Union.[66]

In 1936 or 1937 the CSU affiliated with the TLC[67] and joined Trades and Labor district councils in Toronto and Montreal. Of more immediate importance was the consolidation and growth of the union. Sullivan and a growing number of full-time staff organized seamen up and down the lakes. By the early winter of 1937 the union was ready to have a convention. Seventeen delegates met at the Labour Temple in Toronto. What many of the delegates did not know was that Sullivan and other Communist party members of the union, along with party functionaries, had met secretly in advance at a party 'fraction' meeting. Well before the convention was scheduled to open, this group decided who would run for what union office and what resolutions would be passed. The convention proceeded exactly as planned. Jack Munroe was elected president, Dewar Ferguson and Jack Chapman were elected vice-presidents, and Sullivan became secretary-treasurer. A resolution was passed urging the government of Canada to adopt the International Labor Organization's draft convention on seamen which called for an eight-hour day; the delegates also asked the federal government to amend the Canada Shipping Act to require a wireless on all ships, not just those of 5000 tons or more.[68] An eight-hour day for seamen had been the standard on board American bottoms for some time; a radio on board a commercial ship was a basic safety requirement grasped immediately by sailors but less readily, apparently, by shipping company operators. The convention delegates also decided to open up two new union offices: one at the Lakehead, the other at the Welland Canal. Both offices were quickly established.

Whether different candidates would have been elected to union office had the Communist party not meddled in the union's internal affairs is uncertain. Each of the elected executive members was a well-known rank-and-file leader, fully qualified by background and experience to hold union office. The resolutions passed by the delegates would likely have been passed by a convention of seamen anywhere in North America. This suggests that the goals and objectives of the Communist party and the CSU were not far apart. In 1937, perhaps, they were not. However, political parties, of whatever stripe, have political objectives. Most trade unions and union members have economic objectives. The objective of the Communist Party of Canada in 1936 was the installation of a Soviet-style system of government. The objective of most union members, then and now, is higher wages, a better, safer workplace, and the opportunity to participate in the government of their industrial lives. Very few seamen were ideologically sympathetic to the Communist party and, notwithstanding great efforts on the part of the party, an even smaller number were actually Communists.[69] If asked, Communist party leaders made no mention of their political agenda. Instead, they pointed to their impressive work in organizing labour, at a time when supporters were few and labour needed all the help it could get. Only time would tell whether the Communist party, to retain control of the union and its members, was soft-pedalling its political objectives and advancing economic ones. In the meantime, it was clear that the union's economic objectives could only be achieved through strength. Strength comes through numbers; numbers come through organizing. In the months following this first convention, the union and its supporters began aggressively to organize.

Small companies were quickly brought under union contract,[70] but the CSU was interested in catching big fish. Sullivan therefore contacted officials of the International Longshoremen's Union, an AFL affiliate, to enlist their assistance in forcing the major Canadian shipping companies to the bargaining table. The Longshoremen offered their help.

By refusing to unload the ships of a particular shipping company, pressure could be brought to bear on that carrier, anxious to fulfil its contracts and get the maximum use out of its bottoms. This type of activity is known as secondary picketing. It is and was illegal; it is also extremely effective.

Often, long before the illegal picketing is enjoined by the courts, serious damage to the employer has been done or the union has won. The decision to proceed with a secondary picket is usually based on a calculation of the relative strength of the parties. But it can also be based on a complete and utter lack of strength, a desperate gamble by a union with little to lose and everything to gain. That was the case here.

The CSU had signed up members on board most of the large shipping lines, and, in particular, on Canada Steamship Lines. However, it was getting nowhere in its attempts to negotiate a written collective agreement and formal recognition from these large companies. Without the latter, a union has no status to represent its members. Without the former setting out in detail the terms and conditions of employment, workers have few meaningful rights, whether statutory or through common law. It was therefore crucial that the CSU win a written contract and win it from the largest company on the lakes. That was Canada Steamship Lines, and the Longshoremen agreed not to unload or service their ships arriving in Buffalo until word to the contrary was received from the officers of the CSU.

The plan went off without a hitch. When the SS *Emperor* arrived at the port of Buffalo, not long after the shipping season began, it was declared 'black' by the Longshoremen. What that meant was that no union member in port would touch it. The press was advised that the picket was the result of the refusal of certain Canadian companies to deal with the CSU. Ships of other Canadian lines soon met similar treatment. The Canadian shipping companies, which had never before experienced the strength of union solidarity, capitulated. Sullivan was invited to the office of the president of the Canada Steamship Lines. Within hours an oral contract was reached, providing for a moderate salary increase and union recognition. The secondary picketing in the United States was called off.[71]

This was supposed to be the break the union had been waiting for. However, with the exception of the Quebec and Ontario Steamship Company, which was also brought under oral contract, most of the remaining shipping companies refused to recognize the CSU. A number of these companies grouped themselves into an ad hoc organization to deal with the upsurge in union activity. This organization refused even to meet with the CSU officers. The union, representing an ever-increasing number of lake sailors, had no choice but to call a strike.[72]

Twenty-two companies, representing most ships on the lakes, were advised that their unlicensed crews would, on midnight 22 September, 'hit the beach.' The CSU was not making an idle threat; it was prepared to fight a long strike and had obtained $5000 from the Communist Party of

Canada to finance it. [73] The timing could not have been better; at the end of September shipments are rushed out to the Great Lakes–St Lawrence River waterway system to avoid the annual freeze-up. Just hours before the strike was scheduled to start the companies set to be struck conceded. Jack Munroe, the president of the CSU, met with company representatives and negotiated a significant wage increase. Improvements in working conditions were also won. But neither these gains, nor the recognition of the union's status, was incorporated into a written collective agreement. The strike was a victory, but only as long as the companies were as good as their word. The real test would come in the following year when the terms and conditions of the oral agreement came into effect. In the meantime there was a great deal to do. Sullivan joined the executive board of the Montreal Trades and Labour Council [74] and, one year later, starting what would prove to be a meteoric rise in the Canadian labour movement, was elected vice-president. [75]

These developments were reported with some sense of accomplishment to the delegates attending the CSU's second convention in the winter of 1938. This convention, along with every other convention during the life of this union, was preceded by a Communist party 'fraction' meeting at which the convention agenda was thoroughly discussed. The main party objective at this convention was to replace Jack Munroe, who had proved a reluctant follower of party orders. Moreover, he had allowed his drinking to interfere with his work, as was vividly illustrated at the convention when, as prearranged, party members, attending as delegates, launched him on a bender. Munroe was thoroughly discredited in the eyes of those delegates not already committed to his designated replacement, Pat Sullivan. [76] Sullivan was elected president, Dewar Ferguson vice-president, and Tom Houtman, a popular rank-and-file member of the union who was not a Communist party member, secretary-treasurer.

The convention delegates also passed a number of resolutions. They condemned Japan for its invasion of China; requested that the federal government disallow Quebec's anti-Communist Padlock Act which enabled the attorney general of Quebec to padlock the premises of any organization he declared to be subversive; and called on the government to pursue an independent, almost certainly meaning pro-Soviet, foreign policy. [77] Less out of the ordinary was the delegates' approval of resolutions calling for an eight-hour day, wage increases to American levels, [78] and the organization of coastal and deep-sea ships and fishing fleets sailing from the east coast. [79] None of these latter resolutions seemed beyond the union's grasp. In just a few short years it had organized the greater part of the Great Lakes fleet and was signing up new members every day. From all appearances the CSU was a democratic militant seamen's union run by and for its members. [80] The union began to enjoy an enviable reputation and, more importantly, the loyalty of Canadian seamen. In these circumstances only the most foolhardy shipping companies would violate the verbal agreements reached the previous year and attempt to destroy the union.

Nevertheless, this is what a number of them tried to do two months before the start of the 1938 shipping season. With the shipping companies' encouragement, the McMaster outfit, the National Seamen's Association, made a move. 'Right and left,' McMaster signed contracts for startled sailors who knew little of what was being done 'for' them, and by February 1938 he claimed to have sewn up 140 ships and 5000 seamen. [81] The agreement with the association apparently provided for a union shop on board all the contracted ships. [82] A union shop, which is now a standard provision in collective agreements, means that all bargaining unit employees of a contracted employer must pay dues to the union. These dues are deducted by the employer and remitted directly to the union. It is a provision designed to stabilize collective bargaining by providing unions with financial and institutional security. If the National Seamen's Association were allowed to get away with this backdoor deal, the CSU would be seriously crippled, if not, as the employers intended, destroyed.

The CSU leadership got wind of this scheme and realized the serious threat it represented. Because it was the beginning of the shipping season and ships were spread out along the lakes, there was no way of mounting an effective picket line. The union had no choice but to order its members to do whatever they could to get on board the ships belonging to companies which had signed contracts with the National Seamen's Association. The move was successful and the ships infiltrated. [83] This was only a temporary measure. The CSU was the representative of these sailors and wanted legal recognition. As was now manifest, only a strike, by demonstrating the members' resolve, could obtain recognition for their union.

On 15 April 1938 the CSU called a strike. Responding to the rallying cry of 'Unions of our own choice,' CSU members walked off some fifty struck ships and prevented strikebreakers from boarding them. The shipping companies were incensed. Captain R. Scott Misener, president of several concerns including both the Colonial and Sarnia companies, predicted confidently to the press that the members of his crews wanted nothing to do with the Canadian Seamen's Union. [84] Misener was mistaken. Within three days of the start of the strike, representatives of the struck companies agreed to meet with CSU officials. In return for calling off the strike the union obtained the companies' promise that they would not discriminate against CSU members. The CSU experience with shipping company promises was not very good, nor was this settlement. The union should have insisted on, and held out for, the same terms these same companies were willing to give the National Seamen's Association. However, it did not, and not long into the shipping season one of the smaller companies involved apparently violated its undertaking.

On 4 June three crew members of the *Red Cloud*, a ship belonging to the North American Transport Company, were discharged, according to the CSU, because of their union affiliation. The next day the entire unlicensed crew of the *Red Cloud*, along with the unlicensed crew of the *Damia*, a ship belonging to Inland Lines, left their ships. The walkout was illegal and ordinarily would have attracted little attention. However, at the time of the walkout, whether by chance or design, the *Damia* was smack in the middle of Lock No 2 of the Cornwall Canal. Shipping up and down the lakes ground to a halt and officials of the Department of Transport rushed to the scene and ordered that the *Damia* be moved. They were ignored. The minister of labour appointed M.E. McG. Quirk, under the Industrial Disputes Investigation Act, as a commissioner to investigate the incident. Quirk was also ignored. Company operators who were living up to the terms of their agreement with the CSU then pleaded with Sullivan to stop the tie-up. Sullivan told them that as soon as the shipping companies involved acceded to the CSU's demands the troubles would be over.[85] The other companies made sure that North American Transport and Inland Lines got the message.

Shortly thereafter an agreement was reached which provided that the three discharged crew members would be reinstated if it were shown that they had been unjustly dismissed. It was also provided, once again, that there would be no further discrimination against union members. The union in turn agreed not to discriminate against North American Transport, Inland Lines, and a third company called Mohawk Transportation, and not to intimidate or coerce any member of their ships' crews who was a member of some other union or of no union.[86] This agreement, which granted neither party anything not now guaranteed by law, settled what turned out to be a rather unremarkable affair. The event had, however, demonstrated to the shipping companies and the government alike the power the union could and would illegally exert over the entire shipping industry.

The *Damia* incident gave the CSU an aura of strength, which it exploited to the hilt. Negotiations for a real contract began in late June 1938 with Canada Steamship Lines. After five weeks of talks, the negotiations broke down. On 5 August Sullivan advised the Department of Labour that a strike was imminent. Since none of the mandatory investigation and conciliation provisions of the Industrial Disputes Investigation Act had been complied with, the scheduled strike was illegal. Sullivan may have been bluffing, but three days later Canada Steamship Lines signed a contract. It was a historic agreement. The company recognized for the first time that the CSU was the 'exclusive representative of all its employees,'[87] and formally agreed that the working day on board lake ships would not exceed twelve hours.[88] Also recognized was the right of the union and its members to appoint ships' delegates to help administer grievances on board ship, the right of union delegates to board ships in port, and preferential hiring of union members. The agreement, which further provided for a general increase in wages, was to run until 1 April 1940. It contained a provision providing for its automatic renewal unless notice to the contrary from either party was received sixty days in advance of the scheduled expiry. Within days, most of the members of the ad hoc employers' association signed similar contracts with the union.[89] As a result of these developments, more than 80 per cent of all the shipping companies on the lakes were brought under written contract with the union.

The CSU then began to take a leading role in both the maritime industrial relations field and the activities of the TLC. At the September 1938 TLC convention, CSU delegates showed up in full force. Also attending was Pat Ryan of the International Longshoremen's Association and a member of the AFL committee charged with salvaging the rapidly deteriorating International Seamen's Union. Plans had been made to form a new union, the Seafarers' International Union, at the annual AFL convention scheduled the following month. Ryan told Sullivan that the AFL wished to promote unity in the maritime field, if at all possible, through the creation of one union for unlicensed seamen. This was a goal which Sullivan claimed to endorse. The CSU had everything to gain by maintaining good relations with AFL leaders, especially, as the recent Buffalo experience demonstrated, those operating in the maritime field. As a show of support, the CSU made a nominal payment to affiliate with a proposed AFL seamen's organizing committee.[90] Soon after the formation of the SIU, the CSU received notification that it had been accepted as an affiliate. Although the CSU was by this time an affiliate in good standing of the TLC, it furthered both the union's interests and those of the Communist party to maintain good relations with the SIU in the United States. The SIU was so preoccupied with a fight for members and contracts with its rival, the

National Maritime Union, that it had little time to involve itself in the affairs of its Canadian affiliate.

The CSU held its own convention in Windsor in February 1939. The secretary-treasurer, Tom Houtman, an innocent victim of a rumour that he was a fascist, was defeated for office by Communist party member Jack Chapman. [91] No other changes were made in the union executive, which was now composed entirely of members of the Communist party. After taking care of this ugly piece of business, the achievements of the past year were proudly reviewed, and with good reason. It was, however, clear to all the delegates that notwithstanding everything that had been won, important goals remained: the organization of sailors on board coastal, deep-sea, and fishing ships; the institution of the eight-hour day on the Great Lakes; and the establishment of a union-run hiring hall for the placement of unemployed workers. [92]

The 1938 agreements had, in fact, only given CSU members a preference in hiring. They did not provide that only union members could be hired. The recent McMaster experience demonstrated that the shipping companies were not at all averse to signing sweetheart deals with organizations which had no members, and which bore little resemblance to a real union. In fact, this is the way they seemed to prefer it. The shipping industry was adamantly opposed to the establishment of anything even approximating a hiring hall. The right of a captain to hire his crew was considered sacrosanct. There was, apparently, little room for negotiation.

Not that any negotiation was necessary for the 1939 shipping season. The contracts signed the previous year were for two-year terms, and there were twelve months left. The 1938 contracts provided for binding arbitration of all disputes between the union and the companies and seemed to be working. This was of enormous assistance to the CSU, which had turned its attention to the east coast where many new members were being signed up, including hundreds of fishermen and fishhandlers in Nova Scotia. The CSU was also busy preparing for the September 1939 TLC convention.

As Salsberg had realized years earlier, once the CSU affiliated with the TLC it could promote Communist party labour policy. In September 1939 Salsberg's dream came true. CSU delegates worked actively, along with many non-Communist trade unionists, to avoid the expulsion of the Committee for Industrial Organization unions from the TLC. Originally founded as a committee of the AFL to organize industrial unions, the committee was now expelled from the AFL and established itself as a rival body for American unions, the Congress of Industrial Organization. A number of CIO unions had been established in Canada by Canadians, many of whom were former members of the Worker's Unity League. These unions affiliated with the TLC. However, after the AFL expelled the CIO unions from its congress, it brought strong pressure on the TLC to do the same. While sounding, perhaps, more complicated than it was, the AFL request was, at its root, another demand that the TLC come into line.

The opponents of the AFL demand believed that organized labour in Canada could only suffer from a split in the ranks between the older craft unions and the rapidly growing modern industrial unions. There was relatively little bickering and disharmony among the various TLC affiliates. Why then, it was asked, should American differences and policies be imposed on Canadians? CSU delegates also pointed out to the convention that their union received assistance from the CIO and its affiliated unions operating in the United States, and that the expulsion of the Canadian CIO unions threatened that co-operation.[93] None of these arguments prevailed. The leadership of the AFL international unions affiliated with the TLC, acting on orders from the United States, was determined to expel the CIO unions and, voting as a block, succeeded.

The expelled unions joined forces with the All-Canadian Congress of Labour to form the Canadian Congress of Labour. Since the first president of the CCL, Aaron Mosher, hated Communists[94] and supported the Co-operative Commonwealth Federation, the defeat in the fight against the expulsion of the CIO unions appeared at the time disastrous for the Communist party. Appearances were deceiving, however, and the party was able to recover from this apparent setback and controlled, by the end of the Second World War, unions comprising more than one-third of the total CCL membership. In the meantime, it was obvious to party functionaries that the fight against expulsion might have been fought and won had Communist party members and sympathizers been wielding real power and influence over the decision-making of the TLC. That, Communist party leaders hoped, would come with time.

2
The War Years, 1939–45

The day after Hitler started the Second World War, Pat Sullivan gave a speech affirming the devotion of the Canadian Seamen's Union to the cause of unity.[1] To most Canadians, including the overwhelming majority of sailors on board Canadian ships, unity meant Canada at Britain's side in the fight against the Nazis. To members of the Communist party the cause of unity meant something quite different. Just prior to the outbreak of war the Soviet Union and Nazi Germany signed a Treaty of Non-Aggression and Friendship. Dutifully, soon after Canada declared war against Germany, leading Canadian Communists, on instructions from the Comintern, denounced the government and campaigned under the slogan 'Withdraw Canada from the Imperialist War.'[2] Until the Soviet Union was invaded by Germany in June 1941, Canadian Communists did what they could to frustrate the Canadian war effort. The German attack against the Soviet Union caused Communist parties in Canada, the United States, and elsewhere to re-evaluate the war. Its character had changed, the Comintern announced, from an 'imperialist war' to a 'just anti-fascist war.' The Communist Party of Canada then called on the labour movement and 'progressive' forces in Canada to unite their efforts in support of every measure of the Canadian government to fight the war and 'render effective aid to the Soviet Union.'[3]

The self-interested policy reversal of the Comintern and its affiliated organizations around the world did not, however, occur until some two years after the start of the war. In the meantime, although its activities became increasingly restricted, the Communist Party of Canada did what it could to undermine the war effort. In this context, the first major labour dispute of the war was viewed by many Canadians as unpatriotic, the result of Communist party opposition to the war. The CSU was involved in the strike, but the union was the victim of the dispute, not its perpetrator.

Following the February 1939 convention, CSU organizers were sent east to begin an organizing drive on the coast. Charles Murray, a member of the Communist party, was assigned responsibility for the organization of Nova Scotia fishermen, a job which he performed with considerable success. On 15 August 1939 fishermen working out of Lockeport, Nova Scotia, voted to become Local No 1 of the Canadian Fishermen's Union, an affiliate of the CSU. Later that day, the fishhandlers employed at the town's two fish plants voted to become Local No 2. Representatives of the two locals approached both fishing companies in mid-October to begin negotiations. Under Nova Scotia law, the companies had certain obligations to recognize and deal with the union. The union representatives were, however, advised by the managers of both fish plants that they would close their companies rather than deal with a union. On 21 October 1939 both companies made good on their threat and, without further discussion or notice, locked all the employees out.[4] The employees and townspeople were shocked.

Lockeport is a tiny hamlet approximately one hundred miles south of Halifax with, in 1939, a population of 1400. Most men made their livings in one of two ways: fishing or fishhandling. When 650 fishermen and fishhandlers joined the CSU affiliate in the late summer of 1939, they did so because of the desperation of their plight. At issue was union recognition and badly needed improvements in salary and working conditions.[5] On 23 October 1939 Pat Sullivan arrived in Lockeport to take charge of the lockout.

After addressing union members, Sullivan, Murray, and local leaders headed to Halifax to meet with Premier Angus MacDonald. This meeting, which took place on 25 October, did not go well. The premier wanted to know whether the CSU interest in the fishermen of Lockeport was prompted by a desire to improve the conditions of the men or to advance the cause of the Communist party. This question would have been proper enough had there been any evidence that the strike was politically motivated. There was none. The dispute was a classic example of employer intimidation of employees attempting to exercise statutory rights. Nevertheless, the premier, convinced that the CSU leadership was interested in furthering Communist party goals, sent the deputy minister of labour to Lockeport to mediate the dispute rather than deal with the real issue before him – the refusal of the two fish plants to bargain in good faith with the union.[6]

Back in Lockeport, the fishermen and fishhandlers set up picket lines to prevent produce stored at either plant from being removed. In early November the deputy minister of labour arrived but was unsuccessful in his attempt to resolve the dispute. The companies were prepared to keep the workers locked out indefinitely and had the economic resources to do it. However, on 9 November 1939 the union bought an old unused Lockeport fish plant and called on the community for its support to turn the fish plant into a co-operative. By 14 November ships were sailing and fish was being processed. Steelworkers and miners in Cape Breton promised to buy the fish, which also found markets through unions in the Annapolis Valley, elsewhere in Canada, and in the United States. The federal government dispatched E.M.McG. Quirk to Lockeport to mediate the dispute, but the seasoned conciliator quickly realized that neither party was prepared to budge and, after a few days, returned to Ottawa. An uneasy peace settled over the town.[7]

On 22 November the Town Council, dominated by councillors who owned interests in the two fishing plants, passed a resolution requesting the opinion of the provincial attorney general as to whether the picketing of the fish plants was lawful. J.H. MacQuarrie replied that it was not. Mr Locke, the mayor of the town and owner of one of the two plants, asked MacQuarrie for enough police to clear away the picketers. MacQuarrie agreed. Nova Scotia did not have its own provincial police force but utilized the services of the Royal Canadian Mounted Police. On 9 December MacQuarrie ordered the Mounties to assemble a force to dispatch to Lockeport.[8] On Sunday, 10 December, the two plants announced they would be reopening the next day, apparently with the assistance of strikebreakers, and the Mounties would be on hand to render assistance.[9]

Early the next morning over 700 men from Lockeport and the vicinity assembled on the railway tracks leading to one of the Lockeport plants. The company plan was to bring a train into its yard, load it with stored fish, and send it to market. The union was determined to prevent the train from entering the yard. Moments before the train was scheduled to arrive, a detachment of approximately fifty Mounties paraded down the track, two abreast, and ordered the picketers to disperse. They did not, and a melee ensued. The police were clearly outnumbered and, faced with the refusal of the townspeople to step aside, withdrew. That night further reinforcements arrived, but no further attempt was made to clear the picketers by force.[10]

The confrontation climaxed the eight-week-long dispute. The people of Lockeport were among the most conservative and law-abiding citizens in the country. On 14 December Premier MacDonald announced in Halifax that under the Nova Scotia Trade Union Act the picketers enjoyed no legal rights because their union had not applied for certification until after the lockout began. Certification means that a trade union has been recognized in law by a labour relations board as the statutory bargaining agent for a particular group of workers. Unions may also, to similar legal effect, be voluntarily recognized by an employer. It was common in Nova Scotia for unions not to obtain certification, but the news from the premier that their union was 'illegal' disheartened the Lockeport workers. At a meeting convened that day, union representatives agreed in principle to a settlement of the dispute. [11]

That settlement provided for an immediate end to the picketing and a return to work. The two companies agreed to rehire all their former employees without discrimination and to recognize a fishhandlers' union. The union co-operative was shut down, the employees returned to work, and the detachment of Mounties was sent home. [12] In fact, the union activists were not rehired and the company refused to recognize the union. They did, however, recognize a union led by the five employees who had crossed the picket line during the dispute. It was an ignoble end to a noble struggle. [13] Before the dispute was finally settled, 5000 working days were lost [14] and critics charged that it had been engineered by the CSU to undermine the war effort. There is, however, no evidence that the Lockeport lockout was motivated by anything other than legitimate trade union considerations. Unfortunately, the same cannot be as assuredly said about the first seamen's strike of the war.

Sixty days before the two-year Great Lakes agreements signed in 1938 were due to expire, the CSU notified the contracted companies that the union intended to terminate the existing contract and negotiate a new one. The CSU was perfectly entitled to bargain for new agreements, as were the employers. There was nothing extraordinary or improper about the union's bargaining demands, which included a wage increase, the eight-hour day, additional manning on board most ships, a right to have a union representative appointed or elected from among the crew of each ship, a right of access to contracted ships by union representatives, and, most important of all, a hiring hall. [15]

The union expected that the contract negotiations would be with the same ad hoc employer's organization which negotiated the 1938 agreements. To its dismay it learned that the employers' organization had disbanded and that negotiations would take place with individual employers. [16] The companies stalled the negotiations and the contract expired without a successor being reached. The union was therefore legally obliged to have recourse to the compulsory conciliation provisions of the Industrial Disputes Investigation Act. However, as the 1940 shipping season was about to begin, the CSU feared that the opportunities for delay available under that act would enable the employers to force the union to submit to dictated terms or force the opening of the shipping season with its members deprived of the protection of a union agreement. Declaring that the labour law legislation was never intended to compel workers to become employed on terms to which they had not agreed,[17] Sullivan decided to call a strike. The CSU was advised by the Department of Labour that any strike would be illegal, but decided to go ahead. At midnight on 14 April, 6000 seamen left their jobs, tying up more than 200 ships.[18] Great Lakes shipping was paralysed.

The illegal walkout was marred by violence as shipping companies endeavoured to replace their striking crews. This resulted in the arrest of numerous CSU members including a union vice-president.[19] The CSU was ordered to end the strike, but only after the personal intervention of the minister of labour did the union instruct its members to return to their ships. An understanding was reached which provided for an immediate wage increase of $7.50 a month and reference of all other outstanding matters to a Board of Investigation and Conciliation, as provided for in the Industrial Disputes Investigation Act.[20] A tripartite board was convened under Justice C.P. McTague. Two lawyers, F. Wilkinson and J.L. Cohen, were appointed to the board, representing the employer and union interests, respectively.

The board held prolonged hearings and on 26 June issued an interim report. While the report was extremely favourable to the union, it ignored the institution of a hiring hall. It did, however, recommend that most of the other CSU demands be met. It urged the employers to recognize the CSU as the sole bargaining agent for all unlicensed seamen, preferentially hire CSU members, raise wages, increase the number of seamen on board each ship and thereby decrease the workload, acknowledge the right of the union to have a representative appointed or elected from each crew, and allow a union staff officer to board contracted ships while they were in port.[21] The report also recommended that a Maritime Adjustment Board comprising a union representative, an employer's representative, and a representative of the minister of labour be established to settle future grievances. Pending issue of a final report, it was suggested that a contract incorporating these terms and running until 15 March 1942 be signed.[22]

The bitterest pill for the companies to swallow in this non-compulsory conciliation board report was recognition of the right of an outside union representative to board ship to see to union matters. From the CSU's point of view, this provision was indispensable. Only through representatives with reasonably unrestricted access to contracted ships could the union properly represent its members. Despite their displeasure with this recommendation, a number of shipping companies immediately signed contracts with the CSU, incorporating the bulk of the McTague Report.[23]

All things considered, the report was a fair compromise and probably came close to approximating what the parties would have achieved by vigorous collective bargaining, had it taken place. The recommendations in the report were not, however, compulsory. According to the theory of the Industrial Disputes Investigation Act, these non-binding reports were to have a strong persuasive effect on the parties, who would feel morally bound to implement their terms. The theory, however, differed considerably from the practice.

N.M. Paterson and Sons did not sign with the CSU until the end of the shipping season, while some companies, particularly those in the Misener organization, completely ignored the report.[24] At the end of January 1941 McTague published a final report and recommended that those ten companies which had not yet recognized and concluded agreements with the CSU do so immediately. Five of the recalcitrant companies complied; the other five refused. The CSU was then lawfully entitled to strike those companies with which it was unable to conclude an agreement, and it did so beginning on 11 April 1941. The union claimed one strike goal: to effect the recommendations of the McTague Report.

The strike affected the operation of some fifty ships employing approximately 600 seamen, only a small part of the Great Lakes fleet. Captain Scott Misener asked the minister of labour to declare the CSU 'subversive' and 'illegal.' The minister rejected the request and, to his credit, said that there was only one person to blame for the strike: Captain Misener. However, after less than a week, the strike fizzled out and died. Contracts were not signed with the hold-outs.[25] Misener's open contempt for the McTague Report demonstrated the urgent need for reform of the Industrial Disputes Investigation Act. It allowed Misener to flout its provisions with impunity and entitled the CSU to go on strike at a time of grave national peril.

At the very time that Hitler was conquering Europe, Canadian Great Lakes shipping was in chaos. Canada's overseas allies depended on her for vital war supplies and viewed with concern the disruption in shipping. The opposition of the Communist Party of Canada to the war had already manifested itself in numerous ways and the seamen's strike was seen as just another attempt to thwart the allied war effort. There are good reasons for believing that this was the case.[26] Beginning in September

1939 the Mounties placed the top CSU leadership under surveillance.[27] Within months the RCMP confirmed that the union's leaders, but not most union members, belonged to the Communist party. Undercover agents reported at different times throughout 1939 and 1940 that the Communist party planned to use the Great Lakes ships to smuggle in banned literature from the United States, and, more importantly, that seamen who were Communist party members had been instructed to relay timetable, destination, and cargo information to the party leadership.[28] This intelligence was extremely alarming; a handful of strategically placed Communist sailors would enjoy incredible opportunities to commit espionage and sabotage. On the eve of the 1940 strike an undercover agent reported to the RCMP commissioner that the strike was regarded by the Communist party leadership as a 'trial balloon.' If it succeeded, the party planned to launch a wave of strikes through the unions it controlled.[29]

It is virtually certain that the minister of labour or his deputy received a copy of this report,[30] explaining in part the alacrity with which the government responded to the walkout. Fortunately, the strike quickly fizzled out and shipments were only briefly delayed. Other than passing legislation ordering the seamen back to work, there was little the government could have done. It was not illegal in April or May 1940 to be a member of the Communist party, and the undercover evidence gathered by the RCMP was probably insufficient to support any criminal charges. That situation changed, however, in June 1940 when the government decided that the existence and activities of the Communist party had become inimical to the national interest. Accordingly, the Communist party, along with various fascist groups, was banned by order-in-council. Overnight, membership in the Communist party became illegal and leading party members were rounded up and interned. Among them was Pat Sullivan, the president of the CSU.

On 19 June 1940 Sullivan was taken into custody. Along with everyone else picked up after the Communist party was banned, he was detained under the Defence of Canada Regulations, number 21. Regulation 21 entitled the minister of justice, on the advice of the police, to order the arrest and internment of an individual deemed dangerous to national security. An interned individual could object to a special advisory committee and receive reasons for his arrest, but while the committee was empowered to recommend to the minister of justice that an internee be released, the minister was under no obligation to accept the recommendation. These regulations were an extraordinary infringement on the civil rights of an individual, and would have been intolerable had the country not been at war.

After an unsuccessful legal challenge to Sullivan's arrest,[31] CSU legal counsel J.L. Cohen appeared, along with Sullivan, before an advisory committee constituted according to the regulations. The seamen's leader testified, under oath, that he was not a Communist and swore that since the formation of the CSU in 1936 his activities had been devoted solely to the advancement of the labour relations interests of the union and its members.[32] The government saw things somewhat differently. Prior to the hearing, Cohen was advised that Sullivan had been arrested because in 1935–6 he had been on the payroll of the Communist party and in 1937–8 had attended Communist party meetings and discussed CSU affairs. When the hearing was convened, Sullivan was further advised that the arrest had been ordered, in part, because of the 1938 *Damia* strike and blockade of the Cornwall canal. It was not illegal to have been a member of the Communist party before June 1940, or to be on its payroll. But these facts, along with the *Damia* incident, were enough to satisfy the committee that the minister of justice had not acted improperly in ordering Sullivan's detention. The committee did not, therefore, recommend to the minister that Sullivan be released.

Sullivan was one of several Communist CSU officers placed in internment. Cohen claimed that these men had been arrested because they were unionists, not because they were Communists, and he attempted to turn their internments into a cause célèbre.[33] Cohen argued that Sullivan's arrest in June, just as the McTague Board was emerging from the first stage of public hearings, was not, as the Department of Justice asserted, a coincidence,[34] but was instead an untoward manipulation of the Defence of Canada Regulations to assist the shipping companies at a crucial moment. This conclusion was later reinforced, in Cohen's partisan opinion, by the nature of Sullivan's examination before the advisory committee when he was interrogated about a wide range of union activity.[35] There is not, however, any evidence to substantiate this charge, one which could only be made because these internees were both unionists and Communists. The minister of justice, Ernest Lapointe, understood the distinction. Rising in the House of Commons in February 1941, Lapointe stated that some people who were members of a trade union had been interned, not because they were trade unionists, but because they were Communists.[36] Why, he later asked, should a Communist be given immunity merely because he was a member of a trade union?[37] Organized labour did not disagree.

The president of the TLC, Tom Moore, wrote to Cohen that he was satisfied that Sullivan was detained because of the evidence accumulated against him, not because of his union activities.[38] Indeed, there was no evidence that Sullivan's activities as a trade unionist had anything to do with his arrest. It was concern over his past, present, and future activities as a Communist which precipitated the decision to detain him. The timing of the arrest was perhaps unfortunate. But even so, it had absolutely no effect on the McTague Report, which generally favoured the union. The public, moreover, never became interested in the arrests.[39]

Sullivan was interned at a special camp near Petawawa, Ontario. Conditions at Petawawa were good, and most of the Communist inmates eventually became resigned to their fate; that is, until the Soviet Union was invaded by Hitler on 22 June 1941. The Nazi attack caused a re-evaluation of Communist opposition to the war and the internees, and their supporters, renewed their campaign to obtain release in order to assist the government in the prosecution of the war. This sudden burst of support was attributable to patriotism, albeit not to Canada, but to the Soviet Union. In January 1942 Sullivan and fellow CSU executive member Jack Chapman worked out a plan to mobilize the shipping industry and get seamen behind the war effort. As anticipated, this plan did not go unnoticed, and two months later the CSU officers were released.[40]

Sullivan moved quickly to make up for lost time. He was still president of the CSU,[41] and at the 58th TLC convention held in Winnipeg in August 1942 he outlined his 'Victory Program for Shipping.' This plan had been shared earlier with the minister of munitions and supply, C.D. Howe, and the minister of labour, Humphrey Mitchell. It was ostensibly intended to maximize the contribution of the shipping industry and of merchant seamen to the war effort. Actually, the plan was an ill-conceived, hastily constructed program intended to improve an industry which, in fact, was operating quite well. The plan looked and sounded good, but with one major exception, there was not much to it. That exception, however, was a significant one: the CSU made a no-strike pledge which it honoured throughout the rest of the war.[42]

In Canada, during the Second World War, the two major labour congresses adopted different positions on the use of strikes. The TLC, which supported the governing Liberal party, was in favour of a no-strike pledge and at its 1942 convention urged its affiliates to make similar pledges which, by and large, they did. In contrast, the CCL did not adopt a no-strike pledge. The leadership of the CCL, which largely supported the Co-operative Commonwealth Federation, believed that such a pledge was contrary to labour's true interests in light of the wage-control system imposed by the federal government.[43]

For its part, the TLC was assisted in arriving at its decisions by the lobbying efforts of its Communist party–directed affiliates. The Communist Party of Canada also supported the Liberal party and encouraged the government to accelerate military and economic assistance to the Soviet Union. In this context, the Communist party now discouraged strikes and other labour disputes and encouraged full support by organized labour for the war effort. The CSU followed the Communist party line, and its no-strike pledge, made at the beginning of the 1942 convention, paid off handsomely. Forgetting about the 1940 seamen's strike when the war was still 'imperialist,' the delegates to the 1942 TLC convention elected Sullivan, after considerable manoeuvring by Communist party members, as national vice-president. Communists were clearly no longer pariahs. Indeed, just one month later, Sullivan and the premier of Ontario, Mitch Hepburn, shared a platform at a rally at Maple Leaf Gardens welcoming Soviet war heroes.

The prospect of a known Communist sitting for the first time ever on the national executive of the TLC was not unanimously welcomed. Arthur D'Aoust, who was re-elected secretary-treasurer by the same convention which elected Sullivan vice-president, soon resigned, refusing to sit on the same executive board as a Communist. Percy Bengough, the acting president of the TLC, asked Sullivan to take over the vacant position. After consulting with Communist party leadership in Toronto, Sullivan accepted the position and moved to Ottawa.[44]

The position of secretary-treasurer was the second most powerful in the TLC. If Sullivan wanted to keep it, he had to win it at the next convention. To do so, he needed more votes than those controlled by the Communist party. A group of representatives of AFL international unions operating in Canada and affiliated with the TLC learned that Sullivan was to be a candidate and arranged a meeting with him to discuss the concerns his candidacy raised. Whose interests, they wanted to know, would come first, those of the Communist party or those of organized labour? Sullivan assured the AFL representatives, known as Roadmen, that during his tenure the interests of labour would be paramount. The Roadmen believed him, and at the 1943 TLC convention Sullivan was elected. Members of the Communist party were overjoyed. In his powerful position, Sullivan was able to direct the affairs of the convention and the congress in a way which would have been unimaginable just a few years earlier.[45] From the CSU's perspective, these developments were perfectly timed.

The hundreds of merchant ships ordered by the government at the beginning of the war were now coming into service. The CSU wished to establish itself as the bargaining representative of the crews who would be hired to sail them. Sullivan's position as president of the CSU and second-in-command of the TLC gave him an entree to government which he would not have otherwise enjoyed. In November 1943 the Park Steamship Company signed a collective labour agreement with the CSU. The ships of this merchant marine were operated by private companies, but these companies were obligated by their agreement with the Park Steamship Company to adhere to the terms of the CSU contract. The terms were attractive.

The eight-hour day was one term of the contract, as was the right, for the first time ever, of an elected crew member during a deep-sea voyage to present grievances to the captain. This latter provision represented a significant advance in the law of the sea as it recognized that workers on board a ship were entitled to the expeditious resolution of their work-related disputes.[46] The union, in return, formally gave up the right to strike. Terms and conditions of an employment contract are not, however, everything; the job itself is important and work on board these merchant ships, named after Canadian parks, was both difficult and dangerous.

Two classes of 'Parks' were built: 10,000 tonners and 4700 tonners. Most were steam rather than diesel powered because steam engines could be built quickly in large numbers and required less experienced crews to operate. The steam was generated with coal and only a few ships were equipped with a powered force-feed. Without it, the engines were fed by hand and a large crew was required to do the feeding. Sailors found the ships poorly designed. The crew's quarters were aft rather than amidship, making for a bumpy ride. The galleys were inadequately planned and the food, always of great importance during long voyages, was poor because of insufficient refrigerated space.[47] These ships had been built quickly to meet an international emergency and this was reflected in their design.

Unlike their counterparts on the lake boats, the officers and mates of the deep-sea fleet had not, by and large, worked their way up through the ranks.[48] Officers largely came from the United Kingdom, and it was widely rumoured among sailors that they were third-rate, unwanted at home and exiled to Canada. Canadian sailors also found that these British officers had a severe concept of discipline and, to exacerbate the situation, it was based on class and caste.[49] Furthermore, the Parks, like all allied ocean-going ships, were constantly subjected to enemy attack, and the lives of the crews were often in jeopardy. Life on board the Parks was clearly not enjoyable. But these sailors had certain advantages and benefits not available to the seamen on board the Great Lakes ships.

Foremost among them were the manning pools, established by government order in 1941.[50] Set up in key ports, the pools provided seamen with a home away from home. Medically fit seamen and recruits were offered the basic pay of their rank, along with full board and lodging, provided they agreed to accept assignments on ocean-going ships as directed. The benefits to both the sailors and the shipping companies were obvious; a reserve of seamen was always available and ready to sail at a moment's notice.[51] The government also established training schools in Hubbards, Nova Scotia, and Prescott, Ontario. For its merchant seamen, it appeared there was no need the authorities would not meet. The same was not as true with respect to the needs of organized labour.

At the start of the war, the government emphasized industrial peace rather than employee freedoms. It attempted to be an impartial umpire, reconciling the competing interests of labour and management. But that approach could no longer work. In just a few short years, Canada became highly industrialized with more unionized workers than ever before. The existing system proved itself totally incapable of responding to the changes taking place in society. The government was refereeing a game without rules, and management, as the CSU had seen on more than one occasion, was not under any legal obligation to play. Employers took every advantage of this situation, and labour-related disputes multiplied.[52]

Labour wanted enforceable rights, and it made known its readiness to fight for them. Although the TLC made a no-strike pledge, it demanded that organized labour's legitimate place in society be recognized. The government, well aware of the tremendous contribution organized labour was making to the prosecution of the war, was persuaded to agree. Beginning in June 1940 Ottawa, through a series of orders-in-council, set in motion a process which slowly but surely reformed the industrial relations system. In February 1944 a Bill of Rights for labour embodied in Privy Council Order 1003 was passed. This order climaxed what had turned out to be a four-year period of reform. It declared, for the first time, that workers had a legal right to join a union and to bargain collectively. It established a labour relations board to govern the exercise of this right, and recognized and prohibited certain unfair labour practices of both employers and unions.[53] The legitimacy of collective bargaining in Canadian society had been entrenched.

Few unions benefited more by these changes than the CSU. They gave the CSU some legal muscle in its dealings with employers, which complemented its greatly increased numerical strength. The CSU was the only union recognized by the Park Steamship Company to represent unlicensed seamen on its ships, and almost the entire Great Lakes fleet was under CSU contract. A new two-year Great Lakes agreement was reached without any problems in 1943.[54] Pat Sullivan, just a few years after his internment, had become one of the most powerful and influential union leaders in the country. The union had never been stronger, or more respected. The only dark spot on the horizon was a simmering conflict with the leadership of the AFL and its seamen's union, the SIU.

In 1944 Sullivan and Ferguson were invited to the SIU convention in New Orleans and asked to give an accounting of the activities of their union. The SIU leaders had learned that the CSU was dominated by the Communist party, a situation the anti-Communist leaders of the SIU would not tolerate. Sullivan and Ferguson were not treated as brother unionists, but as subordinates. The two men were given a list of demands and were ordered to implement them immediately. In brief, the SIU told the CSU to begin paying per capita tax and to denounce the Communist party as a dual and hostile political organization which was detrimental to the union movement. Sullivan feigned agreement with these demands, but asked for time to bring them before the executive of the CSU.[55]

The CSU executive had no intention of giving effect to any of these orders, and in due course so informed the SIU. The consequences were predictable enough but the CSU no longer cared. The CSU had affiliated with the International Seamen's Union only to ensure affiliation with the TLC. With Sullivan as TLC secretary-treasurer, the CSU's place in that congress could not have been more secure. The CSU had also come to be listed with the TLC as a national union. As such, it was not subject to the control of any organization other than the congress.[56] As expected, the SIU revoked the CSU affiliation and launched a campaign to expel the CSU from the TLC and its district councils. A widely distributed open letter from SIU president Harry Lundeberg explained why the CSU had been disaffiliated and called upon TLC affiliates, particularly the AFL international unions, to give support. At the November 1944 AFL Convention a resolution was passed providing that the SIU had jurisdiction over Canadian seamen and declaring the CSU a dual and hostile organization. The AFL had no legal right to give any union jurisdiction over seamen in Canada; the TLC had already done so. The resolution was passed in any event. It was further resolved that the TLC and its affiliates should cease to recognize the CSU and begin to recognize the SIU.[57]

TLC representatives, both at the local and national levels, were perturbed by the SIU–AFL intrusion. The president of the TLC, Percy Bengough, wrote AFL president William Green and stated simply that it would be ridiculous to expel the many-thousand member strong CSU to seat the SIU, whose representation in Canada was limited to a local with 300 members on the west coast. Bengough wanted to know why the TLC should take in this 'corporal's guard' which had never bothered to affiliate itself with the TLC.[58] 'From the day they were chartered by this Congress,' the TLC president wrote, 'the CSU has loyally supported the principles and policies of this Congress and has done a creditable job in organizing and improving the standard of living of Canadian seamen.'[59] Bengough was personally incensed by the actions of both the SIU and the AFL. Vilifying an affiliated union and an officer of the congress was not only impudent, but was, according to the TLC president, no way to build friendly relations.[60] The Americans did not get the message and Lundeberg formally requested SIU affiliation in July 1945.[61] The request was denied. Bengough advised the SIU to turn its Canadian membership over to the CSU and try to work out some basis for co-operating with that union.[62] The SIU refused and the controversy quieted down. It was the most serious dispute between the AFL and TLC in years. Soon enough it would return.

3
The Great Lakes Strike of 1946

Any problems created by the falling-out between the CSU and the SIU were quickly forgotten at the end of the war. Other more pressing matters demanded attention. The war years had been a period of great gain but enormous sacrifice for most Canadian workers. Great Lakes sailors, in particular, had sacrificed more than they had gained. Their wages had improved considerably since 1939, but they still worked a twelve-hour day. Attempts made during the war to negotiate an agreement with the Great Lakes shipping companies, providing that six months after the war's end the eight-hour day would be voluntarily introduced, had failed. The companies were well aware that the CSU had made a no-strike pledge and they had no reason to agree to this proposal. The no-strike pledge lapsed in August 1945 when Japan surrendered, and the CSU put the shipping companies on notice that the eight-hour day, fifty-six-hour week could no longer wait.

The two-year 1944 contract was set to expire at the end of July 1946. Negotiations for a new contract began in 1945 between the CSU and the Dominion Marine Association, the organization of Great Lakes shipping companies which generally confined its activities to lobbying on behalf of its members. Occasionally the association became involved with labour relations and, in this set of negotiations, it acted as the bargaining representative of almost all the Great Lakes shipping companies. Talks held in the spring and fall were fruitless, and the parties agreed to adjourn negotiations until the new year. In the meantime, the CSU held a convention and delegates voted 'unanimously' in favour of the executive calling a strike if the shipping companies did not agree to the eight-hour day or if the government did not impose it by law.[1] The Communist party remained firmly in control. Of the almost one hundred delegates in attendance, approximately thirty were party members.[2]

A number of resolutions were also passed by the convention delegates.

One of these resolutions declared that CSU-manned ships should not carry arms to support what it termed Dutch imperialism in Java.[3] Harry Davis, a well-known Communist party member from Montreal who had spent little, if any, time at sea, was elected acting president.[4] Other party members, including a number of recruits, were also elected to the executive.[5]

When the negotiations with the shipping companies resumed in the late winter, the Dominion Marine Association took the position that the companies could not afford to pay the increase in wages an eight-hour day entailed. Extra sailors not only meant higher labour costs, but required, on most ships, expensive modifications to the crew's quarters, leaving less space for cargo.[6] Other union demands, including wage increases, overtime, and holiday pay, were likewise out of the question. The shipping companies made an offer which did not address the CSU demands, and the union withdrew from the talks.[7]

Under the collective bargaining regime established by Privy Council Order 1003, the union's refusal to negotiate and its subsequent scheduling of a strike vote were probably unlawful as an abrogation of the duty to bargain in good faith. Legally, the union was obliged to apply for the appointment of a Board of Conciliation which would then have held hearings and issued a non-binding report. The CSU's experience with this process, even when favourable to the union, was frustrating; and union officials had no intention of leaving what was an uncompromisable issue to the non-binding recommendation of a conciliation board. Only a strike, legal or not, could resolve the matter one way or the other.

For the first time ever, the CSU could count on public support. The union's slogan during the war, 'We deliver the goods,' had proved correct. Rank-and-file seamen were the object of public respect and gratitude.[8] The demand for an eight-hour day was also one which attracted government support. It was long overdue. Minister of Labour Mitchell met with Dominion Marine Association representatives in March 1946 and told them he could not countenance the twelve-hour day. Few members of parliament could, and it was pointed out in the House of Commons that American shipping companies had accepted the eight-hour day for some years. By and large, the government favoured the eight-hour day as it promoted employment which contributed to federal postwar reconstruction. However, Mitchell announced that he was not prepared to legislate an eight-hour day for Canadian seamen. Immediately, the CSU held a strike vote and on 15 April the membership voted overwhelmingly in favour of going on strike. Unless its demands were met, a strike would start on 3 June 1946.[9]

The Dominion Marine Association did not have much experience in labour relations but it knew how to run an advertising campaign. In an attempt to attract public support, advertisements were placed in most major newspapers setting out the 'facts' of the dispute. According to the association, few workers had it better than the seamen who worked the Great Lakes ships. President George Donovan told the *Globe and Mail* that working twelve hours a day on board a ship was different from working twelve hours in a factory. The difference, he explained, was that a ship was like a 'home.'[10] The CSU complained bitterly about this and other advertisements which it considered misleading.[11]

It appeared that the CSU and the Dominion Marine Association were deadlocked and nothing could prevent the strike. Then, in late May, a small number of shipping companies offered to accept the principle of an eight-hour day, fifty-six-hour week, along with a small salary increase. But the CSU would not settle for the 'principle' of the eight-hour day, particularly as it did not stipulate the method by which the eight hours worked would be spread over a twenty-four hour period. The offer was rejected.[12]

Events accelerated on 24 May when the captain of the Canada Steamship Lines vessel *City of Montreal* refused a CSU official, who wished to conduct union business, permission to board. As soon as the CSU crew learned what had happened they gathered their belongings and left the ship, ostensibly 'to attend a prayer meeting.' The captain hired some non-union men and took steps to have his former sailors arrested as deserters.[13] Nothing could stop the strike now and two days later, on 26 May, CSU members up and down the lakes went on strike, shutting down inland shipping. Almost immediately reports of violence began to circulate as a number of shipping companies attempted to replace their striking workers with strikebreakers. In one particularly bloody episode early in June a number of companies tried to free some of their ships in the Cornwall area from CSU pickets. A special trainload carrying more than 600 strikebreakers was sent from Montreal and, expecting the worst, Canadian army Colonel R.E.A. Morton readied his troops to move in if necessary. Fighting did break out, but never to the extent that the troops were required. The Dominion Marine Association began another series of advertisements. 'The real issue,' the association said, was not the eight-hour day but 'law or lawlessness.'[14]

That was certainly true, but, like the earlier advertisements, it told only part of the story.[15] Allegations persist, and indeed among former CSU members it has become legendary that the Royal Canadian Mounted Police, Ontario and Quebec provincial police, and the Canadian National

Railway Police were all heavily involved in the strike, providing protection and other services to strikebreakers.[16] That there were strikebreakers is undeniable. Mitchell told the House of Commons, midway through the dispute, that he was not aware of any instance in which the National Employment Service provided strikebreakers. But, he continued, if a company requested a worker, the service would pass the request on to available and interested men.[17] This was an astonishing statement for Mitchell to have made. Before entering Parliament, he was an active trade unionist, and if there is anything inimical to the labour movement it is strikebreaking. The minister of labour perhaps revealed his real feelings several days later when he said that the 'communist crowd' in Canada did not want strikes to settle. He went on to say that if 'they' wanted a battle, 'well, the battle is on.'[18] Mitchell was generally right that the Communist party, in yet another policy reversal, no longer wanted strikes to settle. But he was wrong in this case. Two days after his statement the Department of Labour proposed a formula for settling the strike which was immediately accepted by the CSU.[19] The proposal called for the rehiring by the companies of all the striking workers except those convicted of criminal charges arising out of the strike. It was further provided that the institution of the eight-hour day would be referred to the Labour Relations Board and, in the interim, certain minimum numbers of sailors, depending on the ship, would be hired. All other outstanding matters were to be referred to conciliation. On 18 June almost all of the shipping companies represented by the Dominion Marine Association rejected the proposal.[20]

Shipping had now been tied up for three weeks. It was clear that only the government could end the dispute and, as had been rumoured for over a week,[21] it decided to do so. Under the authority of the National Emergency Transitional Powers Act, the Privy Council passed Order 2556 and took over all Great Lakes shipping. Captain Eric S. Brand was appointed controller of shipping. In effect, Brand was given legal control over the inland shipping companies. Although the owners and managers could continue to operate their enterprises, they were now to do so under Brand's general direction and control.

The government of Canada usually legislates striking workers back to work if it decides that a strike is detrimental to the public interest. Placing a private company under controllership, especially during peacetime, is rare. However, there was considerable government regulation of the economy both during and after the war. In the war years the purpose of the regulation was to mobilize resources behind the war effort. After the surrender of Germany and Japan, the objective of the regulatory effort

became the promotion of employment and the curbing of inflation. A prolonged shipping strike would be detrimental to these goals, particularly
where the main object of the strike, the eight-hour day, was itself seen as
instrumental to the success of the government's postwar economic efforts.
The controllership was announced in the House of Commons on 21 June
and the shipping companies were informed that as of 9:00 AM, 24 June,
Captain Brand was in charge. [22]

Also announced was the appointment of the Honourable Mr Justice
S.E. Richards of the Manitoba Court of Appeal as a commissioner to
investigate and conciliate during the controllership. It was now official
government policy that there be an eight-hour day for Great Lakes seamen, and the Labour Relations Board soon issued a 'Finding and Direction' so declaring. Of the major shipping companies, only the Upper
Lakes and St Lawrence Transportation Company and the Quebec and
Ontario Transportation Company were unaffected by the appointment of
the controller of shipping. Both of these lines had earlier accepted the
Department of Labour proposal and signed memoranda of understanding
to that effect with the CSU. Their ships began sailing the day the controllership was announced. [23]

Brand, a former British navy officer, served with the Royal Canadian
Navy during the war. In Naval Intelligence, he became fully acquainted
with merchant shipping; his responsibilities included scheduling merchant convoys. After his appointment as controller, Brand made a broadcast on national radio in which he asked for the co-operation of all parties
and ordered the striking seamen back to work. Within days he had moved
to Toronto and established a general headquarters. [24]

Shipping was in serious disarray following the twenty-eight-day strike.
Over 2500 seamen had walked off or been locked out of more than 150
ships. Altogether, 45,000 working days had been lost. Countless seamen
had been arrested – a few under the Criminal Code for various picket-line
offences, most with desertion under the Canada Shipping Act – revealing
once again the severity and inapplicability of that statute to an industrial
dispute. [25] A number of companies also took advantage of another provision of the Canada Shipping Act which entitled them to turn over all the
wages owing to a 'deserter' to the receiver general of Canada. [26]

Captain Brand looked upon the numerous outstanding charges with
great concern. First of all, they made the industry look lawless. In fact,
virtually all of the charges were the result of private prosecutions initiated
by various shipping companies. Brand wished to restore peace to the
industry and, as much as possible, foster a sense of goodwill. For three
weeks he attempted to persuade the companies which had laid the deser-

tion charges to withdraw them, releasing to the sailors any monies owing. The companies involved refused to comply with the request, failing to realize that if they did not withdraw the charges, Brand, exercising his wide powers as controller, would do it for them. This is exactly what took place and, by the middle of July, the majority of the 'deserters' received their withheld pay. To Brand's regret, what could have been a concilia-tory gesture caused further bad feelings.[27] These were not the only ones.

On 27 June Captain Reoch, then the operating manager of Canada Steamship Lines, and Captain Misener requested to see Brand 'alone.' The controller refused and told the two men that if they wanted to see him they were welcome to do so, but they could not dictate the terms. A meeting was held and, to Brand's utter astonishment, Reoch told him that 40 per cent of the men in his company belonged to Captain McMaster's National Seamen's Association. It was the policy of Canada Steamship Lines, Reoch explained, 'to do everything possible to remove the Cana-dian Seamen's Union from their position as bargaining agents for the men.'[28] For his part, Misener told Brand that he would not under any cir-cumstances sign a contract with the CSU.[29] Brand ordered them from his office. The next day he issued a general instruction to the effect that any man employed before 24 May who had returned to his ship on 24 June could not be discharged without his permission. Brand learned several days later that Canada Steamship Lines was not implementing this order. Concluding that the only way the company would obey the law was if forced to do so, Brand decided to take a drastic step.

On 6 July Captain J.E. Matheson was, by order-in-council, appointed deputy controller of shipping and sent to Montreal. Five days later he moved into the offices of Canada Steamship Lines, taking physical con-trol. With Matheson in place, Brand reasoned, his directions could be enforced. The difficulties with that company, however, still did not abate and Brand was forced to take further action. In co-operation with the Department of Labour, the controller arranged for fifteen additional inspectors to be assigned to Montreal, where they boarded each Canada Steamship Lines vessel and ensured that no members of the National Sea-men's Association were placed on board.[30] This task proved much easier than removing the strikebreakers who had made their way on board the ships during the strike. Both Canada Steamship Lines and the Misener companies were informed that all men hired contrary to Brand's instruc-tions were to be dismissed with seven days' notice. Both companies refused. Brand suspected that the two companies were stalling until 31 July, when the existing collective agreement with the CSU expired. What advantage, if any, this would have given the companies under controller-ship is unclear. Nevertheless, at the end of July another Privy Council order was passed giving the controller the authority to extend the terms of any collective agreement he wished.[31] By August, Canada Steamship Lines, presumably finally realizing that further resistance was pointless, agreed to hire according to the CSU preferential hiring clause. As a sign of his good faith, Brand removed the deputy controller from the Canada Steamship Lines offices.[32]

Meanwhile, Mr Justice Richards had been holding meetings with the Dominion Marine Association, the different shipping companies, and the CSU. In August 1946 he was able to issue an interim report containing a draft collective agreement which, as well as providing for the eight-hour day, was extremely favourable to the union.[33] The draft agreement also provided that 'all unlicensed personnel shall be hired through the offices of the union,' and 'the actual selecting and dismissal of seamen shall be at the discretion of the Master or Chief Engineer.'[34] What meaning these two contradictory provisions should be given caused a flurry of excitement for the union and great alarm in the offices of the deputy minister of labour and the different shipping companies which believed that this draft contract brought the industry to within one step of a union-run hiring hall, and that nothing could be worse than that.[35]

The Seamen's Section of the National Employment Service was strengthened on orders from Ottawa, and the shipping companies advised that seamen could be hired directly from the service. It was hoped that this government 'cushion' would prevent the establishment of a union hiring hall, as employers would turn to the National Employment Service for seamen. However, the practice quickly developed of turning to the CSU for sailors and, within a short time, the union-controlled hiring hall quietly came into being.[36] Most of the companies agreed to sign collective agreements along the lines of the one recommended in the Richards report, and Great Lakes shipping returned to an even keel, almost.[37]

On the morning of 26 August 1946 Reoch and Misener, joined by Captain McEwan of N.M. Paterson and Sons, held a private meeting in Toronto. Canada Steamship Lines, the Misener organization, and N.M. Paterson and Sons were the only companies left of any size which had not signed the new collective agreement (and were under no legal obligation to do so), although Canada Steamship Lines had agreed to implement its terms. That afternoon, representatives of these three companies presented national CSU secretary Gerry McManus with a contract which they had devised and which their companies were prepared to sign. Apparently, they also encouraged McManus to establish a new union and promised him financial support. Both the contract and payoff were rejected.[38]

The other shipping companies would not have tolerated the CSU making a backdoor and sweetheart deal with Canada Steamship Lines, the

Misener organization, and N.M. Paterson and Sons after they had signed agreements which fully implemented the terms of the Richards report. In attempting to bribe McManus the companies misjudged the CSU officer but, as later developments will show, not by much. The CSU asked for permission from the Labour Relations Board to prosecute the Misener companies and Canada Steamship Lines for their offering of a bribe. Consent was, however, refused because the application requesting it was out of time, and the board was of the view that no useful industrial relations purpose would be served by granting it.[39] The parties were once again at an impasse.

News of these developments reached Brand, and further efforts to conciliate were made. Brand had the power to sign collective agreements on behalf of a company, but he preferred to exercise it as little as possible. After intensive talks, a compromise was reached. Instead of signing a contract, the CSU and these three companies executed and registered with the Department of Labour an undertaking to abide by the terms and conditions of the Richards report. The undertaking was not an enforceable collective agreement and differed in two fundamental respects from the contract reached with the other shipping companies: it provided that the companies would only be required to recognize the CSU for the 1948 shipping season if the union won a government-supervised representation vote, and that the company involved was under no obligation to dismiss any unlicensed crew member who refused to pay union dues.[40] It was obvious to Brand and the CSU leaders that this undertaking not only embodied inferior terms but was itself a potential source of future disruption in the shipping industry. Nevertheless, it brought immediate peace and, not long after this settlement was reached, the Privy Council order establishing the controllership was revoked and Brand's duties, performed at all times with honour and dispatch, came to an end.

The episode came close to exhausting the union financially. At the end of the strike it was more than $10,000 in debt.[41] This explains, perhaps, why the union officers agreed to execute undertakings with the Department of Labour rather than holding out for a real collective agreement. Like the Lockeport lockout, the 1946 strike was as just a strike as organized labour can have. It is possible that the Communist party supported it for its own purposes; shipments of grain and other supplies urgently needed in Europe were delayed while European Communists consolidated their positions. But there is absolutely no evidence, in the RCMP Papers or elsewhere, that the Communist party instigated the dispute. For all intents and purposes it was a real trade union strike, and it was one which made CSU members proud of their union and confident about its future.

4
Communist Revelations and Repercussions

One month before the 1947 navigation season opened, the CSU was dealt a blow so serious and unexpected that it was never able fully to recover. In the middle of March, Pat Sullivan called a press conference and confessed his longstanding and long-denied membership in the Communist Party of Canada, by now renamed the Labour Progressive party. With considerable detail, and in classic cold-war rhetoric, Sullivan outlined to a startled country the extent to which the Communist party had infiltrated the labour movement in general and the CSU in particular. Sullivan's renunciation of the Communist party, coming not long after Igor Gouzenko's defection and revelations about the existence of a Soviet spy ring in Canada, created a sensation. The press and the union's enemies had a field day. The TLC advised seamen to change their skipper and the rest of their officers if they wished, but not to desert the ship. Joe Salsberg, who was by 1947 a Labour Progressive party member of the Ontario Legislature, said 'good bye to bad rubbish' and, soon enough, Sullivan was expelled from union membership. Sullivan, who some CSU members claimed had been bribed by the RCMP, formed a new union, the Canadian Lake Seamen's Union, and affiliated it with a minor Quebec labour congress. He then tried to raid CSU members.[1]

When the 1947 shipping season opened a number of companies, led by the Misener organization, refused to allow union delegates to board their ships on the grounds that they were Communists. As was provided for in the undertaking registered with the Department of Labour, an arbitration board was convened to resolve the dispute. The Misener companies refused to participate, but the board, chaired by the dean of Osgoode Hall Law School, Cecil Wright, proceeded in any event. The character of the union representatives was not, according to Dean Wright, a legitimate matter of company interest. Misener was ordered by the quasi-judicial Board of Arbitration to allow the CSU delegates to board his ships.[2] Having refused to participate in the arbitration process, however, Captain Misener had no intention of implementing the arbitration award and said as much. Indeed, the Misener companies, along with Canada Steamship Lines, had all but made an open declaration of war against the CSU. Captain Reoch wired Prime Minister King in July 1947 and requested that 'the entire communist executive of the CSU be removed from office and replaced by accredited representatives truly representative of seamen.'[3] The next day George Donovan of the Dominion Marine Association contacted Ottawa and asked for a government investigation of the CSU.[4]

The CSU was also pressing the government to take action: it demanded that Ottawa enforce Dean Wright's arbitration award. Following various representations from the CSU, labour minister Mitchell asked Leonard Brockington, a conciliation officer in the Department of Labour, to try to resolve the dispute. Brockington began work in July 1947 and on 22 August 1947 issued a report. There was nothing in the agreement reached with the CSU, Brockington wrote, which permitted a company to exercise any control over the selection of union delegates.[5] Misener now claimed to be prepared to come to an agreement with the CSU and in September a compromise was worked out. Misener agreed to allow the CSU delegates to board his ships provided they swore affidavits that they were not members of the Communist party. It was also agreed that the Misener companies would hold government-supervised certification votes among their unlicensed seamen to decide the issue of union representation and, if the CSU won these votes, the Misener companies would enter into real collective agreements with the union for the 1948 shipping season.

From the union perspective the compromise settlement was a voluntary abrogation of rights it had already won and enjoyed by law. Harry Davis, who had been appointed president of the CSU by the union's executive after Sullivan's departure, attempted to score some political points with an explanation that the union agreed to the deal in the national interest. According to Davis, by accepting the compromise the CSU prevented a strike and interference with both the Canadian economy and 'with shipments of foodstuffs and other necessities of life to the hard-pressed peoples of the British Isles and Europe.'[6] The more plausible explanation is that the CSU decided not to enforce its rights legally in order to avoid the calling of Sullivan as a witness in court.

Initially, it seemed that the union made the right choice. When the first government-supervised certification vote was taken in two Misener companies, Colonial Steamships and Sarnia Steamships, 297 of the 328 votes cast favoured continued CSU representation. But contrary to his agreement, Misener refused to negotiate a written collective agreement for the

1948 shipping season. The September 1947 compromise agreement turned out to be worthless.[7] The CSU had no better luck with Canada Steamship Lines. Unlike the situation with the Misener organization, the CSU had never bothered to obtain formal certification as the collective bargaining agent of the unlicensed employees of Canada Steamship Lines, and, after witnessing the enormous success on board the Misener ships, Canada Steamship Lines officials decided not to permit the certification vote to proceed. They refused to give the Department of Labour, which was in charge of conducting the vote, a list of employees eligible to participate.[8]

The Department of Labour could have acted aggressively, both to enforce the terms of the undertaking filed with it and to protect the process itself. Instead, it did nothing. The minister lamely justified his department's inaction by claiming that steps had been taken to hold a vote, but that these steps failed because the ships were on the move, it was late in the season, and the industry had a high turnover.[9] None of these 'reasons' had prevented the holding of certification votes in the past.

Canada Steamship Lines and the Misener companies had decided not to honour any of their agreements with the union. Not long after the CSU won its certification vote, the Misener companies reverted to their old ways and once again began to deny access to their ships to CSU delegates – even those producing sworn affidavits that they were not Communists.[10] But this was just a minor skirmish with the union. The real battle began on 27 October 1947 when the Misener organization and Canada Steamship Lines contacted the CSU and purported to terminate their legal relationship with the union.

That was something which they could not legally do. The Misener companies and Canada Steamship Lines were legally obliged at least to attempt to negotiate collective agreements with the CSU, and the Labour Relations Board said as much.[11] When the minister of labour appointed a Conciliation Board, however, the two companies refused to have anything to do with it. Instead, continuing their violation of the law, they announced that they had signed contracts with the new Sullivan-led union.[12] Canada Steamship Lines and the Misener organization also took legal action against the Conciliation Board and attempted to get a court to issue an order prohibiting it from continuing to sit. This legal move failed, but the board was forced to disband after it learned that the employee representative was, for technical reasons, ineligible. In the board's place, the minister of labour appointed two industrial disputes inquiry commissions: one to investigate the dispute between the union and Canada Steamship Lines, the other to investigate the CSU–Misener dispute. The Canada Steamship Lines–CSU commission reported in early

June 1948 and found that Canada Steamship Lines had acted in bad faith. With regret, the commissioners were, however, forced to conclude that Canada Steamships was not required by law to bargain with an uncertified bargaining agent.[13] This was a sorry conclusion considering that the CSU had been the voluntarily recognized representative of the employees of Canada Steamship Lines for over a decade. It was also a conclusion which the law should not have permitted and no longer does.

The Misener–CSU commission called the parties together in Toronto on 12 April 1948. Unlike the earlier attempt at conciliation, Captain Misener sent a representative to the proceedings but failed to give him any instructions. With the CSU's consent, the TLC also sent a representative and gave him specific and highly novel instructions: the congress was willing to enter into a contract itself with the Misener organization on behalf of the unlicensed seamen. If accepted, it enabled Misener to save face and obey the law, while at the same time it protected the bargaining rights of hundreds of seamen. But the plan came to naught. Misener rejected it, and the commissioners, Chairman Leonard Brockington and J.D. McNish, issued an interim report on 15 April.[14] They found that the Misener companies had broken the law, breached the 1946 undertaking filed with the Department of Labour, and violated the 1947 compromise agreement. It was, the report said, a deplorable situation. The commissioners sadly concluded that because of the intransigent attitude of the Misener companies there was nothing they could do.[15]

There was also very little the union could do other than concentrate its activity in a strike against the two companies. The strike began with considerable public support. 'Captain Misener's position is most unreasonable,' the *Globe and Mail* editorialized. 'It is not for him, or his fellow executives in the other companies to choose the union representatives of their employees, and certainly not their right to dictate the labour laws of this country.'[16] Violence broke out on numerous picket lines and it was hard to tell which side was more to blame. Canada Steamship Lines issued its officers revolvers, guns, and tear gas to fight the CSU. 'Any Commie rat who comes aboard our ships,' Reoch told the press, 'will get what they are looking for.'[17] Striking one or two companies is much harder than striking the entire industry and, in the end, both the Misener organization and Canada Steamship Lines were able to operate throughout the 1948 shipping season reasonably unhampered.[18]

The CSU appealed, repeatedly, to the Department of Labour for assistance. That department, however, declined to become involved. As far as Mitchell was concerned, he had done everything possible to bring about a resolution of the dispute and no more could be done.[19] Mitchell's claim was, in part, correct. The existing industrial relations legislation was still imbued with a high level of voluntarism and depended in large measure on the good will of both labour and management. When either party was forced to rely on its strict legal rights, the system broke down. There were legal remedies available to a party determined to enforce its rights but, when obtained, these remedies often inadequately redressed the wrong. The new Industrial Relations Disputes Investigation Act was not proclaimed until September 1948. By then, the real battle with Misener and Canada Steamship Lines was over. The government's handling of the entire affair was a disgrace.

The TLC must also shoulder some of the blame. The CSU had been a vehicle of the Communist Party of Canada. It had also been, with some exceptions, a strong militant trade union organization protecting and enhancing the rights of its members. The public exposition of the union's dual character presented its members with an opportunity to chart their unions' future course democratically. There was no way they could do that as long as the incumbent executive, comprised entirely of Communist party members, remained in charge. In these circumstances, the TLC should have taken action. It could have placed the CSU under trusteeship and, through supervised rank-and-file elections, turned it over to the control of its members. [20] The congress, however, failed to act, first in the fall of 1947 and later in 1948. TLC officers remained strong supporters of the union and its officers, and democratic elections were never held. Bengough, missing the point entirely, told the delegates at the union's February 1948 convention that as long as they kept their union in the hands of the membership, no 'boss would be able to put it out of business.' [21] The union was not in the hands of membership, nor had it ever been. It was also threatened more by the Communist party than by any employer, as was illustrated by the appointment of Harry Davis to the union presidency by other Communist party members of the executive. From that point on the uneasy balance within the union between its political and economic ends shifted in favour of the former. Indeed, the shift had already begun.

Just one month earlier, for example, not long after Misener and Canada Steamship Lines began to violate their agreements, the CSU violated one of its own. The union was contractually obligated to supply men from its hiring halls to deep-sea ships. However, when the captain of the SS *Islandside* requested a crew, the union refused to supply any men. The reason was clear. The *Islandside* was bound for China and carried arms to Chiang Kai Shek, to be used in the fight against the Communists. The CSU claimed at first that this had nothing to do with the refusal of sailors to man the ship, but later, realizing that this issue enjoyed no labour or public support, agreed to man the vessel provided that its crew was given life insurance for the 'dangerous' voyage.[22] In this political abuse of its contractual responsibility the CSU signalled not just to Misener and Canada Steamship Lines, but to the entire shipping industry, that it too was prepared to violate contracts and collective agreements whenever such action served its purpose.

After the Sullivan revelations and events of late 1947 and early 1948, the only way to save the CSU was for the TLC temporarily to take it over. TLC president Percy Bengough, however, continued to support the CSU's leaders, instead of taking radical steps on behalf of its members. Bengough's abdication of responsibility and the slow but unmistakable emergence of the CSU as an organization increasingly motivated by political rather than economic aims was, of course, noticed in the labour movement. In particular, the international unions operating in Canada believed that the time was right both to renew the AFL's earlier request that the SIU be admitted by the TLC into affiliation and to curb what they perceived to be nationalist tendencies among the TLC leadership. Frank Hall, the Canadian leader of the International Brotherhood of Railway and Steamship Clerks and a life-long anti-Communist, led the campaign. It began inauspiciously enough.

Hall clashed with the CSU in early 1948 over what might have been a misunderstanding between his union and the seamen's union at the Lakehead. Hall claimed that the CSU attempted to induce his members to go out on an illegal strike, and he was furious.[23] Soon enough he wrote TLC president Bengough and demanded action. After not getting a reply, Hall contacted the international president of his own union and suggested that steps be taken to encourage the SIU to come and take over its jurisdictional responsibilities in Canada. These responsibilities had been 'assigned' to the SIU by the AFL at its 1944 convention following the refusal of the CSU to come into line. So long as Pat Sullivan was Number Two man at the TLC and the CSU remained a respectable member of organized labour, it would have been foolhardy for the SIU to attempt to exercise its 'jurisdiction.' Sullivan was now gone and the CSU had fallen into disrepute. This was the opportunity the SIU had been waiting for.[24]

Early in August 1948 two SIU representatives arrived in Canada. After advising them of recent developments, Hall set up a meeting between them and Captains Reoch and Misener. Both Misener and Canada Steamship Lines were anxious to be free of the CSU and agreed to recognize the SIU as the bargaining agent of their men if it were able to take over the Sullivan-led Canadian Lakes Seamen's Union. It was obvious by this time that Sullivan's new union would never supplant the CSU. By taking over that union, with its existing contracts, the SIU would obtain an entry to the industry. While hardly a match made in heaven, it suited the immediate needs of the SIU and the two companies. It was a classic backdoor deal.[25]

On 1 September 1948 the merger of the Canadian Lakes Seamen's Union and the Seafarers' International Union was announced. It was a choice between a Communist union and a company union, Hall explained to the press, and 'we choose the lesser evil.' One of the terms of the merger was that Sullivan had to go.[26] The next day, representatives of the international unions operating in Canada met in Ottawa. Hall asked for their support. Rallying around the cause of American internationalism, the Internationals passed a resolution applauding Hall's work.[27]

Percy Bengough thereupon summoned a TLC Executive meeting, which passed two resolutions: the first stated that the CSU was the only bona fide union in Canada and that the SIU was dual; the second declared that Hall had violated the letter and spirit of the TLC Constitution, and expelled the International Brotherhood of Railway and Steamship Clerks from affiliation.[28] As far as Bengough was concerned, Hall's union, and any other affiliate, were welcome to fight Communist influence in the congress, or work towards the replacement of the CSU with the SIU, provided that the procedures in the constitution were observed. When they were not, the congress had no choice but to protect itself and its process.[29] For their part, Hall and the other members of his group charged that the TLC had gone adrift. It was moving, they said, away from its traditional international aspect and was attempting to transform itself into a national union movement and allying itself with Communists to do so. The TLC was warned that if it did not purge itself of Communists and co-operate with the Internationals, the Internationals would leave.[30] Both sides prepared to fight it out at the TLC convention scheduled just a few weeks away.

In the short time between the suspension and the convention, Frank Hall was able to enlist what appeared to be considerable support, particularly among the Internationals; the AFL ordered its paid representatives in Canada to support Hall and fight against the suspension of the International Brotherhood of Railway and Steamship Clerks.[31] At the convention, officials of the international unions voted, almost unanimously, against the actions of the TLC executive. The rank-and-file delegates, however, voted overwhelmingly in favour of the suspension, flabbergasting the Internationals. It also left them with little choice but to make good on their earlier threat and withdraw from the congress, which would likely have destroyed it. Fortunately, a compromise was worked out, whereby the suspension was lifted, Hall was censured, and a resolution was passed condemning Communism in the trade union movement. The CSU was not the only Communist-controlled union affiliated to the TLC, but it was obvious that it was being singled out.[32]

If anything, the convention was a stalemate, with neither side able to claim victory. The Internationals succeeded in obtaining the readmission of Hall's union to the congress, but failed, for the second time in just a few years over the same issue, to exercise their considerable muscle and bring the TLC into line. The defence of the CSU affiliate stood in marked contrast to the numerous occasions in the past when the TLC had invariably acquiesced to AFL instructions and implemented policies which TLC officers found both unwise and distasteful. The expulsion in 1939 of the CIO unions was a recent example of a long history of subservience in the name of internationalism. Other TLC leaders had accepted it; Bengough, it seemed, would not.

At the same time, Bengough loathed the prospect of jeopardizing the relationship of the TLC with the AFL. In February 1949 he led a TLC delegation to Miami for a meeting of the Joint Co-operative Committee of the AFL and TLC to attempt to resolve the difficulties. Matters worsened. The TLC leaders were ignored for a week and then informed that no meeting would take place as the AFL had unilaterally dissolved the committee and set up a tribunal comprised entirely of its own members to look into the controversy. The TLC representatives agreed to appear before the tribunal.

Following the September TLC convention the Internationals, under Hall's leadership, had formed a group with the purpose of cleansing the TLC of Communists. This association had enlisted the AFL's support. An extensive document had been prepared, reiterating and detailing the charges of Communist influence and nationalist tendencies present in the congress. There was something to the first charge, but little to the second.[33] Uncontradicted, however, the Internationals' submission portrayed a most serious state of affairs, demanding immediate action, if only to save the AFL affiliates operating in Canada.

Frank Hall spoke to the tribunal first, reading for almost two hours from a prepared text. Following a noon adjournment, congress representatives were invited to speak, but were given only half an hour to do so. Even then, they were subjected to constant interruption and insults by members of the Executive Council of the AFL.[34] It was not a tribunal but a kangaroo court. The TLC was denied any realistic opportunity to answer the half-truths and found itself judged by a body with absolutely no authority to do so. After being informed that an AFL Select Committee would render a decision, the Canadian unionists were asked to leave the room.[35] In due course, President Bengough was summoned before the AFL tribunal and read an ultimatum.[36] The TLC was ordered to eliminate every vestige of Communist influence in its affairs and advised to amend its constitution so that AFL Internationals enjoyed voting rights relative to the amount of per capita tax they paid. Bengough was also told that the AFL–TLC relationship could only survive 'on the basis of the tried and true principles that have characterized free trade unionism on this continent during the last century.'[37] What that meant needed no explanation.

The AFL demands, seen in the context of the past relationship between the two bodies, were not extraordinary. The TLC had given in on matters of principle many times before. Led by anyone other than Bengough, the TLC would have more than likely done so again, with the Canadian delegation hurrying back to Canada and making enough changes to save face, satisfy the AFL, and restore peace. This time the TLC was not prepared to capitulate to all of the AFL demands.[38]

Amendments to the constitution increasing the voting power of the Internationals were out of the question. The TLC was, however, willing to take certain steps to reduce the influence of Communist unionists in its movement: all TLC affiliates were advised not to elect any known Communists to union office.[39] Officers of Internationals operating in Canada were also invited to a meeting to discuss the AFL demands. This was a conciliatory and highly political gesture, and one which the TLC made clear should not be interpreted as a sign of weakness. Claiming to be 'proud of' the 'splendid relationship' between it and most Internationals, the TLC, in a warning of its own, went on to say that any International operating in Canada which flaunted the policies of the congress would find itself severed from affiliation, with its jurisdiction handed over to a national union. Conceding somewhat optimistically that the consequences of such action would 'present many difficulties,' the congress was prepared, if necessary, to face them. The TLC was, Bengough said, 'battling for principles and convictions upon which our Congress was built and without which no free trade unions can exist.'[40] The congress, at long last, had made a declaration of independence.

At issue was the right of the TLC to exercise full jurisdiction over all labour matters relating to its affiliates, both national and international unions, in Canada. Very simply, it was the right of Canadian labour to govern its own affairs free from outside interference. It was a battle that had to be fought and won. However, it was highly questionable whether independence and autonomy could be won through fighting to protect the CSU. The TLC leaders thought they had no option other than to support the CSU affiliate. They believed they could not sacrifice the CSU to American internationalism and simultaneously claim autonomy for themselves, and they were right. But they could have just as easily asserted their right to autonomy by placing the CSU under trusteeship and inviting a revitalized democratic seamen's union to continue in affiliation. Positive steps of this kind would have proved that the Canadians were not only masters in their own house, but were wise and competent as well. More likely than not, had action of this kind been taken, the AFL interference, if even attempted, could have been dealt with quickly, quietly, and without the external controversy so damaging to organized labour. TLC autonomy would have been proved by action, not words.

Instead, the TLC decided to support its affiliate and, with each day, that support became more and more untenable. By adopting this position, the TLC also delayed taking action against Communists in the labour movement generally. Not only had the Cold War begun, but events of the past decade both at home and overseas left no doubt that communism was directly antithetical to unionism: wherever Communists took power, they destroyed free trade unions. The purge had to come and, provided it was carried out democratically and constitutionally, it was to be welcomed. The rival CCL certainly realized as much.[41]

In all this controversy, the issue of nationalism versus internationalism was little more than a red herring. What really mattered was who exercised jurisdiction over organized labour in Canada: union leaders in the United States or union leaders at home. There could only be one answer to that question, and in late 1948 and early 1949 Percy Bengough tried to give it. That Bengough, supported by the other congress leaders, attempted to do so is to his credit. This was one of the first times that a leader of the TLC stood up, claimed for the TLC and Canadian workers what was rightfully theirs, and did not back down. But acting for all the right reasons is not enough, if the right choices are not also made. In this case, they were not. Bengough called a meeting with the Internationals after rejecting the AFL ultimatum. That meeting did not take place for a long time. It did not need to. Just a short while later Bengough was forced to begin acceding to the AFL demands, demands which his own earlier inaction had made inevitable and which, in part, retarded recognition of Canadian labour autonomy until the TLC merged with the CCL almost a decade later. The CSU was the TLC's undoing.

5
The Demise of the CSU

Long before the 1946 strike for the eight-hour day, the problems with the Misener organization and Canada Steamship Lines, and the dispute over who ran the TLC, the CSU realized that, as a union, it was in trouble. The future of the deep-sea fleet was in doubt. Membership in the CSU jumped during the war by almost five thousand and most of the new members were employed on the deep-sea ships. Anything that threatened the fleet threatened these jobs and the union.

By 1945 the government of Canada had title to more than 250 merchant ships. Almost 150 were owned by the Park Steamship Company; the rest were under charter to the British Ministry of Transport. It was a sizeable fleet by any standard, and, in the aftermath of the war, the fourth largest in the world. Its future concerned both the union and the government. In 1943, as part of the government's general postwar planning, a Merchant Shipping Policy Committee was appointed to make recommendations for the merchant marine after the war. The committee considered a full gamut of options available to the government and recommended that Canadian shipping should in peacetime be owned and operated by private companies, with only limited government involvement.[1] This recommendation made a great deal of sense because Canadian deep-sea shipping had throughout the Second World War been run by private concerns under contract with the Park Steamship Company. More importantly, the recommendation reflected the government's purpose in building the fleet: to help win the war.[2]

As early as its February 1944 convention, CSU delegates passed a resolution calling for the postwar maintenance of the fleet.[3] In May 1944 and again in September 1945 the CSU outlined in formal presentations the immediate steps it believed should be taken to ensure the long-term viability of the Canadian flag merchant marine.[4] The initial proposal called on the government 'immediately [to] adjust its shipbuilding program and go into construction of faster well-constructed vessels, with modern crew's accommodations, able to carry both cargo and passengers.'[5] There was no question that the slow, expensive-to-operate Canadian Parks would be uncompetitive after the European shipping industry re-established itself. With considerable foresight, the union recommended the construction of an all-service ship which could compete on both the St Lawrence River system and in the ocean trade, following expected improvements to the inland canal system. The second, more extensive 'National Shipping Policy for Canada' also called for a protectionist shipping policy, improvements in working standards for seamen, and, most novel of all, a CSU place on the Board of Directors of all commissions and bodies concerned with shipping.[6]

As positive as the union's suggestions might have been, they were not to be. The Park Steamship Company was eventually wound up and the ships themselves profitably sold.[7] The return of the industry to private control spelled the end of certain benefits enjoyed by seamen throughout the war. First to go, in July 1946, were the manning pools. A potentially more serious change in the deep-sea part of the industry was the end of bargaining with the government and the beginning of bargaining with private shipping companies. In these circumstances, the first postwar collective agreement was crucial. The deep-sea sailors did not have to fight for the eight-hour day, or to end any other manifestly unjust conditions of employment, but they had to make credible gains at the bargaining table to show the shipping companies that they would not be taken advantage of. To the union's relief, the Shipping Federation of Canada, an organization that had been created at the turn of the century to conduct labour relations on behalf of its members, led the negotiations, in 1946, for the various private employers. After some hard bargaining, the union was able to obtain an extremely favourable collective agreement. The one-year contract raised wages, increased overtime rates, and recognized the union-controlled hiring hall.[8]

The improvement in wages did not represent any hardship to the shipping companies. There was a tremendous postwar demand for shipping, and the Canadian flag bottoms were in constant use. By 1948, however, when the deep-sea contract came up for renewal, signs pointing to the demise of the fleet as it then existed were unmistakable. British and foreign flag ships of advanced design began to compete on the high seas with the Parks. These new ships were, on average, one-third faster, equipped with more efficient cargo-handling gear, and more economic to operate. They were also cheaper to build and finance than the war-built bottoms. In fact, the Canadian ships could not even compete against ships of exactly the same class in other merchant navies. For example, a 10,000-ton Park in the Canadian fleet cost, excluding fuel and depreciation, $810.50 a day to operate. A similar ship under British registry cost almost $300 less to run. Higher Canadian wages accounted for most of the difference.[9] To exacerbate the situation further, currency and import controls and, after 1947, the Marshall Plan, the generous program of postwar American assistance to the nations of Western Europe, put pressure on British and European countries to handle as much as possible of their own shipping and save their money for reconstruction. As part of this reconstruction effort, the United States gave away hundreds of its own war-built 'Liberty' ships which could also be operated less expensively by foreign crews.[10]

The increased competition caused a decline in the fortunes of Canadian deep-sea shipping companies and, prior to the expiry of the 1946 one-year agreement, they made it clear to the CSU that there was no more money to go around. The minister of labour appointed a conciliation officer, who was able to mediate and avoid a threatened strike though the CSU was forced to sign individual collective agreements with the almost thirty different companies operating the Parks.[11] The new one-year agreement was a disappointment, but at least the union and its members did not lose anything by it. Negotiations for its renewal began in the fall of 1948.

It quickly became clear that the majority of employers had no interest in signing anything with the Communist-tainted CSU. Labour minister Humphrey Mitchell appointed a conciliation officer, who proved unable to bring the parties together, and then appointed a Board of Conciliation.[12] Chaired by the Honourable Mr Justice J.O. Wilson of the Supreme Court of British Columbia, the tripartite board met first in Montreal in November 1948 and later in January and February 1949. The proceedings were not conciliatory, but the board was able to agree unanimously on a proposed settlement to the deadlock.[13] Under the proposed collective agreement, wages and benefits remained the same but certain important non-monetary clauses were changed. In particular, the proposed contract contained a clause entitling the companies to exclude Communists from their ships. The companies had been advised that the United States Department of Immigration intended to pay particular attention to ships crewed by the CSU and refuse entry to any suspected Communist.[14] The contract also proposed the elimination of the union hiring hall, with its responsibilities transferred to the government-run National Employment Service. After the *Islandside* incident, shipping companies had no interest in leaving their source of labour supply to the CSU. The draft collective agreement was unacceptable to the CSU, and the Department of Labour was so advised.[15]

TLC leaders advised the CSU to accept the board's report and to insist that the different shipping companies sign contracts embodying its terms. The rival SIU, which had already taken over the Canadian Lakes Seamen's Union and two important CSU Great Lakes contracts, was waiting in the wings and would happily sign any agreement with the shipping companies to obtain the deep-sea sailors bargaining rights. The jobs of CSU members would be protected and the union would be able to consolidate its position, both on the deep-sea side of the industry and on the Great Lakes. Furthermore, there was almost no possibility of the CSU winning a strike.[16] The TLC could not have given better advice.

The CSU, however, rejected both the advice and the report.[17] What the TLC had predicted immediately came to pass. J. Arthur Mathewson, legal counsel to the Shipping Federation of Canada, secretly left Canada for San Francisco to sign an agreement with the SIU. Harry Lundeberg, the president of the Seafarers' International Union of North America, agreed to sign an industry-wide contract with the Shipping Federation of Canada. SIU organizers had been working on the east coast since August 1948 and had not been able to win any bargaining rights. Now the American union was being offered them on a silver platter. It was both unethical and arguably unlawful, in these circumstances, to sign a contract with a union which was not the bargaining representative of any employees, but that question was not as clear in 1949 as it is now. At Mathewson's request, Lundeberg also agreed to send his top assistant, Harold Chamberlain Banks, to Halifax to lead the drive against the CSU.[18]

On 21 March 1949 the CSU learned unofficially what it should have expected: the Shipping Federation of Canada, on behalf of most shipping companies, including the government-owned Canadian National Steamships, had signed contracts with the SIU. CSU leaders immediately called a sit-in strike, and the first ship to be hit was the Canadian National Steamship *Lady Rodney*, moored in the Halifax harbour.[19] Before the sit-in strike spread to other ships in Canadian east coast ports, the companies which had signed contracts with the SIU expelled CSU members from their bottoms. They knew, as did the CSU, that if the sit-in strike spread, it would be difficult to remove the CSU members and replace them with SIU strikebreakers. On 31 March 1949 the Shipping Federation of Canada revealed publicly for the first time that it had signed contracts with the SIU on behalf of the deep-sea shipping companies. Later that day CSU president Harry Davis ordered the union's 3000 ocean sailors, working ninety ships around the world, to leave their ships. These men had no choice but to mount pickets and do everything they could to see the strike through. The number of deep-sea berths had, in just a few years, dramatically declined. The seamen knew that if this strike was lost, so were their jobs.

When Davis announced the world-wide shipping strike, a violation of both the Canada Shipping Act and the unwritten law of the sea, Ottawa was obliged to make every effort, as quickly as possible, to bring the strike to an end. An earlier cabinet decision to adopt a hands-off approach was reversed and the Royal Canadian Mounted Police instructed to give any necessary assistance to the shipping companies to board strikebreakers and free the picketed ships.[20] The *Lady Rodney* was the first ship to receive official assistance. On Friday, 8 April 1949, at three o'clock in the morning, a special train with 200 strikebreakers, including sixty American SIU members who had flown up from the United States, pulled into a railway siding near the struck ship. Only a small number of picketers were on duty. The strikebreakers were well-protected: with them were over one hundred armed officers of the Canadian National Railways Police, along with members of the RCMP. The police, all wearing helmets, formed a cordon around the strikebreakers, many of whom were carrying sawed-off axe handles, and began to escort them aboard the *Lady Rodney* and two other ships, the *Canadian Challenger* and the *Canadian Constructor*. Before they got there, many of the strikebreakers availed themselves of the opportunity the police protection provided and attacked the CSU picketers. At the same time, officers on board the struck ships turned steam hoses against CSU members. A fierce battle ensued, and the odds were not evened until later in the morning when CSU reinforcements arrived. By then, the strikebreakers were all on board ship. But that did not stop the fighting. Rocks flew from both directions and the battle showed every sign of continuing until shots were fired from one of the ships and six CSU members were wounded. The picketers dispersed and the three ships left their moorings and pulled out to sea.[21]

Violence is hardly unknown on the waterfront, but this episode was extraordinary. The police permitted the SIU strikebreakers to launch and continue for hours a vicious, merciless assault against a vastly outnumbered group of picketers who were exercising a legal right to strike. When TLC president Percy Bengough learned about it, he demanded a judicial inquiry. No such inquiry ever took place, nor did an investigation promised by the federal Department of Citizenship and Immigration on how the sixty American SIU members came to be admitted into Canada and placed on board Canadian ships.[22] The incident marked the end of any serious picketing in Canada.[23] Other maritime unions, such as those representing longshoremen, which had initially supported the CSU, reversed their stand and, without further delay, the SIU was able to man and sail all the deep-sea ships in Canada at the time the strike began. The strike at home was lost; by 20 May twenty-six Canadian ships had sailed from Montreal and east coast ports with SIU crews. But the overseas battle had just begun.[24]

Harry Davis travelled to England and Europe to enlist support for the deep-sea strike. The Communist-controlled World Federation of Trade Unions naturally promised its support, but so did the non-Communist International Confederation of Free Trade Unions. Most Canadian shipping was to Britain and the militant British dockers declared the *Beaverbrae* black when it arrived in England on 4 April. The crew were in due course expelled and Communist party member Bud Doucette, along with Harry Davis's brother Jack Popovitch, formed a Central Strike Committee to co-ordinate CSU strike activity throughout the British Isles.[25] Similar events began to take place all around the world. In some ports the striking CSU members obtained tremendous assistance from local unionists, convinced they were assisting the Canadians in defending vital trade union issues; in other ports, local authorities immediately arrested or deported the striking seamen. CSU members ordered deported from Europe were, as British subjects, sent to the United Kingdom. Once they arrived in London they were assigned duties by the Central Strike Committee, which at one point was responsible for feeding and housing almost 400 CSU members. The strike continued intermittently and particularly affected the ports of Avonmouth and Liverpool, commanding the attention of the prime minister and the Cabinet Emergencies Committee.[26]

In Canada the fight continued as a battle of words between the government and the CSU. Both sides were able to score points but one simple fact remained: the strike was serving no trade union purpose. The union should have taken steps to preserve the jobs of its members, for it was obvious that the strike could not be won. Instead, the CSU did what it could to perpetuate the strike, demonstrating that it had no more concern for Canadian sailors than the most notorious employer. Money collected by Communist and other 'progressive' groups all over the Western world for the striking seamen arrested and imprisoned in foreign ports seldom reached the intended recipients. The contributions were either kept by the group which collected it, or given to the London-based strike committee to be used for propaganda and administrative purposes. The striking seamen knew nothing of this act of treachery.[27] The CSU meanwhile encouraged its men to fight a cause which was both lost and not in their interests. It was an enormous act of betrayal.

Slowly but surely this simple truth gained adherents in the labour movement. In late April the International Confederation of Free Trade

Unions announced that it was withdrawing its support.[28] In May the International Transport Workers' Federation made a similar determination and suspended the CSU from membership. The Communist World Federation of Trade Unions, in contrast, remained stalwart in its support of the strike and called on dockers and seamen to continue their struggle and to refuse to transport arms.[29] Canadian seamen were being used – in the interests of the Soviet Union.

By the end of May, Bengough and the TLC decided to do what they could to bring the fiasco to an end. A meeting was held with the officers of the CSU, who were informed that the TLC would no longer continue to support the strike. Bengough urged the CSU leaders to call off the strike and resign. Then, Bengough explained, steps could be taken to repatriate the hundreds of Canadian seamen stranded in foreign ports. The CSU leaders apparently agreed, but the next day they reversed their decision. The TLC, already advised that fourteen different affiliated Internationals would withdraw should steps not be taken against the CSU, was left with no choice but to suspend the union. That was done on 3 June 1949.[30]

In Britain, on 27 June, following several weeks of relative calm, and three weeks after the CSU suspension, another dockers' strike began. This time it was in London; like the earlier strike, it was precipitated by the decision of local employers to lock out their employees unless they worked the two Canadian ships in port, one of which, the *Beaverbrae*, had been sitting idle since the beginning of April. By early July approximately ten thousand dockers were on strike. More than one hundred ships were idled and Britons, who still faced rationing, were forced to witness the spectacle of fresh fruit and vegetables left to rot because there was no one to empty the ships.[31] Once again, the dockers were advised by members of the London-based CSU Central Strike Committee that the CSU was engaged in a fight for vital trade union principles. As Philip Noel-Baker, secretary of state for Commonwealth relations, correctly observed, 'our good-hearted dockers have been duped by Communist lies.'[32] On 11 July the government declared a state of emergency.[33]

Arrangements were made to bring up to 35,000 British troops to work the London docks, joining the 2500 dispatched immediately after the king signed the state of emergency declaration. This proved unnecessary when the dockers voted on 22 July to return to work after learning that the CSU had, at last, called off the strike.[34] Why the CSU suddenly decided to do this is something of a mystery. It is possible that British and Canadian Communist party leaders feared a final showdown with the British government. If the government had been forced to deploy thousands of troops to unload the ships, it would have turned public opinion against the dockers and made it all the more difficult for them next time they went out on strike. It is also possible, although not very likely, that the CSU called off the strike to demonstrate its goodwill at the same time as it was submitting to the Department of Labour a four-point plan for ending the dispute.

Two other plans had earlier been proposed. All three plans shared one common characteristic: they were not realistic. In brief, they contemplated a return to the status quo before the strike. All three plans were rejected by both the government and the Shipping Federation of Canada.[35] The CSU had been thoroughly discredited and all the deep-sea ships were sailing with SIU crews. CSU president Davis bravely declared that the strike would continue 'until victory is achieved,'[36] but the strike was in fact over and the CSU was finished.

By the time Davis called the overseas strike off in July 1949, the deep-sea shipping industry was, except for a small CSU local on the west coast, firmly under SIU control. Great Lakes shipping was another matter. Canada Steamship Lines and the Misener companies had signed contracts with the SIU before the opening of the 1949 shipping season. Other companies had not, and continued to run their ships with CSU crews. In many cases the relationship was in name only; the CSU, preoccupied with running the deep-sea strike, had little time to concern itself with the Great Lakes industry. The SIU, having signed with the Misener companies and Canada Steamship Lines, also wanted to sign up the rest of the inland fleet. Unlike the CSU, it had both the time and resources to do so. In March 1949 the SIU asked for the help of the president of the International Longshoremen's Association, Joe Ryan.

Ryan wrote all the shipping companies operating in Canada and informed them that American longshoremen would be very disturbed by a company giving aid and comfort to the Communist CSU. What Ryan meant subsequently became clear when he followed the letter up with a telegram asking the shipping companies to inform him whether their crews were free from Communist domination. This was necessary, Ryan explained, 'in order that loading and unloading instructions may be given to my people.'[37] Only longshoremen can unload ships and Ryan controlled most of them on the American side of the Great Lakes. The dangers of not co-operating with the SIU and continuing to co-operate with the CSU became obvious as ships carrying CSU crews were harassed and tied up in American ports. Ships carrying SIU crews were, at the same time, treated with courtesy and dispatch.

The refusal of the American longshoremen to unload the Canadian ships was a violation of both American and international law. The Canadian shipping companies complained to the Department of Labour, and asked the minister to take whatever steps were necessary to protect their rights. Instead, the department assisted them in coming to terms with the SIU. Hal Banks, the SIU's international representative, was called in for a meeting with labour minister Mitchell and deputy minister Arthur Mac-Namara. Subsequently, some shipping companies such as N.M. Paterson and Sons reached an agreement with Banks and the SIU. The Paterson company agreed to hire 'reliable' licensed crews, and the company agreed to meet in January and February with SIU representatives to see if a collective agreement could be arranged for 1950. The meeting took place and a contract was reached.[38] The arrangement was unlawful. It was up to the employees of N.M. Paterson and Sons to decide, without employer interference, what union, if any, they wished to represent them. N.M. Paterson and Sons, whose founder was a senator, was not the only shipping company to make peace with the SIU in this way.[39] There was one company, however, which decided to buck the SIU and the Department of Labour and do what it thought was right: Upper Lakes and St Lawrence Transportation Limited.[40]

Founded in 1932 by Toronto businessman Gordon C. Leitch and operated with the assistance of his son Jack, 'Upper Lakes' was being harassed and boycotted as much as any other Great Lakes shipping company with CSU crews. Gordon Leitch did not like being threatened by the Longshoremen, the SIU, or anyone else. Nor did he relish the thought that Communists were working on his ships. He turned to Upper Lakes' director of personnel, Tom Houtman, for advice.[41] Houtman was none other than the former CSU executive member who lost his union position as a result of Communist party intrigues prior to the Second World War. After learning of the SIU's demand that Upper Lakes repudiate its contract with the CSU, Houtman canvassed the men and reported to Leitch that if a certification vote was taken on board Upper Lakes ships, the CSU would win hands down. Signing a contract with the SIU in these circumstances, he advised, would be improper.[42] Upper Lakes was in an unenviable position, one which was not made any easier when the company learned that the CSU was willing to sign a contract for the 1950 shipping season with terms even more favourable than those in the 1949 agreement. Not knowing what would happen next, the company decided to stall the SIU. The boycotts did not abate, and Upper Lakes made it through the remainder of the shipping season only with the greatest of difficulty.

The CSU's suspension in July from the TLC did not help matters, nor would its subsequent expulsion. Accordingly, Communist party leaders ordered the CSU to withdraw voluntarily from the TLC before it met at its annual fall convention. Their strategy was clear: resignation would prevent a floor fight over the CSU, a fight which could only hurt other Communist-influenced affiliates remaining in good standing.[43] The strategy failed. Although the union resigned from the TLC on 1 September 1949,[44] the congress decided formally to expel the union at its convention later in the month. Both the Internationals and, to a lesser extent, Bengough and the other TLC leaders wanted to have a full airing-out of the CSU issue and, more importantly, the place of Communists in the trade union movement.

Frank Hall told the delegates that the CSU was under the complete domination of the Communist party, which was in turn under the complete domination of the Soviet Union.[45] One year earlier when Hall made similar charges, they were rebuffed as camouflage for what was said to be a poorly disguised attempt to take over the TLC and deliver it to the American labour movement. By September 1949 perceptions had changed so radically that not only was Hall roundly applauded but the expulsion resolution was passed by a huge margin, 702:77. 'T.L.C. Leftists Run for Cover as Reds Ousted,' the *Montreal Gazette* headline reported, and it was true. Scared of exposure, a number of delegates did not appear at the convention during the vote. Others attempted to leave before it started but were prevented from doing so.[46]

It was an important convention and signalled the beginning of the end of the Communist party's influence in Canadian labour. The TLC was taking action against Communist-directed trade unions, as was the Canadian Congress of Labour, the other major Canadian labour organization. In 1949 the CCL took a similar position when it disaffiliated the United Electrical Workers, which was under the control of the Communist party. These developments, which were paralleled in the United States, were considered by the mainstream of the trade union movement as essential to the continuation of organized labour as an autonomous and democratic constituent of Canadian society. In forcing the TLC to begin the necessary job of cleaning up its own house, Frank Hall had both scored a major victory and performed an essential service. However, in so far as the TLC was concerned, the jury was still out on the SIU. It would not be admitted into affiliation for quite some time. The TLC had 'reviewed with thoroughness the circumstances under which the SIU intruded into this strike, its willingness and readiness to man the ships of the men on strike with inexperienced crews, with the full support of the struck companies, to say nothing of the questionable methods used.'[47] As far as the TLC was concerned, the SIU had no place, for the moment, in the Canadian labour movement.

The CSU had almost no place left in the Canadian labour movement. In a bid for survival, the west coast branch of the CSU, on 15 October, renamed itself and broke away from the union. Several days later the CSU announced that it had called off the 1949 strike. This announcement misrepresented one more time the causes of the strike.[48] The union's name was mud and, before the end of 1949, it was changed to the Canadian Brotherhood of Seamen, although it was still referred to as the CSU. Davis, Ferguson, and McManus remained in charge. At its 1950 convention the old gang was re-elected and passed various resolutions, including one which called for the scrapping of the Marshall Plan. At the end of the convention, Davis announced to the press that the CSU would be applying for readmission to the TLC within the year.[49] The idea was preposterous. Only a few Great Lakes companies remained under contract and, of these, Upper Lakes was the largest. The CSU attempted, for what it was worth, to negotiate a new agreement with Upper Lakes for the 1950 season.

Meetings were held[50] and a conciliation officer appointed, but nothing was accomplished before the opening of navigation. Upper Lakes rehired its employees from the previous year and paid them the going rate, but there was no union agreement. In the meantime, the SIU had not lost interest in Upper Lakes. At one meeting Hal Banks informed the Upper Lakes management that the Department of Labour was blessing his efforts.[51] When Upper Lakes again refused to sign a contract with the SIU, Banks telegraphed the minister of labour and informed him that Upper Lakes would not be serviced by any workers belonging to any AFL affiliate because it had not lived up to its agreement with the SIU.[52] There was, of course, no such agreement. Upper Lakes obtained a court injunction restraining Banks, Frank Hall, and every Canadian International from proceeding with the boycott.[53] It did not help.

Midway through the summer the company's position changed when the conciliation officer reported to the Department of Labour that he had been unable to resolve the Upper Lakes–CSU dispute. The minister decided that there was no purpose to be served by appointing a conciliation board. The effect of this decision was to end any legal obligations between the company and the union. Upper Lakes was still not prepared to sign an agreement with the SIU and asked the Department of Labour to conduct a certification vote among its employees. 'We consider it imperative,' Upper Lakes manager Captain Bruce Angus wrote the deputy minister of labour, 'that the men indicate to us that it is their wish to be represented by the SIU before we enter into negotiations with representatives of this union with a view to entering into a contract.'[54] This was a reasonable and honourable request, but for reasons not at all inconsistent with the department's conduct over the past two years the request was rejected.[55] Upper Lakes was now in a serious predicament. It was no longer legally obligated to the CSU, and its deference to its employees' representation wishes was not only futile but costing it dearly; it was the only major shipping company on the lakes that continued to be boycotted and harassed. The company had to reach an agreement with the SIU or face bankruptcy.

Meetings were held with Hal Banks in the fall of 1950 and a Memorandum of Understanding signed. The memorandum was, in essence, a capitulation to the SIU demands. It provided that the SIU could supply the company with the names of individuals it considered unsuitable for employment on the Great Lakes. Upper Lakes, subject to its own investigation, was obligated to discharge these individuals if they were already employed. All new employees had to be 'cleared' through the SIU hiring hall.[56] What exactly these conditions would mean in practice remained to be seen. For the moment, the memorandum meant that the CSU had lost its remaining important contract.

To make matters worse, in early July the CSU was notified that its suspension from the International Transport Workers' Federation had been confirmed, and that it had been expelled from affiliation. The CSU was, according to the federation, a 'Communist lackey' which had 'uselessly and wickedly' dragged workers around the world into the dispute to support World Communism.[57] The deep-sea strike was undoubtedly intended, if not in whole then certainly in part, to frustrate the Marshall Plan. While the strike had failed to cause serious disruptions on the continent, and thereby create an opportunity for local Communists to consolidate their positions, that possibility had existed and was considered by many observers to be the real reason for the continuation of the dispute. There was no doubt that the CSU, by its conduct, had become inimical to Canada's national and international interests.

Soon enough the British Labour government released its white paper on the dockers' strike which, not surprisingly, was extremely critical of the CSU. According to the report, the strike had cost Britain dearly: over 400,000 working days had been lost, lost to support 'communist fortunes.'[58] Harry Davis, as to be expected, called the white paper 'a packet of lies.'[59]

Nevertheless, the white paper was reviewed during the summer when a small shipping company named Branch Lines Limited made an application to the Labour Relations Board for an order revoking the certification of the CSU. The CSU, it asserted, did not represent the employees in the bargaining unit, and, being Communist-dominated, was not a trade union. There was no evidence that the union had ceased to enjoy the support of the Branch Lines employees, so the board refused to decertify the union on that basis. It was willing, however, to decertify it on the grounds that it was a Communist-dominated organization, and it issued an order so declaring in December 1950. The order was later upheld by the courts.[60]

The CSU was a Communist-dominated organization, but nothing in the recently proclaimed Industrial Relations Disputes Investigation Act entitled the Labour Relations Board or the court to decertify it for that reason. The board's decision was wrong in law, and there is little doubt that the order was politically motivated. As such, it caused considerable general concern in trade union circles. The CCL asked its lawyer, David Lewis, the future leader of the New Democratic party, to prepare a legal opinion on the issue. 'That it is extremely desirable, in the present international situation,' Lewis wrote, 'to oust communist control from Canadian trade unions is obvious to every Canadian democrat. But whether it is wise to do so on grounds and by methods which are questionable in law and flimsy in fact, is another matter.'[61] Percy Bengough was inclined to agree. The right of workers to join or belong to unions of their own choice was, according to the TLC leader, inviolate. However, and this was critical, it was limited 'when a union becomes a communist front organization, fired with the ambition to liquidate and destroy all free trade unions.'[62]

Any remaining doubts were eliminated in November 1950, just weeks before the Labour Relations Board decision was issued. CSU national secretary Gerry McManus, following in Sullivan's tradition, told his story in two consecutive articles in *Maclean's* magazine. The first revealed a conspiracy by the Communist Party of Canada to conduct a campaign of sabotage in the event of a war with the Soviet Union. The second outlined the Communist party's years of behind-the-scenes manipulation and abuse of the Canadian Seamen's Union. 'In strict accuracy,' McManus wrote, 'there is no such thing as a Communist-dominated union. Once it falls under Communist domination a union ceases to be a union. It becomes a branch of the Communist Party.'[63] The Canadian Seamen's Union, which had closed its offices along the lakes in late 1949 and boarded up its Montreal headquarters in early 1950, ceased to exist.

A chapter in Canadian labour history was over and a new one was about to begin. Very little was known about the SIU and even less about its international representative Hal C. Banks. Only time would tell, as minister of trade and commerce C.D. Howe observed, whether it was a wise decision to man Canadian ships with SIU crews.[64]

6
The SIU and Consolidation of Power

Harold (Hal) Chamberlain Banks was born in a small farming community in Iowa named Waterloo on 28 February 1909. One hundred miles away from Des Moines, Waterloo in the late 1920s offered few opportunities and not much of a future. When he was in his teens Banks went west and soon began to ship out of San Francisco. A chance meeting with Harry Lundeberg, president of the SIU of North America and the Sailors' Union of the Pacific, launched Banks on his union career.[1] Tall and muscular, he began to work for Lundeberg and, by the late 1940s, had become his chief assistant and one of the most important men in the union. Banks travelled throughout North America as Lundeberg's emissary.[2]

Before joining the union staff, Banks had a number of encounters with the law. One offence, passing rubber cheques, earned him a three-year stay at the notorious San Quentin prison. In January 1937 Banks was acquitted of a murder charge arising out of a bar-room brawl which ended in the death of another man. Five years later he was arrested for kidnapping, but the charge was dismissed. In 1947 Banks had another brush with the law and was charged with carrying a concealed weapon. In return for a guilty plea, the police reduced the charge to disturbing the peace.[3] Obviously, Banks was not a model citizen.

He was, however, a logical person to lead the SIU's Canadian organization campaign. The leaders of the CSU were partisan, and the SIU campaign needed that same zealous leadership. Like Lundeberg, Banks was staunchly anti-Communist, believing that the Communist party had no place in the trade union movement and that the eradication of its influence by whatever means necessary was more than justified. In the circumstances, this is exactly what the SIU required. The only problem was obtaining Banks's admission to Canada. Immigration officers routinely deny entry to Canada to individuals with criminal records. However, for reasons which have never been properly explained, when Banks arrived at the border in his big Buick at the end of February 1949 he was admitted to Canada with no questions asked. No questions would in fact be asked for several years, until he brought the entire matter under scrutiny by applying for Canadian citizenship.

The SIU's fight against the CSU was aided by the favourable political climate which Banks found in Canada. The authorities extended themselves on numerous occasions on behalf of the SIU and its leader. 'We have the full co-operation of the police,' Banks wrote home at the end of April, 'and I have a permit to carry a gun.'[4] Any co-operation Banks received was largely motivated by his mission in Canada – routing the Communist-dominated CSU. That was a goal the government shared. Since the end of the war one incident after another had convinced Western leaders that the Soviet Union was embarking on a process of expansionism motivated by its desire to control the world. The 1949 deep-sea strike left little doubt about the havoc a Communist-controlled union could wreak in support of Soviet imperialism. Banks and the anti-Communist SIU were welcomed, in this context, as a positive improvement to the CSU. Unfortunately, in its welcome, Ottawa abdicated its responsibility to enforce the rule of law. The Department of Labour, in particular, found itself in a difficult position. On the one hand, it was confronted with a union which had ceased to be a union, while on the other, the industrial relations system itself was brought into question by SIU contracts with the shipping companies. The department did not know a lot about the SIU, but it liked what it knew. A study made in March 1949 revealed that the SIU had, in Canada, called a strike only once since the end of the war, while the CSU had struck on numerous occasions.[5] When the numbers were compared, the SIU record promised industrial stability in the shipping industry. The SIU willingness to sign the same deep-sea contract the CSU had rejected was also viewed positively by both the government and the shipping industry.

During the first stages of the 1949 deep-sea strike, Banks simply replaced striking CSU crews with SIU members from the west coast who were having trouble finding deep-sea berths and with American SIU members brought to Canada specifically for that purpose. As this was only a short-term solution, some CSU sailors had to be retained. Banks, however, believed that the continued presence of CSU partisans, whether Communists or not, on board SIU-contracted ships threatened the ongoing viability of his union, so he forwarded a list containing the names of all individuals of suspect allegiance to union dispatchers with the instructions that under no circumstance should such persons be shipped out. Called the 'Do Not Ship List,' it was a blacklist. Illegal and arbitrary, with the stroke of a pen it deprived men of their right to make a living. Paradoxically, the list was justified as necessary to protect freedom, not destroy it. The federal government assisted Banks in this endeavour.

As early as December 1948 American and Canadian authorities met to discuss contingency plans for the defence of the inland water system in the event of another war. The invasion of South Korea by North Korea in the summer of 1950 resulted in fear of internal Communist sabotage. President Harry Truman signed an order in September invoking the Magnuson ('Trojan Horse') Act, which made security screening of American Great Lakes seamen mandatory.[6] Banks encouraged the Canadian government to establish a similar program. There were, he claimed, Communists on board the ships of the Upper Lakes and St Lawrence Transportation company endangering the security of the country. This warning was not believed. It was patently clear that Banks was motivated more by his desire to displace the CSU from its remaining stronghold than by genuine security concerns. When both the American Department of State[7] and Great Lakes shipping companies[8] made similar requests for a screening program, however, the matter was referred to an interdepartmental security panel, which met throughout the fall of 1950. In January 1951 the panel presented a program to cabinet for approval, and in late February the proposed regulations were promulgated by order-in-council under the Emergency Powers Act.[9] The security screening system was similar to its American counterpart, the only substantial difference being that it was run by the Royal Canadian Mounted Police rather than by a branch of the armed forces.

At the same time that the government was proceeding with the official screening of merchant seamen, Banks began doing it unofficially. Anyone suspected of Communist tendencies was immediately placed on the Do Not Ship List and, by late 1951, Banks's list contained over 2000 names.[10] This unofficial screening took place with the full knowledge of the security panel and the Department of Labour. Almost all of the names on the list were of former CSU members, but no more than three or four hundred members of that union had ever belonged to the Communist party. None the less, the SIU screening program was welcomed as it relieved the RCMP of a considerable workload.[11] Of the 20,000 merchant seamen screened by the RCMP by the end of December 1952, only fifteen were refused security clearance. Banks's unofficial screening was, in part, responsible for this low number, although the number of names on the Do Not Ship List exceeded even the most paranoid estimates of Communist infiltration of the shipping industry. The dimensions of the list and other evidence which began arriving at the Department of Labour shortly after the security panel first started meeting strongly suggested that it was much more than a device to rid the ranks of Communist party members. Indeed, both unsolicited letters from ordinary seamen and official reports from field officers began to tell a tale of corruption which shocked the seasoned veterans of the department. Seamen were being expelled from the union without cause, forced to bribe union officers to obtain a berth, and required to pay high initiation and other fees to remain a member of the SIU. Anyone who raised even the slightest objection was put on the Do Not Ship List. By October 1950 the Department of Labour had accumulated a thick dossier on Hal Banks and the SIU. Unlike the first relatively benign descriptions of the SIU, those contained in this file portrayed quite a different organization.

Initially, nobody at the Department of Labour knew what to make of the letters and the reports. One of the first industrial relations officers to deal with the problem was Bernard Wilson. He believed that the apparent SIU corruption should be quickly arrested, and proposed doing it in one of three ways: by calling Banks to Ottawa for an informal discussion; by appointing a commissioner under the Industrial Relations Disputes Investigation Act to investigate the SIU; or by tipping off the newspapers.[12] All three of Wilson's recommendations were rejected.[13] It was believed that, unsavoury as it was, the SIU was better than any of its alternatives.[14]

Senior Department of Labour officers had from the beginning helped Banks in signing up the Great Lakes shipping companies. The last of these, Upper Lakes, agreed to terms with Banks in September 1950. The department could not easily have appointed a commission of inquiry to investigate the man and the union they were recommending to the shipping companies. Yet, by December 1950, the department had materials in its possession pointing to massive wrongdoings within the SIU: that the SIU had forced employers to sign contracts by threatening boycotts in the United States; signed agreements with employers without having any members among the employees; coerced employees into membership by threatening their employment; cause other employees to be dismissed from their jobs because of their preference for another union organization; misrepresented to employees representation proceedings before the Labour Relations Board; victimized employees by levying high fees and fines; and engaged in bribery and racketeering in the hiring of seamen.[15] Banks was not concerned. While it was true that lower level departmental employees had serious misgivings about the internal affairs of the SIU, it was the senior level officials who made the decisions. On numerous occasions these men had allied themselves with

Banks and extended him every assistance. In return, Banks was more than happy to assist the authorities when it suited his interests. For example, after the RCMP security screening began, the SIU gave 'first class co-operation.'[16]

The security screening program helped Banks because it clothed his Do Not Ship List with an aura of legitimacy it otherwise would not have had. Whenever asked about the existence of a blacklist, Banks would point to his 'first class co-operation' with the RCMP and claim that the list was necessary to fight Communists. It is highly questionable whether there was ever any real threat from seafaring Communists. Other than going along with a screening program, the only measure adopted by the federal government to address the threat was the erection of a few fences alongside certain canals and the posting of an occasional guard.[17] If the government had really believed there was a danger of sabotage, surely it would have taken more concrete steps to meet the threat.

The early minutes of the security panel reveal a certain lack of enthusiasm for the entire project. However, once the Americans instituted a screening program the Canadians had little choice but to follow suit. As the United States lost interest so did Canada, and in November 1953 the government of Canada decided to discontinue the program. The United States did not object. Nor did Hal Banks.[18] In the guise of fighting Communism, Banks had been able to consolidate power over Canadian seamen. In his own way, Banks appeared to be as great a threat to democratic unionism as were the Communist party leaders of the CSU. Canadian seamen, abandoned by the Department of Labour, were once again at the mercy of their union.

Open revolt was, in the circumstances, out of the question. Reform from within was equally unlikely. For the first two years of its operation in Canada the SIU did not hold membership meetings. In 1951, however, Banks called a union convention. The largely handpicked delegates were welcomed to the Mount Royal Hotel in Montreal by Banks who described the convention as the first truly democratic meeting of maritime workers in Canadian history. After informing the delegates of the recent activities of the union and predicting that the SIU would shortly be admitted into the TLC, Banks explained his job in Canada. He was sent to Canada, he said, by the Executive Board of the SIU to act as the administrator of the Canadian District of the union until it was sufficiently well established to stand on its own feet. Although progress in that direction had been made, Banks advised that immediate autonomy for the Canadian District would be premature. Confident that his view would prevail, the matter was put to a vote.[19] To Banks's considerable surprise, a majority of the delegates to the convention passed a resolution requesting the SIU International to grant the Canadian District immediate autonomy. Distressed by this show of independence, Banks engineered passage of a majority resolution asking the SIU to maintain the status quo. The future of the Canadian District would be decided at the SIU International convention scheduled to take place two months later in San Francisco.[20]

Delegates to that convention, the SIU's fifth, were treated to a most enthusiastic address from Banks, who described in some detail events in Canada since his arrival in February 1949. As far as anybody could tell, Banks had done a splendid job with the Canadian District. The thousands of new members, tens of thousands of dollars in the bank, and contracts with almost all Canadian shipping companies were proof of his success. Before the delegates were given the opportunity to vote on the majority resolution, Leonard J. (Red) McLaughlin, an expatriate New Zealand sailor, member of the Banks inner circle, and guiding mind behind many SIU activities, read the minority resolution. McLaughlin pointed to the worsening international situation and warned that autonomy might lead to a resurgence of Communist party control of the Canadian shipping industry. He also told the delegates that Hal Banks was the only man capable of protecting the Canadian District from this peril. 'If we have to trade in Mr. Banks for autonomy,' McLaughlin said, 'we can get along without the autonomy.'[21] The matter was referred to a convention committee, which duly recommended another year or two of international administration.

Canadian seamen were disappointed to learn that the International convention had adopted the minority resolution rather than the majority one. Banks was delighted and cited the two conventions as examples of membership control and democracy in the Canadian District of the SIU. Few seamen were fooled, but the effect of the convention's actions was demoralizing none the less. As in the past, even a single indiscreet comment was enough to leave a man deprived of his livelihood. Some sailors judged, accurately as it turned out, the futility of the situation and drifted away; only a very few were courageous enough to challenge Banks.

John Droeger was the first. Although an American citizen, Droeger began shipping out of Canada in 1948. He did not welcome the arrival of the SIU and soon came to despise it. In union halls and in informal meetings with sailors, Droeger brought charges of SIU corruption into the open. His charges, as Department of Labour files confirm, left little doubt that the SIU had, as a union, strayed far from a democratic course. Labelled an 'agitator,' Droeger was placed on the Do Not Ship List moments before he was about to set sail on board the *Canadian*

Challenger. A union trial was held,[22] but Droeger was not permitted to attend. His expulsion was confirmed. Theoretically, Droeger could have appealed his expulsion to the SIU International. He also had the option of appealing the expulsion to the courts. While the courts are often reluctant to involve themselves in internal union affairs, Droeger had no difficulty in obtaining the assistance of the Quebec Supreme Court when he filed an application requesting both the judicial review of the decision expelling him from membership and an order reinstating him.

Evidence was adduced in the Montreal courtroom proving conclusively the existence of the Do Not Ship List. In fact, a list dated 1 November 1951, containing more than 2000 names, was produced. The Honourable Mr Justice Frederick Collins ruled that Banks had no constitutional or legal authority to establish the blacklist and he ordered that it be given no effect. He also reinstated Droeger to membership. The ruling was a tremendous victory but provided no restitution to the thousands of men earlier deprived of their jobs. The SIU filed notice of appeal, which had the effect of staying the implementation of that part of the order reinstating Droeger. In the meantime, Droeger was hired by the indefatigable Captain H.N. McMaster. His job: to make life as difficult and as uncomfortable as possible for Banks and the SIU.[23] The appeal decision was given in September 1955 by Quebec's appellate court, the Court of Queen's Bench. The unanimous court decided that Banks and the SIU had no legal right to maintain a Do Not Ship List. The court was also satisfied that Droeger had acted properly in seeking judicial review instead of relying on the union's internal appeal procedure. Although the SIU announced that it would also appeal this decision, its immediate effect was to put Droeger back to work. However, Droeger disappeared and was never heard from again in Canada.

Rumour has it that Banks decided to 'take care of' Droeger once and for all. In fact, after Droeger's reinstatement to the union was upheld, he was assigned by the union hiring hall to a berth on board the *Canadian Constructor*. At its first port of call in the United States men in dark suits came on board and dragged Droeger away. The men were agents of the Federal Bureau of Investigation and they had a warrant for Droeger's arrest. He was a draft dodger and had been shipping out of Canadian ports because he was afraid to ship out of American ports. The reason he was never heard from again is because he went to prison. After his release he did not return to Canada.[24] Few SIU members knew what really happened to Droeger, and union members who strayed out of line were warned to 'remember John Droeger.'[25] Usually this simple warning, speaking volumes, was enough.

'Troublemakers' were dealt with quickly and efficiently. Even when an entire ship's crew revolted against Banks's control, the SIU boss was able to put all the crew members on the Do Not Ship List without fear of adverse consequences. As long as Banks's hand-picked leadership remained loyal to him, there was very little ordinary SIU members could do. Loyalty and a willingness to follow instructions were characteristics shared by all the union's employees. In return, they enjoyed better salaries and lifestyles than any of the members they were there to represent. It was the kind of arrangement which could go on forever, provided that Banks and the employees realized there were mutual obligations involved. When Banks lost sight of this balance, shortly after the Droeger affair began, he set into motion the one serious challenge to his leadership. It was begun by an officer of the SIU, James Todd.

Todd joined the SIU on the west coast in 1946 and shipped out until 1949, when he went to work for the union in Vancouver as a patrolman – the contact between the union officers and its members. In 1949 Banks summoned Todd to Montreal to help with the organizing campaign. The two men did not get along well and Todd was shunted off from one port to another until May 1952 when, without warning or explanation, he was dismissed. [26]

Together with another dissatisfied SIU member named Jack Brydson, Todd circulated a petition calling for reforms not unlike those earlier demanded by Droeger. Todd had been a union officer for years and many seamen rallied behind him. Apparently over eight hundred SIU members risked their livelihoods and subscribed to the petition. This was quite remarkable, revealing the enormous discontent in the union. In August 1952 Todd and Brydson, now joined by a former editor of the SIU newspaper *The Canadian Sailor*, published an appeal to the SIU International. It advocated Banks's immediate dismissal and replacement, pending elections, by a member of the Canadian District Executive. The appeal also requested an independent audit of union finances and an end to the Do Not Ship List. It was an open declaration of war and could not be ignored. [27] In late September 1952 Todd was given two or three days' notice that a hearing was about to be convened to consider the matter. The entire union was watching.

When Todd arrived at the SIU Hall he found SIU International vice-president Paul Hall, Morris Weisberger, an SIU International officer, and Hal Banks sitting together at a head table. He was stunned to learn that these men were going to hear and decide his charges, which were read to the 'tribunal.' None of the allegations were explored. Instead, the accuser became the accused. The only conduct examined was Todd's, and the 'inquiry' lasted from 3:00 PM on 3 October until 2:00 AM the next day. At its conclusion, union members in the audience gave Banks a resounding vote of confidence. The following day, a general union meeting was held and members passed a resolution condemning Todd for his actions, which, the resolution said, 'unwarrantedly reflected unfavourably on the Canadian District membership and our International.'[28] It was a farce.

Nevertheless, the Todd affair demonstrated that Banks could count on the support of the SIU International when faced with a rank-and-file revolt. That support was not without reservations and misgivings. Hall and Weisberger were prepared to stand up for Banks, but they also let him know privately that changes had to be introduced. This was made clear at the SIU's Sixth Biennial Convention held in March 1953.[29] Their report, which was accepted by the convention, recommended that all full-book members who had been placed on the blacklist be given the opportunity to have a union trial presided over by five rank-and-file members. (Any seaman who had passed a probationary membership period of eighteen months was known as a full-book member.) 'The next step,' Hall told the delegates, 'is to provide for ... complete freedom and independent action to our Canadian brothers in keeping with the traditions of democracy practiced in our International.'[30]

The Canadian District had been admitted into affiliation by the TLC in September 1951, and it held the bargaining rights for almost all unlicensed seamen in Canada. Under Banks's leadership, impressive gains in wages and working conditions were beginning to be made. Whatever concerns delegates may have held about the Canadian District had been alleviated. They voted by a large majority in favour of granting autonomy. By the end of the year the Canadian District had obtained a constitution and the SIU International administration was allowed to expire. Elections of a kind were held and SIU of Canada was, more or less, on its own.

With its dirty laundry cleaned, or at least hidden away, the SIU began to look like the union many Canadian seamen had hoped it would be. In so far as the shipping companies were concerned, Banks and the SIU were tough bargainers. A study prepared by the Department of Labour of contracts negotiated by the SIU revealed that it had materially improved the lot of Canadian seamen.[31] In many administrative respects the union was adequately run. Banks hired some competent union employees and insisted that all union officers and employees, with the notable exception of himself, maintain high standards in their use of union funds and in the administration of union rules. However, none of the promised reforms were made to the union's internal administration. Blacklisted seamen were never afforded the opportunity of a fair union trial and the Do Not

Ship List remained as an almost official instrument of Banks's control. As that control strenghtened, resort to the blacklist became increasingly unnecessary. Over 3000 men had been purged between 1949 and 1952. Countless others had left the traditionally high-turnover industry of their own accord. Only a foolhardy few continued to buck Banks, and with predictable results.

Those seamen who stayed out of Banks's way benefited by the reduction in ranks. There were not enough jobs to go around. In 1952 the SIU had only thirty deep-sea ships under contract. When contrasted with almost 200 ships contracted for in 1949, this figure reveals the huge toll in jobs taken by the government's decision not to support a Canadian fleet. The deep-sea part of the shipping industry was heading towards extinction. Union demands had something to do with it, such as those made prior to the SIU's 1953 strike,[32] but this was only a small part of the story. Without massive government financial support, the deep-sea fleet was doomed, SIU or no SIU. It was convenient to point the finger at the American-born leader of the Canadian SIU – and some suggested that Banks had been sent to Canada primarily to deliver Canadian deep-sea shipping to American interests – but the decision not to support a Canadian fleet had been made long before Banks arrived.[33] Neither Banks nor the SIU was to blame for the loss of jobs or the scuttle of the fleet. The *Globe and Mail*, to its embarrassment, had this fact driven home when the Supreme Court of Canada upheld a lower court decision which found that the newspaper had libelled Banks by suggesting he was at fault for the loss of the fleet.[34] At worst, the union's wage and other demands accelerated the inevitable.

The Great Lakes part of the industry was in much better shape and was the key to the union's long-term survival. A short time after bringing all the major Great Lakes shipping companies under contract, Banks launched a campaign to sign up the remaining small companies and crush the union's rivals, insignificant though they were. The remaining shipping companies were easily persuaded to join the SIU. Presenting a slightly more difficult challenge were the rival seamen's organizations. Banks's first takeover object was Captain McMaster's National Seamen's Association.[35] McMaster met with Banks and 'sold' him his members. In return for money, McMaster agreed to transfer his members and contracts to the SIU. This merger, which added approximately 1000 new members to the SIU roster, was arranged without the advice or consent of the men involved. Many of them suffered as a result.[36] Banks had no interest in these sailors; what he wanted was to control their jobs through the SIU's hiring hall. All of the former members of the McMaster association were allowed, at first, to remain on the job. However, as each voyage ended and they appeared at the SIU hiring hall for reassignment, many of these sailors found they had been placed on the Do Not Ship List.[37] These men were victims.

Banks's takeover of the National Seamen's Association was one of three such coups.[38] The only seamen's union of any size remaining outside the SIU orbit was the West Coast Seamen's Union. That organization, composed of and run largely by former CSU members, would be brought under the SIU umbrella before the end of the decade. With the exception of the Canadian Brotherhood of Railroad Transport and General Workers union, which had contracts for Canadian National ferries between railhead links, and men employed on some minor railway-related shipping companies, the SIU represented all the unlicensed seamen in Canada.

The union was a formidable one. At the same time, misgivings about Banks at the Department of Labour did not disappear, although any departmental ambivalence continued to favour the SIU and its leader.[39] The federal government also looked kindly on Banks. After entering Canada as a visitor, his permission to remain in the country was repeatedly extended until May 1952, when he applied for landed immigrant status. In the normal course of events, Banks, like other applicants, would have been required to reveal whether or not he had a criminal record. The existence of a criminal record usually results in the rejection of a particular application. The federal government was, of course, well aware of Banks's criminal past; it had been for years. To approve landed immigrant status for Banks, the Department of Citizenship and Immigration had to be 'officially' unaware of his convictions, including a recent one in Canada for possession of 36,000 illegally imported cigarettes. It was a prickly problem and one that was resolved by furnishing Banks with an application that asked no 'official' questions about his criminal past.[40] The application was, in these circumstances, successful. Shortly thereafter Banks was appointed by labour minister Milton Gregg as a Canadian representative to an International Labour Organization conference scheduled in Geneva.

Milton Gregg liked Banks; he enjoyed his company and considered him a colourful character.[41] The Geneva appointment was a prestigious one, and carried with it a certain recognition and respect from the government. It was also one which was severely criticized in the House of Commons.[42] After Banks left the country, it was suggested by the Co-operative Commonwealth Federation that he not be allowed to return.[43] It is not clear what the CCF had in mind; as a landed immigrant Banks had every right to return to Canada. The only way that right could be abridged was by due processs of law. On 25 February 1954 the cabinet considered the matter. Following reports from Gregg and minister of citizenship and immigration Walter Harris, the cabinet agreed to abide by any decision Harris thought was best. Harris referred the case to a Board of Inquiry. Citizenship judge Jean St Onge, sitting as a Board of Inquiry under the Immigration Act, ordered Banks deported from Canada.[44]

Banks, like anyone else ordered deported from the country, was entitled to appeal this decision to the minister of citizenship and immigration, and he did so successfully. On his last day as minister (before taking over the Finance portfolio), Harris reversed St Onge's decision.[45] What was really puzzling about the decision was that it had been discussed in cabinet.[46] George Drew, the leader of the opposition, wondered aloud about the 'many mysteries' associated with the case. He was, he said, at a loss to know what was going on.[47] Banks was extremely pleased with the result. 'You can't beat a combination of ability, brains and resourcefulness,' he told a reporter.[48]

The cabinet's intercession on Banks's behalf following his appointment as a Canadian delegate to an international conference in Geneva created the impression that the government supported Banks and gave legitimacy to his leadership. Gregg went so far as to attend SIU conventions and praise Banks to SIU delegates.[49] By doing so, the impression of government support was confirmed. The same impression, to the same effect, was left by the TLC.

Acceptance of the Canadian District of the SIU into affiliation was, after the CSU fiasco, inevitable. As Bengough belatedly realized, the Communist-directed CSU was not a cause worth championing in a fight with the AFL over Canadian autonomy. After reaching this inescapable conclusion, Bengough moved quickly and tried to repair the damage. The TLC suspended, then expelled, the CSU. At the same time Bengough issued a communiqué deploring the SIU's organizing tactics and warning that the SIU International should not expect immediate affiliation to the TLC. But this warning, as subsequent events illustrate, was nothing more than an attempt to save face.

In September 1950, just prior to the TLC Convention which approved the Executive Council decision to suspend the CSU, Bengough held a meeting with representatives of various international unions led by Frank Hall. This was the meeting called by Bengough in the spring of 1949 after he rejected the AFL demands that the TLC come into line. It was supposed to be a showdown with the Internationals; instead, when it finally took place, it was a capitulation to most of their demands. All areas of controversy appear to have been resolved in their favour.[50] The following spring the TLC Executive Council admitted the SIU into affiliation, awarding it jurisdiction over all seamen in Canada. This decision was approved at the congress's annual convention in September 1951. The SIU was now a full-fledged member of the congress. It was also the most disreputable.

Percy Bengough was aware of this situation. He had an excellent relationship with the Department of Labour and was kept fully informed of goings-on within the SIU.[51] Bengough claimed that the TLC was powerless to take action.[52] His successor to the TLC presidency, Claude Jodoin, did not feel much differently. Jodoin came from the International Ladies Garment Workers' Union, a union which had in the United States, over the years, received tremendous support from the SIU. Furthermore, the new TLC president had a personal admiration for Banks and was grateful to him for the SIU support which had helped propel him to the TLC presidency.[53] At the SIU's Seventh Biennial Convention in Montreal, held in 1955, Jodoin was invited to give the keynote address. 'The co-operation you have shown the Canadian Labour Movement,' Jodoin said, 'not only in establishing your own organization, which is a credit to the organized labour movement in Canada, but in helping other organizations establish themselves, with all of the troubles and difficulties you had, is certainly gratifying as far as we are concerned ... God bless your organization in its future endeavours.'[54]

The new president of the TLC may have owed a political debt to Banks, but this was really too much. Along with Milton Gregg, who also appeared at this convention, Jodoin was well aware of the true state of affairs in the SIU; just one month earlier the Do Not Ship List had been tendered in evidence in the Droeger case. To be sure, a number of outward improvements in the union's structure had been made. An election of a sort had been held, union members had adopted a constitution and passed the National Shipping Rules, a set of rules which in theory provided a comprehensive code for the administration of the union. These were positive signs and made Jodoin's presence on stage a little more understandable. But as an explanation for his uncritical support of Banks and the SIU, these developments provide only part of the answer. The rest of the explanation is not salutary.

Jodoin did not dare to take action. Doing so, he feared, would result in a division between national and international unions – that same division which just a few years earlier had threatened to destroy the TLC. Furthermore, moving decisively against Banks and his excesses could not be done quietly. Any attempt to restrain Banks's racketeering would immediately bring the SIU into the public eye and, rightly or wrongly, discredit organized labour. Provided the problems in the SIU were kept under control – and there was reason to believe that some changes had been made – there was no sense in rocking the boat. Banks could not have agreed more. With his position in the labour movement firmly entrenched, he could devote his energies to the shipping companies.

Unlike the deep-sea shipping companies, those operating on the Great Lakes had never banded together to deal collectively with organized labour. Their Dominion Marine Association was concerned with everything but labour relations. On occasion, for example just before the Second World War and during the 1946 Great Lakes strike, the inland companies co-ordinated their labour relations activities and co-operated to a certain extent. But they never did so formally or for very long; any arrangements expired with whatever crisis they were initiated to meet. The lack of co-operation among the employers in this industry can be explained by their fiercely competitive nature. So long as the companies believed they were better off negotiating their own agreements, they had absolutely no economic interest in working together. Their attitude changed after the SIU began organizing their bottoms.

To the companies' consternation, they found that the SIU was a militant union. Initially, the union was prepared to sign almost anything to get its men on board the ships. However, once the agreements were signed, the union adopted an attitude of business as usual. The SIU believed that the collective agreement should be enforced and improved. The Great Lakes shipping companies, realizing they had jumped from the 'CSU frying pan' into the 'SIU fire,'[55] organized an association to deal with the union collectively. Early in 1953, just before negotiations for the upcoming shipping season were about to begin, the Association of Lake Carriers was born. All of the major shipping companies joined.[56]

The association's first president was J.M. McWaters, an executive with one of the Misener companies. McWaters led the association in its first round of bargaining with the union. Protracted negotiations were held over the summer and failed to result in any agreement. The parties then went into mandatory conciliation, which also failed. By September 1953 the union realized it had better flex its muscle or the shipping season would be over without any improvements having been made. A strike was announced, scheduled to begin on 21 September. The union's timing could not have been better.

None of the shipping companies wanted their bottoms stranded in the upper Great Lakes by winter freeze-up. Just hours before the strike was about to start, the association capitulated and agreed to most of the union demands. The work week was reduced and wages improved. The new agreement's major contribution was, however, something unheard of in the shipping industry: an employee welfare plan, funded by both employee and employer contributions.[57] Details of that plan were to be worked out between the companies and the union over the winter.

Jack Leitch of Upper Lakes tried to enlist the co-operation of Captain Scott Misener and T.R. (Rodgie) McLagan, president of Canada Steamship Lines, to ensure that the plan was professionally set up and administered.[58] Neither the union nor any of the companies had the expertise to operate a major welfare plan which provided for sick pay, medical expenses, and hospital coverage, and direction by a third party would guarantee its impartial administration. Both of these reasons should have appealed to the SIU as well, but Banks advised the companies that the SIU was opposed to an independently run plan. The union wanted to exercise as much control over the plan as possible.[59] When the other shipping companies, in particular Canada Steamship Lines, refused to co-operate with Leitch and Upper Lakes, the result was a compromise arrangement which, in the end, gave Banks almost everything he wished.

Three trustees were to administer the plan, one nominated by the union, one by the shipping companies, with a chairman agreeable to both. The three trustees owed a legal duty to administer the welfare plan honestly, conscientiously, and in accordance with appropriate actuarial principles. In practice, however, Banks nominated a plan administrator who exercised day-to-day control over the plan and who, without exception, was approved by the trustees. As the largest contributor to the plan, Canada Steamship Lines invariably, but not exclusively, nominated the companies' trustee. The involvement of the other shipping lines was limited to funding the plan. The plan itself, more by good fortune than careful planning, ran well enough, its creation in those days before national health insurance a welcome innovation. What was most interesting about the plan was that no matter what the SIU proposed, the Canada Steamship Lines trustee agreed.[60]

Jack Leitch had also requested the other companies' support in strengthening the association. As it then stood, the association could negotiate collective agreements on behalf of its membership, but there was nothing stopping any one company from reaching a separate deal or signing a contract rejected by the others. The SIU could also call a strike against one company while continuing to work for the others, a practice known as target or pattern bargaining. When the 'target' finally settles, its agreement is a model for the other companies which were fortunate enough to continue operating throughout the strike. The only way around this kind of bargaining is for the companies to decide that a strike against one is a strike against them all. This was at the heart of Leitch's plan. 'I feel,' he wrote, 'we should have an agreement which would provide for a bond to be deposited by each Company, and that the agreement would allow any company which had been hurt as a result of any party to the agreement not living up to the terms to collect for damages up to an amount equal to the total deposited by all or any members to the agreement.'[61] Under this arrangement, any company which refused to lock out its workers in the event of a strike would forfeit its bond. Canada Steamship Lines' rejection of the proposal doomed Leitch's dream of a grand alliance.[62] It also marked the beginning of a gradual withdrawal by Canada Steamship Lines from the association and from co-operation with the other shipping companies. In fact, after 1954, Canada Steamship Lines had no need of the association. Alone among all the shipping companies, it never had another labour problem with the SIU. This excellent relationship was reciprocal.

As the largest company on the Great Lakes, Canada Steamship Lines could enter into collective agreements which other companies could not as readily afford. These agreements became the standard in the industry. While this result was applauded by Canadian sailors, the system was generally not to the advantage of members of the association. The 1955–6 negotiations for a new Great Lakes agreement is a case in point.

Beginning in the fall of 1955, association representatives met with SIU officers to try to work out a new agreement. By winter, the minister of labour appointed a conciliation board under the chairmanship of Judge Walter Little, which issued a report recommending that both the companies and the union make further compromises.[63] As was its right, the union decided to strike and the walkout was set to start on 10 May 1956.[64] Although only two companies were scheduled to be hit by the strike, the association announced its intentions of treating a strike against one company as a strike against them all. Canada Steamship Lines was not party to this plan, but most, if not all, of the other association members were. If the lockout were successful, Great Lakes shipping, with the exception of the ships operated by Canada Steamship Lines, would come to a standstill. Minister of labour Gregg realized that immediate steps were necessary to prevent a strike or lessen its duration. He appointed Carl Goldenberg, a Montreal lawyer and labour arbitrator with excellent Ottawa connections, to try to resolve the dispute.

The strike began on schedule and, as promised, association members, with the exception of Canada Steamship Lines, locked out their crews. Over one hundred ships were, by strike or lockout, involved in the dispute. Goldenberg moved quickly.[65] First he called a meeting at the Windsor Hotel in Montreal between the union and the association. Banks was the last to arrive. Before sitting down, he looked around the room and saw that the shipping companies had not sent any of their senior people to the meeting. He turned around and walked out. Sending subordinates to a meeting was no way to settle the strike. It appeared that the only chance of success was to bring the company presidents and the union boss together for a meeting face to face. Appointed under the Industrial Relations Disputes Investigation Act, Goldenberg had subpoena powers and ordered the company presidents to be present the next day. As it turned out, this order was unnecessary. [66]

That night Goldenberg invited Banks and Rodgie McLagan to a midnight meeting at his Westmount home. Canada Steamship Lines bottoms were not struck, nor had the company locked any of its employees out. But Goldenberg realized that if the SIU and Canada Steamship Lines came to an agreement, the other companies would quickly fall into line. He was right. The settlement to the shutdown was announced by the minister of labour on 18 May. [67] It was another advance for the SIU and its members. [68]

Although pleased that the dispute was settled, members of the association could only consider the outcome of the affair as a failure. The attempt to flex their collective muscle was undermined by a private deal between Canada Steamship Lines and the union. Once that deal was reached, association members had little choice but to follow suit. The economic consequences of fighting the union while competitors continued operating would have been disastrous. Only a completely united association of all the Great Lakes shipping companies stood a chance in an economic contest with the SIU.

Such an association was not in Canada Steamship Lines' interests. If some of the smaller companies were driven to the wall by high labour costs, so much the better. As the number one shipping company, Canada Steamship Lines had little to fear and every reason to co-operate with the union in areas of mutual interest. The 1956 strike and settlement revealed how easily the Great Lakes shipping companies could be divided and conquered.

7
Domination and Discontent

With over 15,000 members, the SIU had become, by the mid-1950s, one of the most important and powerful unions in the country. SIU members worked the Great Lakes fleet, a fleet which every year was transporting an increasing amount of cargo up and down the inland sea. But the ships of this fleet were no different from any others; they could be sailed relatively easily without their union crews. Provided the mates and engineers remained at work, men who had never been at sea could be brought on board and, with little difficulty, turned into sailors. Perfectly legal, this strategy was employed time after time to break strikes and, as in 1949, to replace one union with another.

Banks realized that if he could get the mates or engineers under the SIU flag, strikebreaking would be a thing of the past. In 1950 the SIU announced the creation of the Canadian Marine Engineers' Association and affiliated it to membership. This union was formed to organize the marine engineers. The engineers, however, already had a union of their own, the National Association of Marine Engineers, or NAME, which had existed for over fifty years and, like the SIU, was affiliated with the TLC. The SIU's creation was therefore dual, and the seamen's union was accordingly required by the TLC, as a condition of affiliation, to disband its engineers' organization. Banks complied, begrudgingly. Five years later an opportunity arose to do indirectly what the SIU was forbidden to do directly. It arose because NAME was in disarray.

NAME was divided into two districts: the West Coast District and the Great Lakes and Eastern District. Each district had its own officers and executive and both were subordinate to a National Council, traditionally located in Vancouver.[1] Rivalry and bickering broke out between the two districts and, at the 1955 Eastern District convention, Banks addressed the delegates and offered to affiliate the Eastern District to the SIU. As part of the SIU, he explained, the Eastern District would have the SIU's money and resources available to it while at the same time it could retain its independence and autonomy. The offer was approved by a large majority.[2]

The NAME National Council was displeased to learn about this development, as it cost the union more than half of its membership. Many engineers were also concerned. Management and labour do not belong in the same union: when they merge, chaos results. The National Council, however, did not move swiftly and decisively to bring its constitutionally subordinate Eastern District back into line. It was not until early 1957 that it finally came to the conclusion that something had to be done and a national convention was called.

Not unexpectedly, the Eastern District refused to attend. None the less, the convention proceeded and a new national president, Charles MacKay, was elected. Richard Greaves, a long-time engineer and some-time union officer, was elected national secretary. The new executive was determined to reassert control over the breakaway Eastern District and let it know as much. Meanwhile, when the Eastern District leaders refused to make staff changes ordered by Banks, the affiliation with the SIU came to an end and the Eastern District held its own convention and elected an executive.[3] Although unhappy about this development, Banks was not deterred. The SIU boss had a way of directing adversity into advantage. There was only one way to turn this situation around and that was to assist the National Council in re-establishing its control. Once it did, the SIU would take it over. In August 1957 Banks went to Vancouver to put his plan into effect.

Addressing a meeting of the National Council, Banks claimed to possess documentary proof that the Eastern District engineers were corrupt and had been misusing union funds. He professed horror at this violation of trust and, asserting that all he wanted was a strong engineers' union, offered his help to clean up the mess.[4] At the very least some scepticism about this altruistic offer would have been in order, but the National Council accepted it without question.[5] MacKay and Greaves moved to Montreal and, with SIU staff and money, opened an office around the corner from the SIU hall. They began to fight for the Eastern District's membership. The Eastern District appealed to the president of the Canadian Labour Congress, Claude Jodoin, demanding an end to the 'SIU raid.' The Canadian Labour Congress was formed in 1956 by the merger of the TLC of Canada and the CCL. Since the SIU and NAME had both been associated with the same central labour congress, the TLC, and their respective jurisdictions were a matter of record, it should have been a relatively simple matter for the CLC to order an end to the SIU interference. Jodoin, however, refused to become involved.[6]

After Greaves and MacKay arrived in Montreal, Banks arranged a meeting between them and Rodgie McLagan of Canada Steamship Lines. Banks asked McLagan to begin paying his engineers' union dues to the Greaves- and McKay-led group.[7] The Eastern District, however, had a collective agreement with Canada Steamship Lines which ran until the end of the year. To divert the union dues would be a violation of this contract, to say nothing of a breach of the company's duty to deal only with the legitimate bargaining representative of its men. Unfortunately considerations of this kind had never meant much to Canada Steamship Lines and McLagan did as he was asked.[8] The Eastern District, with more of its engineers employed by Canada Steamship Lines than anywhere else, felt the pinch immediately.[9] Subsequently, the National Council, financed by Banks, initiated a series of lawsuits which pushed the Eastern District to extinction. Because the Eastern District had never done anything constitutionally to sever its relationship with the National Council, it was bound to accept the results of the 1956 convention which it had not attended. That convention had elected MacKay and Greaves to office and, in law, they had control over the Eastern District. The leaders of the Eastern District were finished and Greaves took charge of the Great Lakes engineers.[10]

With his authority to run the Eastern District acknowledged by the courts, Greaves brought some badly needed order to the engineers' association. He also came under Banks's influence and control. The two men became, in a fashion, friends, and Greaves, who was elected president of the National Council in June 1958, began to drop by Banks's office every day for coffee and conversation.[11] With Greaves in charge, there was no need to reaffiliate the Eastern District with the SIU. No affiliate could have been any friendlier. The two unions worked side by side. So long as Greaves remembered his place, even if the interest of the two organizations began to collide, everything would be fine.

This harmony was a great victory for unlicensed seamen. With the engineers on their side, they might lose a strike but they would never lose their jobs. In these circumstances, the SIU did not need to extend its control to the mates, represented by the Canadian Merchant Service Guild. Without the engineers, the mates could not sail a ship. However, Banks was not easily satisfied. In 1957 he also began a run on the mates. By and large, they were even less interested in becoming part of the SIU than were the engineers. Unlike the engineers, most mates had worked their way up through the ranks and guarded their positions jealously. When the raid began, Captain Henry Walsh, one of the guild's representatives, was ordered by its president to repel the attack. Walsh began visiting guild-contracted ships and advised his members not to join the SIU. His activities quickly came to the attention of Hal Banks. When they did, on a certain day in August 1957, Walsh was in trouble.

Banks and Greaves were sitting together in Banks's office, a spacious well-furnished suite on the top floor of the union's headquarters in Montreal, when Banks was shown some papers. All of a sudden he got red in the face and said: 'This son of a bitch, this bastard Walsh ... he's up there in Thorold calling me a thug and a gangster and everything else, and it's time we done something about it. In fact ... I think we will.'[12] Turning to the microphone on his desk which broadcast throughout the SIU hall, Banks said, 'Casper report to Banks office.'[13] Jack Casper was a bruiser from Sacramento, California. Along with two other goons, Casper was ordered to put 'a head' on Walsh. Banks gave the men some money from an SIU strike fund, and the men left Banks's office to look for Walsh. Greaves was present throughout.[14]

Just before midnight the next day Walsh was attacked from behind when leaving his car. He did not see any of his assailants, who gave him a brutal beating. Cowardly and vicious, the SIU thugs left Walsh covered with contusions, abrasions, and bruises from head to foot.[15] The local police were called, and along with the RCMP, conducted a thorough investigation. Naturally they had some ideas about who was behind the attack, but these were only suspicions. In the meantime, the file was not closed.

What Banks thought he could gain, other than revenge, by ordering this attack is a mystery. It certainly did not endear him to the mates, who knew immediately that he was the mastermind behind it. Banks must have realized as much because the union stopped attempting to raid the Canadian Merchant Service Guild. In any event, Banks had what he wanted: the engineers under his belt. He had accomplished a major feat. However, instead of resting on his laurels, he now decided that he wanted to extend his control over the entire shipping industry. This ambition brought the SIU into direct conflict with the Canadian Brotherhood of Railway Transport and General Workers union, and ultimately precipitated Banks's downfall.

With 40,000 members coast to coast, the CBRT was Canada's largest national trade union. It was, for its time, a rarity in the labour movement: strong, successful, and Canadian. Originally a member of the TLC, the CBRT was expelled in the 1920s and joined the All-Canadian Congress of Labour. That congress later merged with the also-expelled CIO unions and formed the Canadian Congress of Labour, which in 1956 merged with the TLC to form the CLC. In theory, the CLC was completely autonomous. Fraternal ties with the AFL and the CIO in the United States, which also merged to form the AFL–CIO, remained, but the CLC was constitutionally independent and, theoretically, exercised full control over organized labour in Canada.

The CCL had never chartered a seamen's union. Accordingly, it was recognized at the 1956 merger convention that the SIU enjoyed exclusive jurisdiction over all Canadian seamen, with one exception: the sailors employed on CPR and CNR ferries serving railhead links. These men were represented by the CBRT. Only a few sailors were involved and the CBRT had no desire to increase their numbers. It was an anomalous situation and would probably have been resolved over time by the transfer of their bargaining rights to where they ultimately belonged, the SIU. The CBRT and SIU came into conflict when Banks decided he could not wait.

In 1955 the CNR ferry service to Cape Breton Island was replaced by a causeway, displacing a number of CBRT members. The union's president, William Smith, negotiated an agreement with the president of the railway, Donald Gordon, that these terminated workers be given job preference on a planned CNR ferry run between Yarmouth, Nova Scotia, and Bar Harbor, Maine. A new ship, the *Bluenose*, was being built at the Davies Shipyard in Quebec for the route. The agreement was approved by minister of labour Milton Gregg.[16] By the late fall of 1955 the *Bluenose* was ready for its sea trials. In its haste to get the ship out of the St Lawrence River before navigation became impossible, the Davies company asked the SIU to supply a crew. It did, and the SIU members sailed the *Bluenose* to Nova Scotia. Banks then took the position that the ship should come under SIU contract since his members were the first to sail it. The following spring when the CBRT made an application to the Labour Relations Board for certification as the bargaining agent of the *Bluenose* crew, the SIU intervened, but to no effect. The SIU then applied to the courts for an injunction restraining the board from certifying the CBRT, but this application was dismissed as soon as it was learned that, at the time of intervention, the SIU had signed up only one member among the *Bluenose* crew. The CBRT was, by unanimous decision, certified as the bargaining agent for the unlicensed crew.[17]

The SIU remained determined and began to raid CBRT members employed on railway ships in Newfoundland and elsewhere. Smith complained to Claude Jodoin. This was the first significant internal dispute the congress had faced since the merger (the NAME dispute would come later), and Jodoin decided to try to settle it informally at a meeting with

Banks and Smith.[18] Banks told Jodoin and Smith in no uncertain terms that his jurisdiction within the CLC covered 'everything that floats,' both officers and crew. He demanded that the CBRT hand its sailors over to him. That was something Smith would not do. Any possibility of subsequently transferring the CBRT bargaining rights to the SIU was now gone. 'Hal,' Smith warned, 'I don't want you to think that our mild manner and desire for a friendly relationship is because we are afraid to fight. We've been in many fights before and we've always come out of them bigger and stronger.'[19] Banks did not back off and the raiding attempts continued. CBRT leaders complained to Jodoin, but their complaints were to little avail. The congress had machinery specifically designed to deal with jurisdictional problems and the CLC constitution prohibited raiding among affiliates at any time. But, as was the case with the NAME dispute, Jodoin did nothing and thereby gave tacit support to Banks.

Indeed, when Banks applied to become a Canadian citizen, Jodoin even testified as a character witness. Banks was of good character and an asset to the Canadian labour movement, he told the Citizenship Court. Judge Paul Fontaine was, however, more impressed by representations made against Banks and rejected his application.[20] Jodoin was well acquainted with the true state of affairs in the SIU, but had once more put himself out for Banks and the union. His testimony in Banks's favour was, along with his refusal to intervene in the NAME dispute and the SIU attempt to raid the CBRT, a shocking abdication of his responsibility to the labour movement. If the president of the CLC would stand up for a thug and a tyrant, what did that say about the congress? Unfortunately, not very much. This was, in any case, the conclusion the officers of the CBRT were coming to, much to their regret.

The CBRT decided to take action of its own. As Smith had earlier warned, his union would not take a raid lying down and it launched a counterattack on the west coast. The CBRT could not have chosen a better spot.[21] After the fall of the CSU a number of its former members moved west, where the CSU affiliate changed its name to the West Coast Seamen's Union. Under the leadership of two former CSU members, Jim Thompson and J.M. (Digger) Smith, the West Coast Seamen's Union grew but did not prosper. In 1956 its membership decided reluctantly to merge with the SIU. The CBRT now made itself available as an alternative union. Elroy Robson, a CBRT vice-president, led the campaign.[22]

Beginning in late 1957, CBRT organizers started to visit SIU-contracted ships, attempting to sign up members. By September 1959 the union had made twenty different applications for certification to the Labour Relations Board for unlicensed crews on ships and lines previously represented by the SIU. Each of these applications was backed up by a lengthy list of new CBRT members. All twenty applications could not be heard at once, but they could be considered one after the other. The Labour Relations Board ordered that the first be held at the end of the month, the second in early October.[23] The CBRT's organizing drive depended on these first two votes; if they were lost, so was the campaign. The first was on board the *Clifford J. Rogers*, a ship of the British Yukon Navigation Company. Only a handful of jobs were at stake but Banks was so desperate to win that he travelled to Skagway, Alaska, to talk to the ship's crew.[24] It did not help. The CBRT won this first vote. Several days later it also won the second.[25] Just as Smith promised, the CBRT was giving the SIU a run for its money. And its campaign was about to be joined by an unexpected recruit.

In the spring or early summer of 1958 Richard Greaves, Banks's pal and the president of NAME, went out west to take charge of NAME affairs – in particular, of an impending ferry strike. Contract negotiations between NAME, the SIU, and the operator of the ferries, the Canadian Pacific Company, had been going on for some time. When conciliation and mediation failed, the SIU announced it was going on strike and, in the middle of May, much of British Columbia's ferry transportation came to a halt.[26] From the outset, Greaves thought the strike was a mistake. In his opinion a better target was the smaller Black Ball Ferry Line, which serviced many of the province's most essential routes.[27] However, the SIU's decision effectively took the matter out of Greaves's hands and the engineers dutifully manned the picket lines. Greaves began to believe that the SIU had no interest in an early resolution to the strike.[28] By bringing all ferry service to a halt, Greaves thought, the matter would come to a head and, in a show of independence, he called a strike against the Black Ball Ferry Line. It was set to begin on 24 June.[29]

Unlike Canadian Pacific, the Black Ball Ferry Line was provincially regulated. When the provincial government learned of the impending strike, it ordered the engineers to remain at work by an order-in-council passed under the Civil Defence Act. This legislation, as its title suggests, was not designed to regulate labour relations.[30] NAME engineers obeyed the stay-at-work order, but, when the government failed to legislate the engineers back to work or force a contract on all the parties through binding arbitration, they went back on strike on Friday, 18 July.[31]

To Greaves's amazement, the pickets were crossed by SIU unlicensed crew. The SIU members were not contractually bound to appear at work, for their union's contract with the Black Ball Ferry Line had also expired, but even if they were, the motivating principle behind the NAME–SIU alliance was to end maritime strikebreaking. By allowing their members to cross the picket line, the SIU signalled to the provincial government that it was not concerned about what happened to the engineers' union. Support, not betrayal, was what the engineers needed.[32] Again, W.A.C. Bennett's government ordered the engineers back to work under the Civil Defence Act.

There were good legal arguments that the use of this act to end a labour dispute was invalid. Greaves initiated a legal challenge which was thwarted by the SIU, launching an action of its own. Alleging that NAME owed it monies, SIU counsel was able to get a court order freezing the engineers' bank account. The SIU lawsuit was crippling.[33] On 24 July legislation was passed requiring the immediate return to work of all striking employees. The next day an administrator was appointed to restore and maintain services. Anxious to restore peace, the administrator marginally increased wages while the other terms and conditions of the collective aggreement remained in effect. Later, new contracts with all the unions were reached. It was an unsatisfactory end to an almost pointless strike.[34]

The entire episode was a rude awakening for Greaves. The SIU's conduct during the strike left no doubt that the engineers' interests could not be served by an alliance with the SIU. '[W]e have many problems,' Greaves wrote NAME secretary-treasurer John Wood at the beginning of August, 'which may be in the best interests of our members, but not in the best interests of the unlicensed and ... it is possible to have honest differences of opinion where we must ... insist on the best interests of our own members.'[35] The two summer strikes were excellent evidence of that. Greaves suggested to Wood that NAME consider a merger with the Canadian Merchant Service Guild. If any merger were to take place, this was the one that made the most sense. Mates and engineers had many interests in common, more than either classification had with the unlicensed crew. The main problem with the proposal was that Banks was sure not to agree, as Greaves learned when he returned to Montreal in September 1958.

The SIU boss refused to see him and Greaves found himself locked out of his own office. John Wood then advised him that a NAME membership meeting had voted in favour of a resolution calling for the amalgamation of the Eastern District with the SIU. The resolution called for the question to be put to the general membership in a vote, and the election was held at the end of the month.[36] Before the election, a large number of blank ballots were brought to Banks's office, where Banks, Wood, and an SIU Montreal port agent named Mike Sheehan marked almost all of them in favour of amalgamation with the SIU. A few engineers, approximately 150 out of the 600 eligible, were then given the opportunity to vote. Their ballots were mixed with the forged ones. To give the election an aura of legitimacy, another membership meeting was held and a four-man tallying committee elected to count the votes. Only one of its four members was aware of the preordained result of the vote. [37] It was a landslide. The final tally showed that the engineers had 'voted' in favour of amalgamating with the SIU by a margin of approximately six to one.

It was not the result Greaves was expecting. He obtained a court injunction preventing the merger from proceeding and an order restraining any of the other NAME officers from conducting union business. In violation of the court order, Wood emptied the NAME bank account and handed the money, almost $10,000, over to the SIU. He then established offices at the SIU hall and began working under the banner 'SIU-Licensed Division.' [38]

Greaves appealed to the CLC. The SIU, he charged, was raiding his membership. Jodoin had no way of knowing that for sure; details of the fixed amalgamation vote would not come out until later. Besides, Jodoin was not going to become involved in an SIU-related dispute unless he was forced to. In the meantime, the CBRT was quite willing to help bridge the gap. [39] At the annual NAME convention in February 1959, the delegates voted in favour of merging with the CBRT. This formalized the close relationship between the two unions which had existed since the previous fall. [40]

At the same time, Banks and the SIU were claiming that the Eastern District of NAME had voted to join the SIU and were now the SIU-Licensed Division. The engineers were confused and did not know who to believe: Banks or Greaves. The fraudulent vote was used by the SIU-Licensed Division to convince the shipping companies to recognize it as the legitimate bargaining representative of the engineers. Canada Steamship Lines signed on the dotted line when asked to do so. Those companies which were more reticent about unlawfully abandoning their contractual agreements with NAME were encouraged to do so by an offer they could not refuse: a reduction in manning for their unlicensed crews at the next round of bargaining. Almost without exception, all the remaining Great Lakes companies signed contracts, either themselves or through the Association of Lake Carriers. They now had two sets of contracts with unions representing the engineers, both set to expire on 31 December 1959. Signing the second agreement was unlawful, and all the companies knew as much.

'This,' John Misener wrote the Department of Labour, 'we realize is against the Labour Relations Act, but, under the circumstances that I have explained to you, we have no alternative but to do so.' [41] The circumstance Misener referred to was a letter of indemnity they had received from the SIU. William Dunkerley, the personnel manager of Canada Steamship Lines, admitted to Greaves that the contract with the SIU-Licensed Division was illegal, but asked the NAME president what he was going to do about it. 'There are no teeth in the labour laws,' Dunkerley said. 'Have a look at the Act. First of all you have to go to the Minister and get permission to prosecute. That will take you a couple of months. We will kick it around here for a year and if necessary take it to the Supreme Court of Canada. This will take about two years.'[42] A challenge in the courts was, however, better than nothing and Greaves, funded by the CBRT, retained one of Canada's top labour lawyers, Maurice Wright, to fight the case.[43]

A small company about to sign a contract with the SIU-Licensed Division, Gulf and Lake Navigation, was the first target of the legal campaign. Despite the apparently bona fide amalgamation of NAME with the SIU, the Labour Relations Board ruled that the SIU-Licensed Division was not entitled to sign contracts on behalf of the engineers. Nothing in the Industrial Relations Disputes Investigation Act entitled a union or a company to sign new contracts which overrode existing ones merely because an amalgamation or merger had taken place. The board ordered Gulf and Lake Navigation to deal only with NAME.[44]

Had the existing NAME contracts expired, the Labour Relations Board decision would undoubtedly have been different. Confusion about this issue might have been partly responsible for the Ontario Supreme Court setting aside, on an SIU application, the Labour Relations Board ruling. For reasons which are not at all clear, Chief Justice McRuer found in February 1959 that the Labour Relations Board did not have the jurisdiction to direct Gulf and Lake Navigation to bargain with an uncertified bargaining agent. The chief justice may have been correct in law, but he was mistaken as to the facts. NAME was certified; it had been for years.[45] It was an unfortunate decision, giving neither side the clear victory which was needed to resolve the question without further ado. Unresolved, the matter dragged on until early 1960, when NAME and the SIU-Licensed Division contracts came up for renewal.

At that time, Greaves wrote the new president of the Association of Lake Carriers, John N. Paterson, and advised him that NAME was the lawful representative of the engineers. Paterson, in turn, contacted the Labour Relations Board for advice and was told that NAME was the engineers' certified bargaining agent. Thereupon the association, in late October 1960, entered into a new contract with NAME, running until 31 December 1962.[46]

In early November 1960 Banks learned about the contract and called a strike against the Paterson and Misener lines. Under the terms of an existing collective agreement, all strikes were unlawful. The SIU persisted in any event, and the other association members tied up their ships.[47] The shipping companies were incensed and the association demanded that the government take action.[48] Minister of labour Michael Starr called Banks and told him to end the strike or face the consequences.[49] Banks said, disingenuously, that he was doing what he could.[50] Had he chosen to, Banks could have ended the strike immediately. Instead, he let it continue a few more days before ordering his men back to work. By then the shipping season was almost over. The loss of the engineers to NAME and the CBRT was a major defeat. Banks, however, could not or would not accept the setback as he was determined to control the maritime engineers. Toward the end of the year, the SIU-Licensed Division made an application to the Labour Relations Board for certification as the collective bargaining representative of the marine engineers.[51]

It was not SIU practice to apply for certification. By avoiding the certification process, the SIU avoided scrutiny of its activities and practices by the Labour Relations Board. Considering what that investigation might have revealed, Banks's practice made considerable sense.[52] Apparently in this case, he decided it was worth the gamble. Hearings to decide whether the SIU-Licensed Division or NAME was the engineers' union began in December 1960 and carried on into the new year. John Wood, Greaves's erstwhile friend and president of the SIU-Licensed Division, was the star witness, testifying at some length about the 'democratic' amalgamation referendum. Although it heard no evidence contradicting Wood, the Labour Relations Board decided that the entire matter would be best resolved by holding a representation vote. Conducted by the Department of Labour, the SIU-Licensed Division apparently won hands down on board the ships of all companies except for Upper Lakes.[53] What this result meant was that all the engineers except those employed by Upper Lakes would be represented by the SIU; Upper Lakes engineers would be represented by NAME. Just then, however, Banks fired John Wood, the president of the SIU-Licensed Division.[54]

The timing was an error. Along with another recently dismissed SIU employee, Mike Sheehan, Wood had first-hand knowledge about the initial amalgamation vote. The two men went to the Labour Relations Board and disclosed the ballot rigging. In the middle of June 1961 the board convened a special hearing, with Wood the star witness. This time he told the truth. His testimony was corroborated and augmented by Mike Sheehan.[55] The Labour Relations Board was appalled. The SIU was making a mockery of it and the industrial relations system. C. Rhodes Smith, the chairman of the board, had no intention of letting the SIU or any other union get away with that. If he did, despite a possibility of unfairness to the engineers who had freely voted for the SIU, the entire system would be placed in jeopardy. The other members of the five-man board, representing both labour and management, agreed. Unanimously they decided to dismiss all the SIU-Licensed Division's applications for certification, notwithstanding the result of the earlier certification vote.[56]

The SIU-Licensed Division attempted to get Smith's decision judicially reviewed. The attempt failed. In law, NAME was now the bargaining agent of the engineers by virtue of the agreement it signed on their behalf with the Association of Lake Carriers in October 1960. Unfortunately, neither that agreement, nor the more recent Labour Relations Board decision, was of any value. With the exception of Upper Lakes, all the large shipping companies proceeded to enter into contracts with the SIU-Licensed Division.[57] It was as if the industrial relations system did not exist. In fact, if not in law, the SIU-Licensed Division was now the collective bargaining representative of almost all the marine engineers. Only the relatively few engineers employed on ships of the Upper Lakes line remained outside the SIU-Licensed Division's umbrella. There was no reason to believe that Banks would tolerate that state of affairs, at least for very long.

8
The SIU at Bay

After NAME filed formal raiding charges against the SIU in October 1958 and again in February 1959, CLC president Claude Jodoin could no longer postpone taking action. Hearings were held, and the congress executive heard representations from all the unions involved, including the SIU. The SIU was ordered in April 1959 to stop its raid on NAME and restore to it all of its collective agreements. This order was backed up by a warning that failure to obey within thirty days would result in the suspension of the SIU's affiliation.[1] Banks ignored the CLC demand to withdraw from the engineers' field[2] and, as warned, the SIU was suspended from the CLC. It was given an opportunity to appeal the suspension at the CLC's next convention approximately one year later, but failed to do so. Accordingly, in late April 1960 the SIU was expelled from affiliation.[3] This move was not unopposed. Jodoin urged the delegates to suspend the SIU for six months rather than permanently.[4] His appeal was rejected. The SIU was now publicly what it had been privately for more than a decade: a renegade.

The suspension and subsequent expulsion from the CLC did not interfere in any significant way with the SIU's day-to-day operations. The CBRT's attempt to displace the union on the west coast had shown early promise of success, but by early 1960 the contest denigrated into a stalemate. While the CBRT was able to win some contracts, the SIU was able to hold onto most. On the Great Lakes the situation was a little different. In late 1958 the CBRT and the SIU began a fight over which union was to represent the employees of the St Lawrence Seaway, scheduled to open in June 1959.

Recent multi-million-dollar renovations had vastly improved the inland waterway's capacity.[5] If SIU members ran the locks, Banks reasoned, they could be counted on to assist sailors in the event of a dispute with an employer. Any shipping company, for example, which hired a strikebreaking crew would find that its ships were always last in line to be moved through the locks, if they were moved at all. Strategically, the plan was brilliant. The SIU filed a number of certification applications covering the employees at various locks and canals. The CBRT also filed a certification application. However, instead of seeking certification place by place, the CBRT applied for system-wide certification. From the employers' perspective, this application made the most collective bargaining sense. But the choice of which union belonged to the workers, and the Labour Relations Board ordered a vote. [6]

Both sides campaigned over the winter of 1959. When the election was held early in the summer the CBRT won, hands down. Banks declared that the vote was fixed, and falsely charged the Labour Board with entering into a 'conspiracy' to destroy him. [7] The charge was sure not to endear the SIU boss to the Labour Relations Board, as he subsequently found out during his attempt to obtain certification for the SIU's group of engineers. The SIU had been dealt another setback. Nevertheless, with a virtual monopoly of unlicensed members and with the majority of engineers, the SIU remained intact. In 1961 the CBRT decided to end its attack against the SIU. Costs were growing and there was no way of telling how long the fight might last. [8] The CLC, CBRT, shipping companies, and, for the first time, the federal government were watching to see what would happen next.

Ottawa's interest in Banks and the SIU, until the Liberal government was defeated in 1957, was one of benign tolerance. First Humphrey Mitchell and then Milton Gregg were made aware of some of the less attractive aspects of Banks's rule, but made no serious steps to curb the abuses. If anything, the government helped to perpetuate his regime through displays of public and other support. Granting Banks landed immigrant status, appointing him a Canadian representative to a conference in Geneva, and the decision by the minister of citizenship and immigration to overturn the deportation order of a Board of Inquiry were just three of the more startling examples of government intervention on his behalf. And, as with his relationship with Jodoin, Banks made the most out of his Ottawa connections. What was in it for the government, and for Jodoin, is difficult to see. Significantly enough, the relationship did not survive the transition of power.

Michael Starr was appointed minister of labour by Prime Minister John Diefenbaker. Unlike his predecessor, Starr was absolutely appalled when he learned about the Do Not Ship List. He ordered Bernard Wilson and Arthur Brown, also with the Department of Labour, to meet with Department of Transport officials to devise a way to outlaw the blacklist.

All that was required was an amendment to Department of Transport Regulations prohibiting the Do Not Ship List and, perhaps for good measure, another regulation transferring the hiring hall to the National Employment Service. But the minister of transport, George Hees, refused to take any action unless ordered to do so by the federal cabinet.[9] The matter was, apparently, never referred to cabinet.[10] Even so, the government looked into the matter. E. Davie Fulton, Diefenbaker's brilliant minister of justice, demanded an immediate and thorough investigation of the SIU.[11] RCMP superintendent C.H. Nicholson assigned one of his top men to the case, Staff-Sergeant A.J. Carroll.

Carroll realized that this investigation required discretion. It was politically important that there be no suggestion that the police or the government were interfering in trade union affairs. Yet within a short period of time, he was able to present a voluminous report on the SIU to Commissioner Nicholson.[12] A copy of the report was forwarded to Fulton. Unfortunately, only portions of Carroll's report and all other relevant RCMP papers have declassified, but they paint, nevertheless, a sordid if by now well-known tableau.[13] Of the Do Not Ship List, Carroll stated, 'The placing of a man's name on this list means that he can never work at his trade again.'[14] Equally as serious was Banks's almost wanton disregard of the criminal law. 'Criminal acts are being resorted to in connection with the activities of the SIU in such a way that the ordinary machinery of law enforcement cannot cope with them.'[15] Nicholson strongly urged Fulton to take action.[16]

Governments, however, like the courts, are loath to interfere in the internal affairs of voluntary organizations, particularly trade unions. If Fulton decided to take action against the SIU, he had, in the face of the CLC's abdication of its responsibility, to have excellent reasons, both legal and political. Almost nothing in Carroll's report was new. What evidence there was, such as the details of the beating of Captain Walsh, was insufficient to support a criminal prosecution. A report prepared for the minister of justice in July 1959 summed up the problem: 'the material gathered together at this very preliminary stage does not link any senior officer of the SIU with anything criminal and does not suggest any major misuse of union funds.'[17] In light of the initial report and this assessment, the only thing Fulton could do, in so far as criminal proceedings were concerned, was order the RCMP to monitor the situation and keep him advised.[18] After the SIU was suspended from the CLC, however, Ottawa had no excuse but to act. If there was insufficient evidence to justify laying criminal charges, an industrial inquiry commission should have been appointed; there was more than enough evidence to justify that. But for reasons which defy explanation, repeated demands for an investigation were rejected – until, that is, the CBRT and CLC, with a little help from Jack Leitch, left Diefenbaker and Fulton no other choice.

As Leitch expected, Upper Lakes began to encounter difficulties following his refusal to sign a contract with the SIU-Licensed Division. Prayer meetings and boycotts by unions friendly to the SIU in American ports were just two of the tactics brought to bear on Upper Lakes. Leitch nevertheless honoured his contract with the SIU, but began to look for a way out. Ironically, Banks gave Leitch the opportunity he was looking for.

In 1959 a wholly owned subsidiary of Upper Lakes named Island Shipping bought a tanker in Wales and sailed it to Upper Lakes's Port Weller Dry Docks near St Catharines. Rechristened the *Wheat King*, the tanker was converted into a bulk carrier capable of plying the Great Lakes and deep-sea trade, now possible because of the opening of the St Lawrence Seaway. Island Shipping, unlike Upper Lakes, was an offshore company, registered in Bermuda. Offshore registration is a common device used in the shipping industry to avoid national safety and manning standards and to permit the registering company to hire a foreign, and therefore less expensive, unlicensed crew. Leitch incorporated Island Shipping offshore for tax and other reasons and it was Upper Lakes's intention to man the ship with a Canadian crew under Canadian standards. The *Wheat King* was also fitted with the latest in automated equipment to reduce the number of men its operation required. After these renovations were completed, Upper Lakes asked the SIU to supply it, through the union's hiring hall, with an unlicensed crew. The company was under no obligation to do so.[19]

Under the Industrial Relations Disputes Investigation Act, the SIU was the voluntarily recognized bargaining agent for Upper Lakes. But it had not been recognized by Island Shipping, and that company would have been well within its legal rights to hire the crew of its choice which the SIU would have then been free to organize. In any case, Leitch asked Banks to supply a crew. Upper Lakes and the SIU agreed that the *Wheat King* would sail under a collective agreement similar to that in effect between the union and Federal Commerce, another Canadian company which plied the deep-sea trade.[20]

Everything seemed fine when the SIU unlicensed crew signed their ship's articles on 17 April 1961. Under the command of Captain Christopher Carr, the *Wheat King* was set to sail from Port Weller to Thunder Bay and then on to Great Britain. The *Wheat King* was one of the few Canadian flag deep-sea ships; a successful and economical run was in the interests of both Upper Lakes and the SIU. If it made money, there might be others, providing employment to Canadian seamen. If it failed, so did any hope of revitalizing the Canadian flag deep-sea fleet. The *Wheat King*'s crew could not help but be aware of this. Nevertheless, soon after leaving port, the ship was beset by labour unrest. The Department of Transport, Captain Carr, the officers and engineers on board ship, shore personnel, and Leitch himself were all satisfied that the *Wheat King* was sufficiently manned.[21] Leitch was being harassed for his refusal to sign with the SIU-Licensed Division.[22] Captain Carr dealt with the situation the best he could and, despite the all too frequent disruptions and delays, the ship made it to Thunder Bay, picked up a cargo, and headed down through the Great Lakes en route to England. After clearing Quebec, the ship suddenly developed engine trouble and had to return to Port Levis, opposite Quebec. As soon as the ship was tied up, half of its unlicensed crew, in violation of their signed ship's articles, gathered their belongings and disembarked.[23]

Upper Lakes charged these sailors as deserters and asked the SIU to supply replacements. Shortly before the ship was due to embark on 6 June, all of the *Wheat King*'s unlicensed crew, led by the recently arrived SIU replacements, walked off the ship. They too were charged with desertion and some union officers were charged with enticing desertion. Upper Lakes asked for leave from the Labour Relations Board to prosecute the SIU.[24] Discussions were held with the union, and Leitch, stating for the record once again that he did not believe his ship was undermanned, agreed to hire three additional crew members and withdraw the charges against the deserters. He would not withdraw the charges of inciting desertion against the SIU officers, nor would he withdraw his Labour Relations Board application requesting leave to prosecute. This settlement was a fair one, as the SIU acknowledged by agreeing to its terms and sending its members back to work. On 14 June the ship finally set sail for England.[25]

Two days outside Port Levis the ship again developed engine trouble. Captain Carr suspected sabotage and the ship returned to Port Levis. The crew, as is customary in the industry, were paid off. The crew members were free to go, which most did. The repairs took four days and again Carr asked the SIU hiring hall to supply him with another crew. The union refused. Leitch was advised that a crew would be supplied only if Upper Lakes withdrew its application for leave to prosecute the SIU. The demand was refused. The SIU then set up a picket line around the *Wheat King* and told Leitch that the ship would sit and rot. This was the moment Leitch and the CBRT had been waiting for.[26]

Without the knowledge of Banks, Upper Lakes and the CBRT had been discussing matters of common interest for more than a year.[27] The NAME merger had been effected; a local of the CBRT now represented Upper Lakes engineers. This relationship was amiable, and it was one which Upper Lakes wished to extend to its unlicensed crew. But so long as Upper Lakes was contractually bound to the SIU, the CBRT would not attempt to represent Upper Lakes's unlicensed crew. The expulsion of the SIU from the CLC and the mass desertion of the *Wheat King*'s crew introduced a new element to the affair. By walking off the ship and picketing it, the SIU violated its contract with Upper Lakes. That contract contained a no-strike clause; all disputes during the life of the agreement had to be resolved by binding arbitration. When the union acted unilaterally, Upper Lakes was arguably entitled to repudiate the agreement and hire a new crew. The CBRT was, in these circumstances, willing to organize and represent that new crew. But, unlike the SIU, the CBRT never ran a hiring hall; it was therefore up to Upper Lakes' personnel manager, Tom Houtman, to man the ship.[28]

Houtman went to Montreal to look for a crew. No SIU member would work the ship and the only would-be sailors Houtman could find were a group of unemployed Greek immigrants, most of whom had never sailed before. Houtman engaged these men, each of whom signed a CBRT membership card. The collective agreement which the company and the union reached was not a sweetheart deal; the men received the going rate. That is, once they got on board ship. First they had to get through the SIU pickets.[29] The authorities would not supply the number of police Upper Lakes needed, so the company retained the Montreal-based Citadel Detective Agency. In labour circles, Citadel was notorious for its heavy-handed tactics, although the strikebreaking business was as lawful as any.[30] In the middle of the night on 28 June the newly recruited sailors were escorted on board the *Wheat King*. As soon as they were, the ship disengaged from shore and anchored midstream. The next day it set sail for England. Engine troubles once again interrupted the voyage: one of the engineers was undoubtedly a saboteur. The ship anchored just outside Sept Iles, Quebec. It was 29 June.[31]

At 1:30 the following morning the *Wheat King* was attacked by gunfire. Grabbing a searchlight, the duty mate found the source; a small ship later learned to be under the command of SIU officer Raymond Doucet. Captain Carr, assisted by third mate Jim Hartford, returned the fire. In the ensuing melee one of the attackers, Nigel Dupuis, was seriously wounded. It was the most wanton act of violence to take place on a Canadian waterfront in years. It presented the federal government with an excellent reason to appoint an Industrial Inquiry Commission. The minister of labour declined to do so. The situation would only get worse.[32]

When another ship of the wholly owned Island Shipping line, the *Northern Venture*, arrived in Canada, Upper Lakes took the position that it was not obliged to ask the SIU to supply an unlicensed crew. In law, Leitch would probably have been better off had he made this decision with the *Wheat King*; as it was, the SIU had some legal arguments to advance in favour of the proposition that once a company voluntarily recognizes a union for one of its ships, it is obliged to recognize that union for all of its ships. The SIU demanded that it represent the unlicensed crew. Leitch, however, had no intention of dealing further with that union and invited the CBRT to organize the *Northern Venture*'s crew. As was the case with the *Wheat King*, very few of the men placed on board had ever sailed before.[33] When the *Northern Venture* arrived in Duluth it was immediately declared black by the International Longshoremen's Association, which had been told that the ship was manned by strikebreakers.

The International Longshoremen's Association was, along with the SIU and several other unions, a member of the Maritime Trades Department. The Maritime Trades Department was a department of the AFL–CIO intended to further the interests of maritime unions. Its creation, following the AFL–CIO merger, formalized the often informal co-operation which had existed among maritime unions over the years. From the labour point of view, membership in this type of association was invaluable, as Leitch was finding out.

First days, then weeks passed as the longshoremen in Duluth refused to unload the idled ship. Leitch appealed to the Department of Labour for assistance. It, in turn, asked the undersecretary of state for external affairs, Norman Robertson, to make representations to the American authorities. Whether he did or not, the records do not reveal. If he did, they were useless. The *Northern Venture* did not move and other Upper Lakes ships, arriving in American ports, were similarly treated.[34]

The CBRT was just as incensed as Leitch about the boycott. In the absence of government assistance, the CBRT had no choice but to act. After the *Northern Venture* had been idle for about one month, the CBRT announced, in the middle of August, that if it was not loaded without further delay, CBRT members employed by the St Lawrence Seaway Authority would, in retaliation, not move any American ships.[35] As a result of this announcement, a port of Duluth supervisory crew quickly serviced the ship. It escaped no one's attention that the threatened boycott of American ships in the St Lawrence Seaway produced immediate results. A solution, however, had to be found to the problem. In mid-September 1961 Claude Jodoin wrote AFL–CIO president George Meany and informed him that the CBRT was a legitimate union. Meany was asked to request his affiliates to respect this fact and stop the secondary picketing of Upper Lakes ships in American ports. 'I understand,' Jodoin wrote, 'that the *Northern Venture* is to dock very shortly in Marquette on Lake Superior, and I hope that your good influence can be used with your AFL–CIO Maritime Trades Department to stop this kind of unbelievable nonsense.'[36] Whether Meany passed Jodoin's request on to the Maritime Trades Department is another matter. Its president was Paul Hall, who was also the president of the SIU International. Meany depended on both the MTD and the SIU International for political support and was therefore not likely to use what influence he had merely to assist the CLC in a fight against Hall's Canadian affiliate.[37] When the *Northern Venture* arrived in Marquette, in early October, the longshoremen refused to unload it.

In late October 1961 Trans-Lake Shipping, another Upper Lakes subsidiary, signed a collective agreement covering the unlicensed crew of its *Hilda Marjanna* with a newly formed union, the Canadian Maritime Union. This union was established by the CLC following the decision of the CBRT made earlier in the summer to end its counter raid against the SIU. An independent national union, it was directly affiliated to the CLC. In December the Canadian Maritime Union was certified by the Labour Relations Board to represent the crew.[38] Now anxious to vacate the maritime field, the CBRT promised to turn over its unlicensed crew on board the *Northern Venture* and *Wheat King* to the Canadian Maritime Union. It was expected that the Canadian Maritime Union would soon come to rival the SIU. When it did, the interests of the unlicensed crew would be best served through membership in a larger specialized association.[39]

The CLC gave the fledging union money, as did the United Auto Workers, the United Steel Workers, and the SIU's American rival the National Maritime Union. This show of support augured well for the union's future. Two former Banks associates were placed in charge: Jim Todd and Mike Sheehan. Todd was a good choice. Many years earlier he had won the respect of Canadian seamen in his ill-fated attempt to reform the Canadian District of the Seafarers' International Union. Although he had not been involved in union activities for some time, he had not been forgotten. Sheehan, until his falling-out with Banks in 1960, was one of the SIU president's more constant companions. As such he was hardly steeped in democratic practices. He was suited, however, to organizing SIU ships for the Canadian Maritime Union. The CLC closely supervised the Canadian Maritime Union's officers and finances. When the union obtained a membership, its members would, through a CLC-supervised convention, be able to chart their own course.[40]

In the meantime the 1961 shipping season was over. It had been the most expensive one ever for Upper Lakes. Delays caused by prayer meetings and by picketing in American ports had cost the company tens of thousands of dollars. Many more thousands were paid to the Citadel Detective Agency for various duties, including protecting Upper Lakes property from increasing attacks by vandals.[41] When the 1962 shipping season opened, more of the same could be expected for the company's three non-SIU-manned ships. What would bring matters to a head were the events following the expiry, at the end of 1961, of Upper Lakes's collective agreement with the SIU.

Although never certified as the collective bargaining representative of Upper Lakes's unlicensed employees, the SIU had been voluntarily recognized by the company. Accordingly, when the SIU served notice to begin negotiations for a new contract covering the company's unlicensed crew, Upper Lakes was legally obliged by the Industrial Relations Disputes Investigation Act to bargain with the union in good faith. There is, however, no legal requirement that a company and a union conclude their negotiations with a collective agreement. In this case, Upper Lakes and to a greater extent the SIU, by their conduct in negotiations, ensured that they would be unsuccessful.

As it was legally entitled to do, Upper Lakes appointed the Association of Lakes Carriers as its collective bargaining representative.[42] The SIU for its part submitted a list of demands which were both illegal and absurd. Banks insisted that Upper Lakes transfer to the SIU the collective agreements covering the unlicensed crew on board the company's three non-SIU ships. As two of these ships had been certified to the CBRT and an application by the Canadian Maritime Union was pending for the third, Upper Lakes could not legally fulfil Banks's request. In addition, the SIU asked for salary increases over 60 per cent, at a time when contracts with other shipping companies providing for wage increases averaged less than 5 per cent.[43]

Early in February 1962 Michael Starr appointed a three-man Conciliation Board. After weeks of wrangling with no positive result, the conciliation process required by the Industrial Relations Disputes Investigation Act came to an end. Upper Lakes, as had been earlier and secretly discussed,[44] signed a collective agreement with the Canadian Maritime Union[45] and, within ten days, the union manned seventeen Upper Lakes ships. It was expected that the ships of the Upper Lakes line were just the beginning and that, as the organizing drive got underway, SIU members would desert their union in droves to join the Canadian Maritime Union. This view was shared by the CLC, Upper Lakes, and the departments of labour and external affairs. The Department of External Affairs agreed to emphasize to the American government the legitimacy of the CBRT and Canadian Maritime Union, and the propriety of Upper Lakes signing a collective agreement with them.[46] This latter point was particularly critical.

As expected, the SIU started picketing Upper Lakes ships in Canadian ports and arranged for their boycott in American ports. Lawyers for Upper Lakes in Canada were able to obtain court injunctions in both Ontario and Quebec restraining the picketing. The situation in the United States was considerably different. Maritime Trade Department affiliates began once again to boycott Upper Lakes ships. The International Longshoremen's Association was the main participant, but other Maritime Trade Department affiliates were involved as well. For example, in Chicago a local of the Grain Workers' Union refused to load Upper Lakes ships. Upper Lakes filed a complaint against that union at the National Labor Relations Board and the Grain Workers were ordered to work the ships.[47] When they did not, a United States District Court judge fined the union $17,000 and imposed a further fine of $500 a day so long as it continued to refuse to work the ships. The conclusion that the Grain Workers were being financed by the SIU International is inescapable. In short order, the fine climbed to almost $35,000.[48] Expensive though the fight may have been for the SIU, it was even more expensive for Upper Lakes. Leitch estimated that he lost $5000 every day one of his ships was forced to sit idle in port.[49] By the end of the year, direct losses exceeded $1 million.[50]

A great deal of violence ensued, virtually all of it inspired by the SIU. Union members belonging to the Canadian Maritime Union were beaten up, while CLC and CBRT officials were harassed and their offices occasionally ransacked. This waterfront violence made headlines. By the end of May 1962, in the midst of a federal election campaign, Claude Jodoin had had enough. He wrote to Prime Minister Diefenbaker demanding action.[51] Citing more than a dozen recent examples of intimidation and violence perpetrated against members of the CLC, CBRT, and Canadian Maritime Union, the CLC president insisted that the government of Canada take immediate steps to restore order. The CLC asked the government to investigate these criminal acts, and in what leading CLC officers later described as the most difficult decision the CLC ever made, to undertake a full-scale investigation into the 'whole matter of the structure, policy, operation and finances of the SIU of Canada.'[52] Never before in the history of Canadian organized labour had the federal government been asked by labour itself to investigate a trade union. Ordering such an investigation was well within the power of the federal government, but the minister of justice would only say that he was looking into the matter.[53]

If the government's apparent lack of interest was disappointing, the attitude of the AFL–CIO was infuriating. Word leaked out that the SIU of Canada planned to appeal its expulsion from the CLC to the AFL–CIO. There was a provision of the AFL–CIO constitution which, under a highly questionable interpretation, would allow the SIU to make that appeal. If the SIU succeeded even in arguing its planned appeal, it would mean that the CLC's constitution was meaningless and its autonomy non-existent. Accordingly, Jodoin, in early June, wrote Meany and warned him not to get involved. Meany was prepared to go along with that,[54] but he was not willing to offer any assistance of a practical nature to the Canadian labour centre. For example, when a United Steel Workers Union representative in Duluth asked Meany whether his men should unload Canadian Maritime Union ships, Meany replied that a national policy decision was not 'necessary to point out the simple fact that the SIU is an affiliate in good standing with the AFL–CIO while the Canadian Maritime Union is not.' The reply left little doubt about where the AFL–CIO president's sympathies lay.[55]

George Meany was not entirely to blame. Unloading the Upper Lakes ships in American ports was not just a union problem; it had become a national and international one. In June the Department of External Affairs advised the CLC that a note on the matter had been delivered to the American government.[56] There was little the American authorities could do, however. Until 1963 American law was unsettled as to whether it was the National Labor Relations Board or the District Courts which enjoyed jurisdiction over the labour relations of international shipping in American waters. Before the United States Supreme Court decided the question, the courts and the labour board competed for authority over the matter, often with conflicting results.[57]

In the meantime, Upper Lakes suffered. Not a day went by without one of its ships being delayed in one way or another by SIU-inspired conduct. Of greater concern was the increasing violence on the waterfront. Between late May when Jodoin first wrote Fulton and requested an investigation and the middle of the following month, numerous additional incidents of violence had occurred. The most serious of these took place on 16 June when the president of a St Lawrence Seaway local of the CBRT, John MacNamara, was savagely beaten on the front lawn of his home. Attacked with his own garden shears, MacNamara was lucky to survive. In the end he required more than thirty stitches to close his wounds.[58]

Both Jodoin and, on behalf of the CBRT, Elroy Robson unsuccessfully renewed their appeals for a government inquiry into what Robson aptly described as 'gangsterism' within the ranks of maritime labour.[59] The CBRT in particular faced a dilemma as its members were bearing the brunt of the waterfront warfare. As a union its job was to protect its members, something which the local police authorities could not effectively do in this type of situation. By appointing an investigatory commission, the federal government could bring an end to the more blatant acts of violence by thrusting the entire matter into the public eye. As that was something which the federal government was not willing to do, the CBRT was left with no choice but to force the government's hand.

The CBRT represented all of the employees who worked on the St Lawrence Seaway. Canadian maritime unions had, since the 1930s, realized that by disrupting just one seaway lock the entire inland water transportation system could be brought to a halt. In 1961 just the threat of shutting the Seaway down got the *Northern Venture*, sitting idly in Duluth, moving again. The CBRT, after obtaining its members' consent, decided to close the Seaway and not open it again until the federal government agreed to appoint a commission of inquiry.

What the CBRT proposed to do was illegal. Under its contract with the St Lawrence Seaway Authority, it was prohibited from striking for any reason during the life of the agreement. Nevertheless, the CBRT decided to accept whatever legal consequences might ensue.[60] The CLC was advised and agreed with the plan. Senior CBRT and CLC officials also met privately with R.V. Rankin, the president of the Seaway Authority, and advised him of the action the CBRT was about to take. Significantly, Rankin did not, by way of a mandatory injunction, attempt to restrain the union in advance.[61] Even after the *Globe and Mail* reported on 3 July 1961 that a CBRT boycott of SIU ships was imminent, nothing was done. Two days later, at the Welland Canal, the boycott began.[62]

As soon as it did, William Dodge of the CLC, representatives of the CBRT led by Elroy Robson, and members of the Canadian Maritime Union and Canadian Merchant Service Guild met with the minister of labour. Starr was told that the government could take what action it wished but that the CBRT would not back down until a commission of inquiry was appointed. The next day, the government agreed to do what it should have done a decade earlier and, when it did, the boycott of SIU ships was brought to an end.[63] The government had agreed to appoint a commission of inquiry.[64] What kind of commission remained to be seen.

9
The Norris Commission

Having promised to appoint a commission of inquiry, the first decision the federal government had to make was what kind of commission it should appoint. Years earlier when justice minister Fulton first looked into the matter, his advisers were divided between recommending a royal commission or a board or commissioner of inquiry under the Industrial Relations Disputes Investigation Act. In Canada, royal commissions are generally reserved for matters of national importance. The disruption in shipping was a matter of considerable importance, but hardly warranted a full-scale royal commission. At the same time, a less elaborate commission of inquiry under the act might be of insufficient stature to investigate properly the background to the dispute and to make recommendations which would carry any weight. A compromise between the two was reached. The minister of labour decided to appoint a commission of inquiry, but to appoint as commissioner a man whose stature and prestige would be reflected in the commission he led. That man was one of Canada's few admiralty judges and a justice of the British Columbia Court of Appeal, Thomas G. Norris. On 18 July Norris's appointment was passed by order-in-council.[1]

Norris, who was given a broad mandate to investigate the causes of the dispute, began work immediately.[2] As counsel to the commission he retained well-known Toronto trial lawyer Charles Dubin. On Fulton's recommendation, his former executive assistant, a young Montreal lawyer named Marc Lalonde, was appointed junior commission counsel. An auditor, commission secretary, and court reporters were also hired. Norris called the first meeting of the commission on 7 August in Ottawa. 'The subject matter of this inquiry,' Norris said, 'affects the welfare of all the people of Canada. This is not a mere matter of jurisdictional differences between conflicting unions nor merely of differences between employees.'[3] It was 'unthinkable,' he continued, that the usefulness of the St Lawrence Seaway should be impaired, and he warned that he would not tolerate any industrial disruptions during the course of the commission.[4] It was decided that the CLC, Upper Lakes, and the St Lawrence Seaway Authority would call evidence first and, after they had done so, the SIU would be given an opportunity to call its evidence. This was a mistake.

A commission of inquiry is not a court; it makes investigations, whereas a court holds trials. By allowing Upper Lakes and the CLC to present evidence first, the proceedings would take on an adversarial character, giving the impression that the CLC and Upper Lakes were 'prosecuting' the SIU, which in due course would be entitled to give its 'defence.' Norris should have ordered that all evidence be given through commission counsel, after which all the parties to the hearing would have an equal opportunity to cross-examine any of the commission witnesses. Proceeding in this way would have offered another important advantage. If all witnesses were commission witnesses, Norris would retain control over the hearing and the witnesses called to it. Nevertheless, with these preliminary details arranged, Norris adjourned the inquiry until 14 August, when the commission met in Toronto.

At that time Joe Nuss, a suave young Montreal lawyer speaking on behalf of the SIU, made a motion that Norris attempt to reconcile the parties. Even if Norris had been willing, Upper Lakes and the CLC were not. The SIU motion was doomed to failure and Nuss probably expected as much. Totally unexpected were Norris's comments after hearing the motion. Quoting in Greek, Norris observed that one should beware of Greeks bearing gifts.[5] Following a noon adjournment, the lawyer representing Upper Lakes, Jack Geller, advised Norris that an Upper Lakes ship, the *Gordon C. Leitch*, was being picketed by longshoremen and SIU-operated tugs in Chicago. Norris asked another SIU lawyer, John Ahern, for his comments. Ahern was the batonnier of the Quebec Bar and one of the most respected lawyers in the country. He advised Norris that the Canadian District of the SIU had no control over the longshoremen, but would try to use its influence over its American counterpart. When Ahern sat down, Norris set him straight.

'Mr. Ahern,' he said, 'we might as well at the earliest stage in this inquiry learn that I will have no part of any "Cox" and "Box" business.'[6] When Ahern protested, Norris told him that he was not 'born yesterday' and knew very well that the SIU was using a 'side-wind' in the United States to accomplish its objectives.[7] Norris wanted the boycott of Upper Lakes ships in American ports brought to an immediate end and told all the lawyers present as much. Only the SIU, of course, was in any position to do anything about that, which CLC counsel Maurice Wright attempted to explain. He too was given a tongue lashing. 'Cannot,' Norris said, 'is a word I do not like. Somebody can do something about it all the time, whoever should wear the cap can put it on. I think that a situation is disgraceful where so-called responsible people, whoever they are, are acting like a lot of Sons of Freedom Doukhobors, and that is just what the situation is.'[8] After telling everyone that he was going to get to the truth, the second day of the inquiry was over. It was obvious that this was not going to be an ordinary hearing. But then, Tom Norris was no ordinary judge.

Norris grew up in Victoria and attended a local law college. When the First World War interrupted his legal studies, Norris enlisted, was commissioned in the field, and awarded the Military Cross and Bar for bravery. Upon returning to British Columbia in 1919, he was called to the bar and began to practise law. In 1939 he again responded to the call of duty and served overseas as deputy judge advocate and senior Canadian legal officer in northwest Europe. On his return from overseas, Norris once again went into private practice, but was called upon on numerous occasions to serve as a special prosecutor in sensitive cases. In his private practice, as in his work as a crown attorney, Norris earned a reputation as a champion of the rights of the individual and the rule of law. In 1958 Fulton appointed Norris to the British Columbia Supreme Court and one year later he was elevated to the Court of Appeal. At the time of his appointment to the Industrial Inquiry Commission, Norris had not had enough time to establish a reputation as a jurist.[9]

It was soon obvious that Norris's quick temper and indiscreet remarks on the first day of the inquiry were not an isolated occurrence. Where the SIU was concerned, Norris was all too willing to jump to conclusions before all the facts were in.[10] This was certainly the case with respect to the evidence of some of the victims of the affair – the men who had suffered beatings in the months leading up to the appointment of the inquiry. Their evidence left little doubt that goons associated with the SIU were behind most, if not all, of the attacks. No other explanation made any sense. But the evidence of these witnesses was lacking in one crucial respect: not one of them was able to identify his attackers, and none of the attackers could be linked, other than circumstantially, with the SIU. The testimony was relevant to Norris: in broad terms his mandate required him to look into this part of the disruption in shipping. However, as evidence linking the SIU to the violence, the testimony was not legally probative of anything other than that beatings had taken place. Nevertheless, despite the evidentiary deficiencies of the testimony, Norris found the accounts of violence persuasive and quickly came to some important and damning conclusions about Hal Banks and the SIU.[11]

In addition to calling the victims of violence, Geller elicited the testimony of other witnesses, such as Upper Lakes personnel manager Tom Houtman, who were able to fill the commissioner in on some of the background to the dispute. After Upper Lakes concluded its 'case,' the CLC led its evidence. Maurice Wright had two major goals. First, he wanted to place the illegal boycott of SIU-manned ships by the CBRT at the Welland Canal in its proper context, by demonstrating that the CBRT and the CLC had only resorted to an illegal act after all other options failed. Second, he wanted to adduce evidence about the events themselves which had led to the conflict within the CLC and the ultimate expulsion of the SIU from the Canadian 'House of Labour.' In doing so, Wright wished to convey to the commissioner that on the one hand Norris was dealing with responsible, law-abiding organizations with important roles to play in society and on the other, a hoodlum-run organization which called itself a union, namely the SIU. By calling witnesses familiar with both the CLC and its affiliates, and witnesses well acquainted with the practices of the SIU, a contrast between the two would inevitably be drawn. Wright had a difficult, complicated case to make.

The CLC's first major witness was James Todd. Todd testified about his efforts years earlier to bring about reform in the SIU.[12] He was followed on the witness stand by John Wood and Dick Greaves, who explained the SIU–NAME conflict which itself was responsible in large measure for the overall dispute. However, it was the testimony of one witness in particular, Mike Sheehan, which made the headlines. As one of Banks's former henchmen there was not very much that Sheehan did not know. With considerable Irish charm and a refreshing willingness to confess his own disreputable past, Sheehan told the commission all about Banks's use of violence to keep control. His testimony about the 'pavement treatment' received front-page coverage. This treatment involved placing victims on the sidewalk and jumping up and down on their legs. To a country not accustomed to gangsterism except on American television, the testimony was spectacular.[13] Sheehan was also able to shed light on the internal practices of the SIU and the dispute with Upper Lakes which led to the formation of the Canadian Maritime Union.

Neither Sheehan's evidence, nor that of any of the other witnesses called by Wright, went unchallenged by commission counsel or the SIU. Both Dubin and Lalonde, on behalf of the commission, and Nuss, on behalf of the SIU, cross-examined these witnesses. Nuss had the hardest time of it. His cross-examinations were constantly interrupted by Norris, who regularly, increasingly, and generally without cause criticized his behaviour as counsel. Norris was aggravated and disturbed by the SIU's conduct outside the hearing room. When, for example, CLC vice-president William Dodge was testifying in Montreal, the Maritime Trades Department, which was holding its annual convention in that city, passed a resolution denouncing Dodge as a 'scab.'[14] At the same time, Banks was presented with a gavel made by members of the Carpenters' Union and a plaque made by the Building Trades Union in appreciation of his efforts 'to promote the interests of the trade union movement.'[15] A public attack on a witness giving evidence in a judicial proceeding threatens the integrity of the proceeding itself. The Maritime Trade Department's resolution was stupid, badly timed, and completely incorrect. It made matters difficult for Nuss, a young lawyer struggling to further the instructions of his client in an unenviable situation. It was obvious that the SIU was not taking the commission seriously.

Banks told his members as much at a 3 October 1962 membership meeting. 'It was clearly apparent,' he said, referring to those incidents early on in the hearings when senior SIU counsel Ahern was subjected to some of Norris's critical remarks, 'that the presiding judge was biased.'[16] Later in the month SIU-manned tugs in the Port of Montreal illegally refused to move an Upper Lakes ship, the Red Wing. Unlike most of the more recent Upper Lakes boycotts, this one took place in Canada. Norris sent Banks a telegram demanding that he order his men to live up to their collective agreement. When Banks failed to do so, Norris convened a special hearing and ordered Banks to testify. Banks claimed that he had nothing to do with it and that only the men who worked on the tugs could decide when to end the boycott. Norris did not believe a word of this and told Banks as much.[17] Banks was excused from the witness box and a little while later the tug crews 'voted' to end their boycott. By that time the commercial navigation season in the Port of Montreal was over. So, by 25 October, was the CLC's evidence. In all, Wright had called more than forty witnesses in twenty-three days. He had a few more witnesses remaining to be heard, such as CLC president Jodoin, and they were expected to testify after the SIU had called its evidence. The commission, which had on 22 October removed itself to Montreal, was expected to remain there for the balance of the hearings.

Although the SIU's conduct made it clear that the union had no interest in assisting the commission, inside the hearing room union counsel Joe Nuss attempted to do the best he could for his client. Nuss had several points he wished to explore and matters to bring before the commission. In particular, he wanted to ask about the illegal boycott of the St Lawrence Seaway, about the use of Citadel Detective Agency guards by Upper Lakes, and about what had happened to the jobs of 'hundreds' of its members the SIU said had been locked out by Upper Lakes after it signed a collective agreement with the Canadian Maritime Union. However, judging by the first witnesses the SIU called, the indications were that there was little evidence Nuss could call to make anything out of these complaints, nor to assist him in putting forward a positive SIU 'case.'

The first witness the SIU called was an economist with dubious credentials, who attempted to demonstrate through the use of statistics that the SIU was a responsible, democratically run trade union. A chartered accountant followed, who purported to verify the economist's evidence. Neither man knew what he was talking about.[18] The vice-president of the SIU, Leonard McLaughlin, was considerably more informed about the internal operations of the SIU and began giving evidence on Monday, 5 November. By Friday afternoon there was still no end in sight. McLaughlin was expected to return to the witness box the following week. What was unexpected was the commissioner's announcement, just moments before the hearings adjourned for the weekend, that on Monday they would resume in Ottawa.[19]

Luc Couture, the lawyer representing the St Lawrence Seaway Authority, had learned that the SIU had obtained a prohibition order from a judge of the Quebec Superior Court which, when served, would have had the effect of temporarily preventing Norris from continuing with the hearing. Couture discussed the matter with some of the other lawyers and Norris was advised. The order was based on the allegation that Norris was biased. If served, Norris would have had no choice but to discontinue the hearing and fight the allegations against him in court. Having no intention of so doing, he decided to leave the legal jurisdiction of the province of Quebec before the order was served. If the SIU had a serious case, Norris reasoned, it would have no trouble obtaining a similar order from an Ontario court. Significantly, SIU counsel did not make any attempt to obtain similar relief from the Ontario courts.[20]

When the hearings resumed in Ottawa, Norris gave no explanation for the decision to leave Montreal. He told SIU counsel that too much time had been wasted and he would tolerate no more delays.[21] After Nuss finished examining McLaughlin, he made a formal motion that the commission return to Montreal for the balance of the SIU's case. According to Nuss, the SIU had many more witnesses to call and documents to introduce. The balance of convenience, Nuss explained, favoured the resumption of the hearings in Montreal. Norris asked the other counsel present if they had any objections to the SIU request. Wright, the most senior lawyer present, spoke first.[22]

'My Lord,' Wright began, 'I would like to engage in some plain talk respecting the SIU's submission and I do not intend to exercise any subtlety in putting my submissions to Your Lordship. I regret that I shall have to use some strong language but I consider that the public interest demands that everything that needs to be said should be said. I submit that this application for transfer of the hearings to Montreal is not made in good faith and that good faith is not being exercised by the SIU or counsel for the SIU.'[23] The SIU, Wright continued, was guilty of delay and of abusing and perverting the commission, 'a free institution set up by Parliament,' for purposes of propaganda.[24] 'A halt must be called to these tactics,' he concluded. 'The halt is here. My respectful submission is that we should continue the hearings in Ottawa and get on with this job.'[25] In the unlikely event that Norris did not understand what was behind the SIU motion, Upper Lakes counsel Jack Geller, who spoke immediately following Wright, filled him in. The canny Toronto lawyer noted that senior SIU counsel John Ahern was both a 'master' and a 'specialist' in obtaining writs of prohibition without notice to the other side. 'Now,' Geller said to the commissioner, 'you are invited to return to Montreal to see whether Mr. Ahern will refrain from exercising his considerable charm in pursuing or taking another crack at his specialty.'[26]

Norris declined the invitation and ordered Nuss to go on with his case. The SIU now pursued with vigour what can only be described as a poorly disguised attempt to frustrate the inquiry through prolonging the hearings indefinitely. The only surprising thing about this was how long Norris let it go on. As a part of the union's deliberate plan to delay the proceedings, SIU members were asked at a membership meeting to volunteer to testify. The volunteers were interviewed, and those found suitable were bussed to Ottawa. Forty-nine witnesses were called in this way, ostensibly to give evidence about the democratic character of their trade union. Without exception they were all unsuitable witnesses and their evidence was often more damaging to their union than helpful. The SIU's case was, in fact, almost a complete waste of time. As November ended and December began, the dull parade of useless SIU witnesses continued. However, one or two of these witnesses were actually quite helpful to the commission: in particular, Bernard Boulanger, the administrator of the SIU welfare plan.[27]

This plan had been conceived many years earlier by Banks and was won through contract negotiations. In the years before universal healthcare insurance was introduced and before the expansion of the welfare state, properly administered welfare plans providing a kind of insurance for different medical and other expenses were a godsend. They were also, as investigations of the Teamsters' Union in the United States had revealed, a goldmine to racketeers. Boulanger's evidence, however, revealed that while Banks as both a trustee and union president had not met the requisite standard of care, he had not looted the plan or used it to reward his friends and punish his enemies.[28] By the conclusion of Boulanger's evidence on 20 December, the commission was ready to adjourn for Christmas.

After more than seventy days of hearings, no end was in sight. If the commission proceeded at this rate, it would still be hearing evidence when the shipping season opened in a few months' time. That prospect was viewed, especially by counsel for Upper Lakes and the CLC, with alarm. It was feared that the resumption of commercial navigation would inevitably lead to a resumption of the harassment of Upper Lakes ships and Canadian sailors on both sides of the border. Indeed, it was conceivable that the harassment would get worse. The SIU had no expectations of Norris making a finding favourable to its cause and therefore had little to lose by stepping up its campaign against Upper Lakes, particularly since the American authorities had proved themselves to be unable or unwilling to become involved in ending the illegal boycotts. It was obvious that future disruptions in shipping could only be avoided through a speedy conclusion of the hearing, the issuing of a report, and the implementation of any recommendations.

In these circumstances, Norris decided to expedite the proceedings. Accordingly, when the hearings resumed early in January, it was announced that all future witnesses would be called by the commission, with the parties given an equal opportunity to examine them. This step, commission counsel Dubin explained, was taken because the SIU was wasting too much time. The first commission witness was Hal Chamberlain Banks. The SIU president would be on the stand for nine days.[29]

Preparations for this moment had been going on for some time. Dubin, a thorough, highly experienced trial lawyer, had spent hours putting together his examination, but the real work had taken place throughout the fall as auditor Alan Watson and junior counsel Marc Lalonde poured over documents obtained from SIU headquarters and elsewhere. Dubin was to examine Banks first, followed by lawyers for Upper Lakes, the CLC, and the St Lawrence Seaway Authority.

Dubin wanted to know about Banks's exercise of power, use of union funds, and the background to the dispute. Of these areas, the one where Dubin's questions elicited the most interesting answers concerned Banks's use of union funds. It was, in a word, astonishing. By then it was fairly well known that Banks lived in an expensive home in a fashionable Montreal suburb. It was also well known that he drove a Cadillac convertible. What was not widely known was that the SIU members, through their membership dues, were supplying him annually with a new one, and had been for years. Union members were also paying the bill for Bank'ss penthouse office at the union's Montreal headquarters. Commanding a skyline view of the city, the office was equipped with a private bedroom and bathroom, built-in radios and televisions, remote-controlled draperies, and a loudspeaker system which allowed him to broadcast throughout the union headquarters. Banks himself worked at an impressive circular desk and sat on a chair which visitors invariably described as resting on a dais. Few union members ever had access to this office and even fewer knew anything about it. In fact, ignorance about many of Banks's activities was a characteristic shared by numerous SIU members.

The union members who had been paying his salary, for example, were under the impression that it was $13,000 a year. In fact it was $20,000, but Banks made his wage and those of the other executive members appear less substantial than they actually were by reporting only net income. Either way, $13,000 or $20,000 was a lot of money in the early 1960s, certainly much more than the average salary of $380 a month earned by members of a ship's unlicensed crew. In his testimony before the commission it was also revealed that Banks's salary did not even include his expenses. These too were enormous. Between 1959 and 1962 Banks was reimbursed by the union for expenses of $80,205.73, and vouchers were presented for only 10 per cent of this amount. Banks, whose job unquestionably required him to do a lot of travel, did it in style.[30]

When confronted with hotel receipts made out to 'Mr. & Mrs. Banks,' the SIU leader, who had ended his earlier marriage with New Brunswick-born Helen Lavigne, denied travelling with a woman companion at the union's expense, insisting that the registrations, made out at hotels such as Miami's swank Fountainbleu, were incorrect. What Banks would admit to was travelling from time to time at the union's expense with his nurse, one Miss Josie Charlebois. Banks justified this expense, to the titters of the onlookers, by explaining that Miss Charlebois, a 'practical,' not a 'registered nurse,' travelled with him on his doctor's orders: 'If the doctor tells me to take a nurse with me when I travel, I charge it to the union if I am taking the trip on union business.'[31] It was all above board, Banks said; he was 'not sleeping with her.'[32]

Banks's salary (which had never been properly approved by the union's membership as was required by the union's constitution), the Cadillac, the unsubstantiated expenses, and the questionable travel arrangements were not the only matters which came under scrutiny. Large lump-sum payments for vacations allegedly foregone in the busy early years of organizing the Canadian District, airline tickets made out to members of Banks's entourage having no apparent association with the union, lengthy sojourns at the union's expense in Puerto Rico and elsewhere – in one case ostensibly to assist another union in organizing a brassiere factory, and a myriad of other highly questionable uses of union members' money – were all brought into issue. For each expense that Banks could recall, and there were many he had forgotten, he had an explanation, if not a wholly satisfactory one. For example, he was asked why the union needed to maintain a luxury penthouse suite costing $475 a month in an apartment on Montreal's fashionable Drummond Street. The explanation, according to Banks, was to have 'meetings with people who do not wish to come into the St James Street building.'[33] Who these people were and why they did not want to be seen in the union's headquarters was unfortunately not explored.

Whoever these clandestine visitors were, they must have been important; once they arrived at the Drummond Street penthouse they were hosted in style. The apartment was furnished with two sofas costing $1000 each, a radio-television console costing almost $800, a $238 short-wave radio, another $374 hi fi, there was a maid to look after the guests, groceries in the refrigerator, and fourteen mirrors costing the union members $1082. Of all the expenses, the last was the most peculiar. For what possible reason, Dubin asked Banks, could any apartment need one thousand dollars worth of mirrors? 'Well,' the union boss replied, 'we got a dollar's worth of value for every dollar spent to advance the cause of the union.'[34] Dubin disagreed and suggested to Banks that these expenditures were extravagant, a suggestion which Banks refused to accept.[35]

Dubin also had questions for Banks involving matters other than the union leader's apparent misuse of his members' money. Dubin wanted to know all about the Droeger affair, about Jack Caspar, the enforcer from California who beat up Captain Walsh, and details of other acts of violence. In brief, Banks denied all allegations of wrongdoing. The same held true when he was asked about the notorious Do Not Ship List. That list, Banks willingly admitted, was widely used in 1949 and 1950 when the union was in the midst of its organizing campaign. It had been, Banks said, subsequently discontinued. As the Droeger court case of almost a decade earlier had shown, this was not quite correct. Furthermore, Sheehan and others had already testified about the ongoing use of the blacklist, but it was hard to prove its existence without an actual copy, something which Banks denied existed and Dubin did not have.

When Dubin concluded his cross-examination, Jack Geller and Luc Couture, representing Upper Lakes and the St Lawrence Seaway Authority, respectively, examined Banks. When they finished, CLC counsel Maurice Wright was ready to begin. Assisted by the research director of the CBRT, Harry Crowe, Wright had been preparing for this examination for months. He began by questioning Banks on his use of union funds. Banks was on old ground and answered the questions confidently. Some of the questions, probably by design, were patently ridiculous. For example, Wright asked about the expenditure of $1.29 on Kitty Litter for the union's headquarters mascot. If Wright was attempting to lull Banks into believing that he was dealing with a lightweight, he certainly succeeded. After almost a day of cross-examination, Banks was more than holding his own.[36]

As his evidence continued from one day into the next, the SIU leader answered almost every question. His explanations were often not very believable, but they were not always incredible either. On 17 and 18 January it was a different story. Wright began by asking about the conduct of membership meetings. Was it believable, Wright asked, that Banks's resolutions were always passed unanimously at membership meetings as union minutes indicated? It certainly was, Banks said; 'it is the fact.'[37] Wright next asked about the Do Not Ship List and the Report of Charges. The 'ROC,' Banks explained, was, in contrast to the Do Not Ship List, an information file, one which did not have the same effect as the old Do Not Ship List. Apparently the fact that they looked exactly the same was only coincidental. Banks was then examined on his evidence of just a few days previously, when he denied that the Do Not Ship List was any longer in existence. Banks repeated the denial. Wright had Banks where he wanted him. First he produced an old ragged list and asked Banks if it was a Do Not Ship List. It was, Banks admitted, one of the older ones. Then Wright produced several other lists, eight in all, including lists dated long after the time that Banks set for the discontinuance of the list. Banks had been proven to be a liar. Norris, shaking his head at the bench, quoted from Swinburne: 'all our past bespeaks our future.'[38] Wright's examination was complete.

Overall, the SIU boss's evidence did his cause more harm than good. Indeed, the allegations of impropriety in management of the union were given, ironically enough, further substantiation by Banks on his last day in the witness box. After receiving permission to make a statement, the SIU president told the commission that the union's internal procedures were fair, but that in any event it had been decided to establish an independent tribunal to review disciplinary actions taken against union members. It was too little and too late. Paul Hall had failed to make good the same promise ten years earlier at the Todd trial.[39]

In contrast to Banks, the next witness called to give evidence before the commission was entirely credible. Elroy Robson, a founder of the Ontario Federation of Labour and the chief architect of the CBRT's fight against the SIU, testified about the organization and operation of his union. The CBRT, like the SIU, had a constitution. The difference between the two was that the CBRT strictly observed its constitution. It held regular elections and each member was afforded a full opportunity to participate in the government of the union. Union officers were completely accountable to their membership which, unlike the SIU, took an active and informed interest in the union's operations. Union dues paid by CBRT members were a fraction of the regular and extraordinary dues assessed by the SIU. CBRT officers routinely submitted expense accounts, which were almost entirely substantiated by vouchers, to membership audit committees. The most telling contrast between the two unions was in their treatment of dissident members. The CBRT, a union with more than double the SIU's membership, had in forty years expelled only six persons. 'And I can remember them all,' Robson told the commission, 'we don't need a list.'[40]

Robson's memory was less clear when it came time to answer some questions pertaining to the SIU. Quite properly, Nuss wanted to know about how the *Wheat King* and the *Northern Venture* came to be organized. Somewhat improbably, Robson testified that it was the Greek-speaking crew of the *Wheat King* which contacted the CBRT, not the other way around.[41] Nuss then attempted to illicit information concerning the relationship between Upper Lakes and the CBRT in the fall of 1961. Robson agreed that his union was on a crusade to clear out the SIU, a union not fit 'to associate with organized labour,' but his memory almost failed entirely when he was asked to tell the commission about lunches and other meetings where this crusade was discussed with Upper Lakes[42] and with officials of the Department of Labour.[43]

Evidence of this kind was key to the SIU's interpretation of events, premised as it was on an allegation that Upper Lakes, the CBRT, and, more than likely, the government had joined together in an alliance to destroy the seamen's union. CLC counsel Wright was willing to admit that the CLC and CBRT had begun planning opposition to the SIU as early as 1959. Quite understandably, however, Nuss wanted the details and, when Robson was less than co-operative in providing them, Nuss should have been able to look to the commission for support. Instead, all he got was abuse. Some of it was deserved. When the SIU lawyer began calling

Robson Mr Robeson, presumably alluding to the well-known American Communist opera and folk singer, Norris quite justifiably became annoyed.[44] However, the commissioner should have kept his temper when Nuss was examining Robson on matters of legitimate interest to the SIU. Instead, Norris lost his already limited restraint. The worst outbreak occurred right in the middle of Nuss's cross-examination of Robson, who was finally detailing meetings jointly attended by senior representatives of the CLC, CBRT, Upper Lakes, and the government of Canada. After what was, at most, a technical breach by Nuss of the rules of conduct in examining a witness, and those rules had been broken at one time or another by all the other lawyers present at the inquiry, Norris went, in a word, berserk. In the presence of everyone, the commissioner called Nuss inept and cheeky, accused him of acting like a little boy, advised him to grow up, and impugned his honesty as counsel. As Banks later correctly described it, Nuss took the attack like a man. Following a short recess, Nuss, for the record, objected to Norris's comments and continued with his questioning the best he could.[45] But it was clear to one and all that any opportunity for evidence from Robson about what took place at some of those rather unusual labour-management-government meetings was lost.

Ideally, the commission counsel should have picked up where Nuss left off and dug a little more deeply into this part of the background of the dispute. Neither Dubin nor junior counsel Lalonde chose to do so. However, that is not to say that either man was only interested in delving into details of the controversy that reflected unfavourably on the SIU. This became crystal clear in Dubin's examination of the next witness, CLC president Claude Jodoin, who appeared on 25 January.

Jodoin had to answer questions in public for the first time. The SIU had been the cause of complaints for years. Why was it, Dubin wanted to know, that the CLC did nothing until the dispute broke out with NAME? The answer, Jodoin explained, was that there was no proof. 'I had a few complaints during the time that I was in Montreal,' he said, 'but very few.'[46] This was a lie that Dubin refused to accept. Jodoin and every other ranking officer of the congress were well aware of the SIU's internal activities, and had been for years.[47] Surely, the commission counsel asked, the CLC knew that something was wrong with the SIU? Jodoin replied that he had heard 'rumours.' Did the CLC not investigate these rumours because it wanted to protect a member of the labour family? No, the witness answered. Well, why did you not look into them, Dubin asked? 'Because,' Jodoin explained, 'we did not have any type of proof of any sort. I heard all kinds of rumours. There were two or three hundred on a so-called "Do Not Ship" list. Others said 3000, others said 7000, others 500. There were rumours of that sort. We did not take any action in this case.'[48] Dubin was back to square one. Why had the congress not taken any action? Could it be, Dubin asked again, that Jodoin and his predecessors regarded an attack on an individual labour leader as an attack on labour itself? Proving himself a master of obfuscation, the most Jodoin was prepared to concede was that in certain circumstances that proposition might possibly be true. Whether or not it applied with regard to the SIU, he refused to say.[49] The most the CLC president would admit was that, like everyone, he made mistakes. This admission touched off one of the more amusing incidents of Jodoin's testimony. It began when Dubin asked Jodoin about one of his bigger mistakes: his 1957 testimony in support of Banks's application to become a Canadian citizen. Jodoin's testimony was not entirely truthful, but at least he could make fun of himself. 'That's right,' he told Dubin. 'That is why I told you that when I make errors I make some good ones.'[50] His judgment had changed, but despite a number of attempts by Dubin to find out exactly what made it change, Jodoin's testimony did not become any more forthcoming.

Perhaps more out of frustration than anything else, Dubin asked what the CLC hoped to gain from the inquiry. The best answer Jodoin could come up with was 'the truth.' Dubin pressed him further and as he did it became painfully obvious that Jodoin had given the matter little, if any, thought. Dubin's questions were embarrassing to the congress president and would have continued to be had Maurice Wright not intervened and, more for the benefit of his client than the commission, explained that Jodoin was just one executive council member and that before the commission was over, the CLC would make complete recommendations.[51]

When Joe Nuss was given an opportunity to examine Jodoin several days later, he continued the line of questioning Dubin had begun. Nuss asked Jodoin about his relationship with Banks. It was not, according to Jodoin, much of a relationship at all. Their meetings were infrequent. Both claims were false, as Jodoin later admitted that he had called on Banks at his house, visited him in his office, and run into him at national conventions and other congresses. In short order, Jodoin also acknowledged making glowing tributes to Banks at SIU conventions. This was embarrassing to Jodoin, but the worst was yet to come. What about the rumours of the Do Not Ship list and the Report of Charges? Why, Nuss asked, had Jodoin never done anything about that? Was it not true that all of the allegations which were presently being made against Banks had been made in the past? Had the congress leader on occasion not discussed these concerns with Banks? The answer to each of these questions reflected poorly on both Jodoin and the congress. The CLC president fudged as much as he could. In fact, most of the answers he gave made very little sense. But the substance of his evidence, pieced together from the transcript, could not be more clear.

Jodoin had, he admitted again, heard all sorts of things about Banks and the SIU. He said that they were rumours and that rumours alone did not give him any justification to act: 'if I haven't got any basis for a complaint, a factual one which somebody will back up, it is not the function of the CLC to go and examine an autonomous affiliated organization.'[52] The rumours of a Do Not Ship List, the Todd trial, the Droeger affair, the reports from the Department of Labour, the violence against members, the high dues, the two-tiered system of membership, the earlier events with NAME, all of these were, according to Jodoin's testimony, mere 'rumours.' As such, they were not sufficient to merit an official investigation by the congress to ensure that the rights of the members of an affiliated organization were not being trampled on.

When the congress finally took action it was not because Jodoin had suddenly been furnished with the facts, but because it had no other choice. The facts had always been there for the asking; what had changed was that raiding charges filed by NAME and the violence on the waterfront had publicly exposed the activities of the SIU. Once these activities were exposed, and once the CLC was constitutionally bound to take action, it could no longer affect the studied detachment which had characterized its conduct, and that of the predecessor TLC, for so many years. Had NAME, the CBRT, and Upper Lakes not come into conflict with the SIU, and had the CBRT and Upper Lakes not refused to back down, the 'rumours' would, in all likelihood, have remained exactly that. The CLC and its predecessor had failed to take action for many reasons. Percy Bengough and the TLC feared another confrontation with the AFL and the Internationals so soon after the CSU debacle, while Claude Jodoin, who was intent on entrenching the legitimacy of organized labour in Canadian society, ignored the charges of impropriety in the SIU rather than face the damage to labour's cause their prosecution may have entailed. Both the TLC and the CLC had sacrificed principle to expediency. In the process, the lives of thousands had been damaged. It was not organized labour's finest hour.

Fortunately for Jodoin, his cross-examination by Nuss was shortlived and by noon of 1 February, other than a brief appearance some days later, Jodoin's testimony was over. The commission, however, ground on. John Misener and John Paterson both made appearances, but added little. Several weeks later the testimonies of Norman Reoch and then of Rodgie McLagan were similarly unenlightening.[53] The evidence of Upper Lakes president Jack Leitch was more germane. From the SIU's point of view, now was the chance to ask Leitch all sorts of questions about the use of the Citadel Detective Agency and about its alliance with the CBRT.

In particular, Nuss wanted to know more than just the cost to Upper Lakes of hiring the private detectives; he also wanted to know who was stationed where, for how long, at what times, and under whose instructions. When Upper Lakes counsel raised an objection to these questions, Nuss properly explained that they were relevant. There was a remarkable relationship, according to Nuss, between detectives and violence. The SIU lawyer attempted to explain that in the history of the labour movement there were numerous examples of private detectives being used to frustrate trade union activity, of private detectives committing acts of violence for which unions were blamed. Nuss was suggesting that this might be the case in the SIU–Upper Lakes affair. Accordingly, he wanted to ask Leitch some questions. Norris did not agree.[54]

First the commissioner told Nuss not to make any inflammatory speeches. When the SIU lawyer insisted on being able to ask his questions, Norris not only refused, but added, 'I am ashamed of you.' Nuss continued to make representations as best he could. He was not, he told the commissioner, stating that the detectives did or did not commit acts of violence. All he was saying was that the vast number of detectives involved in the dispute was a salient point and should be taken into consideration. There was absolutely nothing wrong with this line of questioning. In the earliest days of the inquiry, Norris had shown himself more than willing to listen to evidence of violence which inferentially, but not directly, implicated the SIU. He was therefore bound to allow the SIU to elicit evidence of violence that inferentially implicated the Citadel Detective Agency and Upper Lakes. Once the evidence had been adduced, counsel could argue as to what conclusions should be drawn, and Norris, after listening to their submissions and weighing the evidence, could decide for himself which version of events, if any, he believed. But that process could not begin until Nuss's questions were answered. Norris had no right or reason to prevent Nuss from asking these questions, but he ordered the SIU lawyer to begin another line of questioning. Nuss had no choice but to obey.[55]

The commission continued and, with Norris growing more and more impatient by the day, still no end was in sight. The change of procedure announced following the Christmas recess had done little to speed up the inquiry's pace. On 11 March 1963, the 104th day of hearings, the commissioner, completely unexpectedly, told counsel that he was ready to proceed to argument. Nuss objected. The SIU, he said, had not had a sufficient opportunity to adduce evidence. Nuss had supplied commission counsel Dubin with a list of witnesses he wished to have called on behalf of the SIU. But after reviewing the list, Dubin recommended to Norris that only three of the eighteen suggested witnesses actually be called.[56] Now Norris was suggesting that the evidence end and that argument begin. While the other counsel were not as disturbed as Nuss by this sudden change of events, they were just as startled by the commissioner's announcement. Wright, for example, admitted to being 'taken by surprise.'[57]

After learning of Norris's decision to stop hearing evidence, Nuss renewed an earlier SIU request that Norris disqualify himself as commissioner. In brief, Nuss asked Norris to disqualify himself on four major grounds: that the commissioner had restricted the SIU in adducing evidence and examining witnesses; that the rules of evidence were inconsistently applied throughout the hearing to the detriment of the SIU; that the commissioner prejudged certain matters to the detriment of the SIU; and that the commissioner had treated the SIU's lawyer in an abusive manner on numerous occasions throughout the inquiry. These grounds, each of which was supported by at least one example and could have been substantiated by many more, had the effect, according to the SIU submission, of depriving the SIU of a full and thorough opportunity to present its case.[58]

That there was something to the SIU charges is indisputable. They were, however, only part of the story. The SIU had authored many of its own misfortunes and had, indeed, as the scores of totally useless SIU witnesses who testified immediately before the Christmas recess illustrated, attempted on more than one occasion to frustrate the work of the commission. The request that Norris disqualify himself also came too late in the day. Maurice Wright called it 'scandalous.'[59] The urbane Luc Couture, the lawyer representing the St Lawrence Seaway Authority, quoted poetry in Italian: 'You cannot complain of yesterday's black snow,' he translated, 'if you allow today's white snow to fall over it.'[60] The legal point Couture was making so elegantly was that there is a limit to how far back a party to a proceeding can go in alleging an impropriety. If the impropriety was of such a serious nature as to threaten the rights of a litigant, it should have been acted on with dispatch; if counsel chose not to do so, then he was later precluded from making any complaints about it.

Norris denied the motion and asked Upper Lakes lawyer John Geller to begin his argument the following day. However, when the commission reconvened, Nuss announced that the SIU would no longer take part. There was no chance of receiving a fair hearing in closing argument, Nuss said, and therefore the SIU had decided to withdraw.[61] The commission had heard almost 200 witnesses, and had received more than 800 exhibits. Hearings had taken place in Ottawa, Toronto, St Catharines, and Montreal. On the day the SIU withdrew, the commission was meeting for the 105th time and the transcript of evidence was almost 16,000 pages long. The commission had occupied the full-time attention of five lawyers and countless newspaper reporters. The hearings had been front-page news for months. And, except for argument and a report, it was effectively over.

If Jack Geller was taken aback by the short notice Norris gave him to present Upper Lakes argument, there was no sign of it when he got up to speak. Following some general comments about the difficulties in dealing with the SIU over the years, Geller began, in a long, point-by-point, at times impassioned, review of the evidence, to analyse the breakdown of Upper Lakes's relationship with the SIU.[62]

When looked at in its entirety, the evidence, Geller said, led to the conclusion that the SIU had no respect for the law. This situation cried out for change. Upper Lakes would not, however, be making any recommendations as to what that change should be. As Geller explained, his company had no formal relationship with the SIU and, besides, it was up to the CLC to make recommendations on that point. What Upper Lakes did want the commissioner to do was to recommend in his report to the minister of labour that the government of Canada take whatever steps were necessary to ensure that Canadian ships flying Canadian flags with Canadian crews certified by Canada's Labour Relations Board could operate without interference in both Canadian and American waters. After thanking the commissioner for his patience and consideration, the Upper Lakes lawyer took his seat.[63]

Upper Lakes's battle with the SIU had been long and costly. It was not over yet and would not be for some time. Geller's description of the events leading up to the dispute rang true. As the commissioner's report would later reveal, they also struck home. There were omissions, to be sure. Very little was said about how the *Wheat King*'s and *Northern Venture*'s crews became members of the CBRT. Not enough was said about the 1962 meetings with the CLC, meetings which took place at the same time that Upper Lakes was legally bound to attempt to bargain in good faith with the SIU. Nothing was said about the hundreds of seamen, some of whom had worked for Upper Lakes for years, who lost their jobs as a result of the collective agreement signed with the Canadian Maritime Union. But these were matters which one could hardly expect the Upper Lakes lawyer to bring to the commissioner's attention. That was the job of counsel for the

SIU, and that counsel was no longer present at the inquiry.[64] Geller's job, performed with skill and integrity, was now over.

As important as Geller's submissions to the inquiry were, it was the CLC, not Upper Lakes, which had the most to gain or lose by the commissioner's report. Upper Lakes ships were no longer manned by SIU crews and, although there was every expectation that the SIU-inspired harassment would begin anew following the opening in April of commercial navigation, that was something Upper Lakes could now, at least in theory, effectively deal with. Two recent decisions of the Supreme Court of the United States had clarified the jurisdiction of American courts and the National Labor Relations Board over foreign shipping. This removed the legal roadblock which had previously complicated Upper Lakes's attempts to obtain relief from SIU-directed picketing in American ports.[65] The CLC, in contrast, had more riding on the outcome of the inquiry. The hearings had been an unprecedented public display of organized labour's dirty laundry. It was now up to Maurice Wright to put the evidence of the past nine months into context. It was essential that the SIU be seen for what it was: an anomaly within the lawful and democratic trade union movement, not, as some would believe, the tip of an insidious iceberg. Wright had to convince Norris, and the Canadian public, that while the CLC may not have initially acted with dispatch in dealings with Banks and the SIU, when the push came, the CLC had acted properly.[66] The CLC's submissions began on Wednesday morning, 13 March 1963. Wright spoke for the entire day.

The SIU was not a union, Wright explained. A trade union was a free association of workers. That was something the SIU was most assuredly not. 'The SIU, on the record – on the abundant and incontroverted evidence before this Commission – is not a free association of workers. It is a captive legion of dragooned and helpless individuals.'[67] Bogus elections, fixed union meetings, brainwashing and propaganda, violence, intimidation, and the Do Not Ship List were among the instruments of Banks's control. Wright spared few details in his almost spell-binding account of Banks's exercise of power. But the CLC lawyer preserved the bulk of his outrage for the instrument of control he most despised, the insidious and evil Do Not Ship List.

'In 1951,' Wright began, 'there were over 2,000 names on the Do Not Ship list ... In 1962 there were 3,999 names on the Do Not Ship list (Report of Charges Cards they called them) seen by Commission Counsel in the SIU Headquarters Hall ... If we were to say that 10,000 Canadians have been barred from the marine industry by Mr. Banks, we would probably be understating the magnitude of his monstrous crime against

Canadian seamen.'[68] Examination of the different Do Not Ship Lists and
Report of Charges cards revealed that with only very rare exceptions, seamen were expelled from the union solely because Banks or some SIU func-
tionary questioned their loyalty and obedience.[69]

The SIU, Wright explained, was a union quite unlike any other. It 'is
congenitally incapable of making a contribution to the labour movement.
It has no ideas. Its leadership is, in the widest sense, unlettered. Its
spokesmen have not even heard of the names of great labour leaders, past
or present, including the founder of their own union. Their weapons are
clubs, not ideas. They are not of the labour movement – they are a growth
upon it.'[70] What other trade union in Canada, Wright asked, has a Do
Not Ship List? What other trade union goes on year after year without
affording its members any opportunity to attend union conventions?
What other trade union has fallen into the hands of unconscionable
leaders who, in an attempt to gouge as much money as possible from their
members, have such a disproportionate number of members in relation to
available jobs? What other trade union uses violence and fear as a continuing instrument of policy to regulate their members and the industry in
which it operates? 'The SIU is unique unto itself,' Wright said. The SIU was
the problem and, Wright urged, Norris should not lose sight of that fact.[71]

If legislation of general application were passed, the consequences,
according to Wright, would be tragic: 'All unions and their leaders would
comply with such general legislation; all, that is, except the SIU.'[72]
Reforms to the industrial relations system were not what the situation
demanded. The system itself was operating properly and collective bargaining was making an essential contribution in the establishment of the
social principles that guided industrial society. What had no contribution
to make was the SIU and its leaders. 'We have stated,' Wright said, 'that
the SIU is not a part of the Canadian labour movement – it is a growth
upon it. Equally, we submit, that the SIU is not a part of Canadian society
– it is a growth upon it. We submit that Your Lordship should be prepared to recommend whatever social surgery is necessary to relieve both
the trade union movement and society from this growth. There is no place
in our social structure for a hoodlum empire which works hand-in-glove
with certain shipping companies to the advantage of both and to the dis-
advantage of the workers and the general public.'[73] Before telling the
commissioner the specific social surgery the CLC had in mind, Wright
paused and then spoke about the CLC's part in the affair. This was probably the most important part of his address:

The labour movement bears and is most conscious of bearing a heavy burden of
guilt in allowing so intolerable a situation to develop and to continue. It is a burden

of guilt which rests also upon shipping companies and upon Government. The back-door agreements which some of the companies made with Banks gave the SIU a powerful weapon against other shipowners. The practice of entering into collective agreements with both the NAME and the SIU for the same group of employees covering the same period of time, however great the intimidation to which they were exposed was inexcusable and served only to embolden Banks and to convince him that might was right.

Nor can Government escape its share of guilt. This Inquiry has revealed that certain departments of Government knew for some years what was going on in the SIU; yet nothing was done ... The fact that others are responsible equally does not lessen the guilt of the labour movement. The leadership of the labour movement should have known more than it did know. It should have done more than it did, earlier than it did, on the basis of what it did know. And it should have enquired more deeply into what it suspected and heard rumoured. In defence it might be pointed out that the Canadian labour movement is a large and varied operation, or that the Canadian Labour Congress is a 'labour-centre' and not a union, and limited in its supervisory activities. Or more pertinently it might be said ... that decades of hostility from employers, from governments, from society generally have bred into the labour movement an instinctive 'group loyalty.'

Our concern, however, is not defence of the past but protection of the future ... The CLC asked for this Inquiry. It did so because of the pattern of violence along the Great Lakes – an unmistakable pattern of undeniable violence. For the first time there was at hand a significant body of evidence which could be put before a Commission of Inquiry. Not only did the CLC ask for this Inquiry, in concert with affiliated unions in the marine industry, it began to collect and sift evidence, interview potential witnesses, many of whom they found too terrified to testify, and then to lead evidence before this Commission. This activity of the CLC may be looked upon as expiation of guilt by those whose interest is pre-occupied with that question; but for us it is merely a continuation of our determination to take whatever steps are indicated by clear evidence in our possession, to build a strong and clean Canadian labour movement in which there is no place for racketeering or corruption or the domination of unions by hoodlums or by companies.[74]

Having accepted, on behalf of organized labour, responsibility for the affair, Wright could now tell Norris the serious and possibly far-reaching recommendation the CLC wished to make. It was the view of the CLC that the minister of labour should be advised that the SIU was not a bona fide union and that steps be taken 'to ensure that legal and practical efficacy will be given to such a conclusion.'[75] In short, the CLC was suggesting that the SIU be wound up.

It was a suggestion which, from the CLC's point of view, made the most sense. Reform was out of the question, certainly as long as Banks and his lieutenants were around. Besides, the CLC had by now, as Norris knew, set up a union of its own in the maritime field, the Canadian Maritime Union. A message had to go out that there was no place in Canada for unions like the SIU. The CLC had taken the first step in that direction by admitting publicly its own responsibility for the misery inflicted on thousands of seamen by Banks.

Although this admission was at first hesitant, and an attempt was made to share the blame, at the end of the day the CLC, as Wright's submission leaves no doubt, was ready to let the blame lay where it fell: on the shoulders of the congress. Years of moral cowardice and the refusal to make the right decisions had come home to roost. But, as Wright also made clear, this was a thing of the past. It was now time to look to the future. The rest was up to Norris and parliament. After making an additional request that Norris recommend in his report that negotiations be undertaken between the governments of Canada and the United States to ensure peace in the forthcoming shipping season, and following an expression of thanks to the commissioner, Wright took his seat. The inquiry was over.

10
The Norris Report

Other than a few isolated and relatively minor incidents, the waterfront, in both Canada and the United States, had been quiet since the appointment of the Norris Commission in July 1962. However, the SIU withdrawal from the inquiry in early March, just days before the hearings came to a close, ended whatever incentive the union might have once had to preserve labour peace on the Great Lakes. Soon after the 1963 commercial navigation season opened, Peter McGavin, the secretary-treasurer of the AFL–CIO Maritime Trades Department and a long-time supporter of Hal Banks, vowed to resume picketing of Upper Lakes ships in American ports.[1]

As soon as the *Howard L. Shaw*, an Upper Lakes freighter manned by a Canadian Maritime Union crew, arrived in Chicago, it was declared black by American longshoremen and SIU crews on board harbour tugs. Relying on the recent United States Supreme Court decisions, Upper Lakes sought and obtained injunctions against the picketing. The injunctions were ignored and further legal wrangling ensued. Jack Leitch urged the federal government to take some action and the Canadian press editorialized against this continued harassment of Canadian shipping.[2] CLC president Jodoin also urged the government to act.[3] However, it was not until another Upper Lakes ship, the *James Norris*, was shot at in an American port that the recently elected prime minister, Lester B. Pearson, promised the House of Commons he would take action. In particular, Pearson told the members of parliament that he would discuss the issue with President John F. Kennedy at a forthcoming meeting at Hyannisport. There, the two leaders appointed Willard Wirtz, American secretary of labor, his Canadian counterpart, Allan MacEachen, CLC president Claude Jodoin, and AFL–CIO president George Meany to a committee to deal with the problem.[4]

Within days of the Hyannisport meeting the Committee of Four, as it was known, joined by Canadian deputy minister of labour George Haythorne and United States undersecretary of labour James Reynolds, met in Washington. The Canadians began by reviewing the background to the dispute and stated that, under Canada's law, the dispute between Upper Lakes and the SIU was over. The Americans were also advised that Upper Lakes was legally free to negotiate a collective agreement with another union if it wished to do so.[5] The niceties of Canadian labour law were, however, lost on George Meany, who expressed the AFL–CIO's view that the Canadian Maritime Union was a 'scab union.'[6] The next day, when Jodoin, Meany, and SIU president Paul Hall met privately, Hall attacked Jodoin and accused him of working with the shipping companies to destroy the SIU. Hall took this ridiculous charge to the press and announced that the issue was not Hal Banks, who was 'a great field general in the tough waterfront wars, but scabbing by the CLC's Canadian Maritime Union.'[7] Jodoin, enraged by Hall's scandalous statement, returned immediately to Ottawa and told Pearson that all further negotiations with the Americans were off until the harassment of Canadian ships in American waters was brought to an end.[8] The *Shaw* remained stranded in Chicago and relations between the CLC and AFL–CIO reached a new low as Meany and Jodoin became completely estranged. Ironically, it was the release of the Norris Report in early July which brought the two labour leaders together, united in an attempt to avoid the most draconian of the report's recommendations: the imposition of a government trusteeship over all Canadian maritime unions.

The report, published in July 1963, totalled 316 pages. The longest industrial inquiry commission in Canadian history had a report to match. Although the order-in-council appointing Norris set out five fairly specific matters into which the commissioner was to inquire,[9] the report primarily concerned itself with only one: the activities and operations of the SIU and its president, Hal Chamberlain Banks. Much like the inquiry itself, the report and the commissioner's recommendations, expressed in a dramatic, often rhetorical, and always fascinating way, were shocking.[10] Banks had, Norris found, looted union coffers, illegally deprived thousands of Canadian seamen of their livelihoods, run the SIU in a dictatorial manner, countenanced and encouraged violence against the SIU's opponents, and shown disrespect for Canadian law and institutions. The union president was an outlaw, hoodlum, rogue, and villain. The commissioner concluded that all the strife, 'all this lawlessness – the unlawful picketing, the intimidation and violence in Canada and the United States, all the litigation in Canada and the United

States, the international difficulty requiring the attention of the heads of two great nations – is not an effort to right any wrong nor to assist seamen, but is part of an irresponsible campaign to maintain one rapacious violent man, Banks, in power as a dictator.'[11] Accordingly, Norris recommended Banks's deportation from Canada. But this recommendation, along with a number of other recommendations such as appointing special legal counsel to review the evidence adduced before the commission to determine whether criminal charges should be laid against Banks and some of his men, and the transfer of union-controlled hiring halls to government supervision, was subsidiary to the key recommendation of the report: government trusteeship of Canada's maritime unions.

Norris recommended that three trustees with unfettered powers be appointed to operate Canada's maritime unions. The trustees should merge all the maritime unions and, following consultation with a strictly advisory seamen's committee, take whatever steps were necessary to bring about democracy in the newly created union. According to the commissioner, a special Act of Parliament should be passed to establish the trusteeship, and provide for its discontinuance by order-in-council and re-establishment should difficulties in the maritime industrial relations system recur.[12]

The trusteeship recommendation, if implemented, would have meant the complete restructuring of the Canadian maritime industrial relations system. It would also have resulted in government control of trade unions, including trade unions which did not stand accused of any impropriety or misconduct. Not surprisingly, the principal recommendation of the report, if not its general content, met with a mixed reception. So did other aspects of the report. It had remarkably few findings about the shipping companies that had supported Banks. It was undeniable that some of these companies, in particular Canada Steamship Lines, had had a special relationship with the SIU leader for years and had enjoyed labour peace as a result. The evidence also illustrated that most, if not all, of the shipping bosses had at one time or another shown the same cynical disregard for Canadian law as Banks, yet Norris had not made any recommendations to prevent future abuses. The report also failed to make findings concerning the federal government's involvement with the SIU. The Department of Labour had known for years about misdeeds in the SIU. Surely its failure to act deserved some comment and, perhaps more importantly, some recommendations – for example, amendments to the Industrial Relations Disputes Investigation Act which would permit the Labour Relations Board or some other federal agency to take action in the face of union racketeering.[13] These omissions aside, and they were not insignificant, it was the report's principal recommendation, the imposition of a government-controlled trusteeship over the Canadian maritime unions, which attracted the most immediate criticism. It came from both the SIU and the CLC.

The SIU objected to Norris's conduct of the inquiry and to the report itself, both of which it saw, not entirely without reason, as illustrative of bias and a denial of natural justice.[14] For its part, the CLC issued a press release expressing serious reservations over the trusteeship recommendation as it applied to bona fide trade unions.[15] Putting the gangster-led SIU under trusteeship was one thing, but placing legitimate trade unions under the trusteeship suggested by Norris and then merging them with the SIU was something else. An alternative had to be found.

For their part, Conservative members of parliament in the House of Commons demanded almost daily that the government immediately establish a trusteeship along the lines recommended by Norris. Prime Minister Pearson was not, however, prepared to rush into anything. He told the Commons that as much as he understood the need for urgency, there was also a need to act with wisdom.[16] Indeed, shortly after the report was released, the government established a high level interdepartmental committee to study the report and its recommendations.[17] Besides, with the legislative session about to end, there would only have been enough time to pass a general enabling measure. It was decided to postpone action until Parliament reconvened in the fall.

On the eve of the parliamentary recess, labour minister Allan MacEachen announced that the government had decided that when Parliament returned, it would implement the trusteeship recommendation in the Norris Report. MacEachen also told the Commons that of the maritime unions which would be affected by the trusteeship, all but the SIU had, begrudgingly, agreed to co-operate. His statement was followed by an unusual show of parliamentary unity. Tory labour critic Mike Starr commended the government, while the New Democratic Party's T.C. Douglas praised the Grits for their ongoing consultations with the CLC and promised his party's support for the trusteeship.[18] MacEachen's announcement, the ensuing display of parliamentary unanimity, and the delay occasioned by the summer recess were in fact shrewd moves. It provided Canadian and American organized labour with another opportunity to resolve their differences and work out a solution to the maritime situation that would not necessitate the involvement of the federal government. At the same time, MacEachen signalled to labour leaders, and in particular to American labour leaders, that if necessary the Canadian government would do what needed to be done. To its credit, the government spared no effort in the next four months to assist organized labour in restoring order to its house.

Claude Jodoin was still incensed by the treatment he had received during his last visit to Washington when Paul Hall had, with George Meany's apparent blessing, called him a 'scab.' A proud man, Jodoin would not go back to the bargaining table without good reason. Unwittingly, the SIU gave it to him when it sabotaged the *Shaw* in early September.

The *Shaw* had been sitting in the port of Chicago for more than five months. Attention was dramatically redirected to its dilemma when, in the middle of the night on 9 September, an SIU operative planted and detonated a bomb on board the stranded ship. Although the ship was not seriously damaged, the bombing clearly illustrated that there was little the SIU would not do to get its way. In due course, an American SIU member was sentenced to a ten-year prison term for the bombing.[19] Jack Leitch, realizing that this ship would never be unloaded in Chicago, ordered it to Fort William. Although no longer a poignant daily symbol, the bombing of the *Shaw* demonstrated the difficulties faced by Canadian ships in American ports and the fact that troubles on the waterfront were far from over. Organized labour's reputation was increasingly at stake.

Claude Jodoin certainly realized that this was the case. Swallowing his pride, he telegraphed Meany with the request that the AFL–CIO take whatever steps were necessary to bring an end to the violence. The next day, two days after the bombing, Meany replied and asked for 'details.'[20] Prime Minister Pearson was more helpful and made an urgent appeal to American government officials.[21] Pearson's appeal, in marked contrast to Jodoin's, brought about some results. Willard Wirtz flew to Ottawa and, accompanied by a bevy of officials and the American ambassador to Canada, met with many members of the Liberal cabinet. The ministers of labour, justice, transport, external affairs, along with deputy minister of labour Haythorne and assistant deputy minister George Cushing were all in attendance at a long meeting in which various solutions to the problem were explored. It was agreed that a private trusteeship over all the Canadian maritime unions jointly administered by the AFL–CIO and the CLC offered the most promise of a peaceful resolution of the dispute. The meeting concluded with Wirtz and MacEachen agreeing to put the proposal to Meany and Jodoin and to working out the details at another meeting of a slightly modified Committee of Four, scheduled for Boston later in the month.[22]

After the Americans left, Jodoin, William Dodge, and Joe Morris, all members of the Executive Council of the CLC, were invited by MacEachen to a meeting. MacEachen advised them of developments and they agreed to co-operate with the AFL–CIO in establishing a private trusteeship over the Canadian maritime unions. It was obvious that the CLC, even with the support of the government of Canada, could not unilaterally impose a trusteeship over the maritime unions. Any attempt to do so would have been subject to AFL–CIO attack and would likely have resulted in a division within the CLC between national and international unions. A private trusteeship acceptable to the CLC, the AFL–CIO, and the SIU International held the greatest promise of success. The CLC Executive Council decision was not, however, unanimous. [23]

The CBRT was opposed and, days before the Committee of Four was to meet, issued a policy statement. While it reiterated its willingness to have its maritime locals placed under trusteeship, it insisted that only a government trusteeship could bring an end to the waterfront terror. [24] Paul Hall was, for quite different reasons, also opposed. He did not want the SIU Canadian District placed under any form of trusteeship and asked the presidents of international unions affiliated with the CLC to lobby Jodoin against the proposal. Jodoin did not appreciate Hall's efforts and continued with preparations for the Boston meeting. [25]

That meeting was marred by a disagreeable prelude when Jodoin accepted an AFL–CIO invitation to attend a pre-meeting conference limited to trade union leaders. On 24 September, four days before the Committee of Four was scheduled to meet, Jodoin flew to Washington and attended at the offices of the AFL–CIO. He spent most of the day in George Meany's waiting room and, indeed, never did see the American labour boss. Before leaving in disgust, Jodoin was apparently advised that the AFL–CIO was prepared to investigate the operation of the Canadian SIU and, if necessary, impose controls. The offer was too late by years, and totally unacceptable to Jodoin and the CLC. [26] The Boston meeting was scheduled to go ahead as planned.

CLC staff had been working closely with officials of the Department of Labour on a private solution and were able to agree on a unified approach to take to the Americans. A proposed 'Memorandum of Understanding' set out terms of reference for a private trusteeship. Unlike the Norris Report, the memorandum did not envisage the merger of all the maritime unions. Rather, it respected their integrity, but referred to certain steps which needed to be taken to end the disruption in shipping and bring about confidence and democracy in the SIU. The Canadian proposal, made at the first meeting on 28 September, called for a trusteeship of three persons: one named by the CLC, one by the AFL–CIO, and one, a

Canadian, to be named jointly by Meany and Jodoin. These three trustees were to be given wide powers, and their trusteeship was to be established for a specific period, although it could if necessary be extended. The trusteeship was to operate under the auspices of the AFL–CIO and the CLC, with the Canadian minister of labour and the American secretary of labour as co-signatories. It was a good plan and both the CLC and MacEachen and Haythorne were optimistic that the AFL–CIO would accept it.[27] MacEachen promised that if an agreement were reached, the Canadian government would refrain from legislating a trusteeship and would give the privately negotiated solution a reasonable opportunity to work. Despite this incentive, the talks failed to result in an agreement.[28]

The Americans, who appeared as united as the Canadians, objected to the composition of the trusteeship. In particular, they would not accept the requirement that the third trustee, to be jointly nominated by the CLC and the AFL–CIO, be a Canadian. Nor would they agree to that part of the proposal which would have given the trustees the right to remove union officers.[29] After two days of meetings it became apparent that agreement on a private trusteeship could not be reached quickly. The meeting was adjourned with the understanding that close contact among all the parties would be maintained.[30]

In the meantime, the CBRT launched a campaign to scuttle the proposed private trusteeship. William Smith wrote Jodoin and stated unequivocally that any labour-devised trusteeship which was acceptable to Paul Hall was unacceptable to the CBRT. He also reminded Jodoin that the AFL–CIO leaders had called CLC officers scabs and that only when faced with the threat of government intervention were the Americans willing to deal with the CLC. Thoroughly incensed, Smith accused the CLC of demeaning itself and degrading the Canadian labour movement by even considering such a proposal. He then warned Jodoin that should the CLC proceed with a private trusteeship, the CBRT would 'be compelled to make an agonizing reappraisal of its policy of association with the Congress.'[31]

Although Jodoin replied to Smith the next day that he was not influenced by threats, there is no doubt that the resignation of the CBRT would have been disastrous for the CLC. As the largest national union in Canada, and as the union which had spearheaded the fight against Banks, its resignation would have left the CLC polarized on a national versus international basis, probably leading to its disintegration. The CLC accordingly gave its approval to a legislated trusteeship. To allay CLC fears and ensure that the legislation not be considered a precedent, MacEachen promised that any trusteeship legislation would be explicitly temporary in nature. The result was hardly ideal, but the CLC, which had little if any choice, pledged its co-operation. On 9 October MacEachen took the first steps in the House of Commons to introduce and pass a trusteeship measure.[32] The next day, both Meany and Wirtz made statements in Washington, statements which confirmed the resolve of the Canadian government and the CLC to proceed with the imposition of a legislated trusteeship.

Meany told reporters that the Canadian trusteeship proposal was the kind of thing he would expect in Cuba and other totalitarian states. He then called upon AFL–CIO affiliates to support the SIU in its fight against the destruction of free trade unionism in the Canadian maritime industry.[33] Even more incredibly, secretary of labour Wirtz seemed to echo these ridiculous remarks later that day when he issued a statement equally critical of the Canadian legislation.[34] Made at the very time the Parliament of Canada was considering passing legislation to place the Canadian maritime unions under trusteeship, Wirtz's comments could only be interpreted as an unwarranted intrusion into Canadian domestic affairs. Pearson was outraged and, a few days later, told President Kennedy that the government of Canada did not appreciate Wirtz's 'unhelpful intervention' and Meany's 'more than shocking intervention' into Canadian affairs.[35]

On 11 October, with the extraordinary vote of 181 in favour, 4 against, the second reading of the Trusteeship Bill, C-102, was approved and sent to committee.[36] The bill was given third reading following the introduction of amendments, and passed with almost unanimous consent.[37] Under the guidance of Senator David Croll, it passed quickly through the Senate and on 18 October received royal assent.[38] Commonly known as the Trusteeship Act,[39] its preamble made clear that it was an emergency measure, passed under the peace, order, and good government provision of the British North America Act to restore order to maritime industrial relations.

The Trusteeship Act placed the SIU, NAME, Canadian Merchant Service Guild, Canadian Maritime Union, and thirteen CBRT locals under the control of the trustees. With two exceptions, the trustees were not given broad powers, and even those exceptions were restrained compared to the sweeping powers the Norris Report had originally proposed. For example, the trustees were given the power to recommend changes in the different union constitutions, but those changes had to be approved by the membership of the affected union. Similarly, collective bargaining was, under the act, the exclusive prerogative of union members. The trustees were given some custodial powers over union finances and property, but the exercise of those powers was limited by practical and constitutional considerations. By and large, therefore, the Trusteeship Act contemplated a limited type of tenure for the government trustees. There were, as earlier mentioned, two major exceptions.

The first was set out in subsection 7(2)(d) of the act which gave the trustees the power to remove, suspend, and replace by appointment any officer or employee of any of the affected maritime unions. Known as the 'Hal Banks provision,' there was little doubt that it was written with the SIU boss in mind. The second major exception vested in the trustees the management and control of the maritime unions. By subsection 7(1) of the act, the trustees were to 'manage and control each of the maritime unions and do all things necessary or advisable for the return of the management and control of each of the maritime unions to duly elected and responsible officers of such unions at the earliest date consistent with the national and public interest of Canada.'[40] As this subsection was worded imprecisely, it was unclear whether the trustees were to run every detail of the different union's operations, or whether they were, as their other powers suggested, to play a more limited role. The answer to that question would, as it turned out, become clear in time.

For the moment, however, the confusion – and there was legitimate confusion among seamen, unionists, and civil libertarians as to the nature of the trusteeship – fuelled concern about the legislative measure. Pearson responded to these concerns and told Canadian seamen that they had nothing to fear from the trusteeship.[41] In fact, for a very brief period, it appeared that the act would not even be proclaimed, as a last-ditch effort to negotiate a private trusteeship with the AFL–CIO showed some promise of success. However, Hal Banks intervened and scuttled for good any hope of a private trusteeship.[42]

The publicity-conscious SIU boss had been keeping a low profile, but at the same time was taking what steps he could to ensure that trusteeship over his union never came to pass. Soon after the Liberal victory at the polls in April 1963, Banks began actively to lobby against government intervention in the affairs of his union. He hosted a dinner at Ruby Foo's, then a fashionable restaurant in suburban Montreal, attended by at least one cabinet minister and two Liberal members of parliament. Other MPs, apparently some thirty in all, later accepted Banks's invitation to make personal visits to the SIU headquarters to observe firsthand the union's operation.[43] These efforts had no discernible effect on the passage of the trusteeship legislation. It was then that Banks decided to take matters into his own hands.

At a union meeting in Montreal the day before the Trusteeship Act received royal assent, Banks described the act to his members in derogatory terms: 'This law will place Government-appointed trustees in full control of the union's properties, assets, finances, membership and contracts. It will make us virtual slaves under Government trustees with dictatorial and unlimited powers. It will put us in the same position as unions in Russia, East Germany, China and Cuba.'[44] Thoroughly aroused, the seamen present at this meeting voted, as usual, 'unanimously' to go to Ottawa and assert their right to make representations directly to Parliament.[45] Beginning on 18 October, SIU crews all along the Great Lakes began to abandon ship and make their way to Ottawa for a massive protest meeting scheduled to take place on 21 October.

Exactly on time, approximately 2000 seamen converged on Parliament Hill. The protest was an orderly affair. By and large the SIU members showed little enthusiasm until Banks arrived in his gleaming white Cadillac convertible.[46] 'Boys,' Banks shouted to the crowd, 'you look real good.'[47] The SIU members then cheered their president, who told them that contrary to what they may have read in the press, the march was neither a strike nor an illegal walkout. It was, Banks said, a 'demonstration.' In fact, it was an illegal strike. After milling about for a short while longer, most of the strikers left Ottawa for Montreal to attend a mass meeting the next day. In a tremendous and undeniable show of support for Banks, all but fifteen of some 2000 union members present at the meeting voted against returning to work.[48] This vote was not kept secret from the press and it, along with the events of the previous day, made proclamation of the Trusteeship Act inevitable. Pearson telephoned Kennedy and told him that it was essential that he persuade the AFL–CIO to accept the implementation of the Canadian legislation. Kennedy promised to do what he could,[49] and, with that taken care of, the government moved to do what it had tried so hard to avoid: it summoned to Ottawa the three men it had earlier asked to serve on the Board of Trustees. An important chapter in Canadian labour history was over and a new one about to begin.

11
Trusteeship

At 12:00 noon on 23 October 1963 the Trusteeship Act was proclaimed. Immediately afterwards, by order-in-council, the three trustees who had been earlier summoned to Ottawa were appointed. Their names, labour minister MacEachen said in his announcement to the House of Commons, were Victor Dryer, René Lippe, and Charlie Millard. That night the trustees held their first meeting and began what the *Globe and Mail* described as the one of the 'toughest' jobs ever demanded of Canadians. [1]

The chairman of the board was the Honourable Mr Justice Victor Dryer of the Supreme Court of British Columbia. After his call to the bar in 1936, Dryer entered private practice and, at the same time, taught at the University of British Columbia Law School. In the 1950s Dryer acted as special prosecutor in the bribery and conspiracy trial of Robert Sommers, a former provincial cabinet minister. He served in 1955 as assistant counsel in the inquiry into charges of graft and corruption in the Vancouver police, followed by service as counsel to the provincial Royal Commission on Workers' Compensation. In 1963 he was appointed to the bench. His knowledge of labour relations and his wealth of experience as counsel and trial judge made Dryer a splendid choice.

René Lippe, from every appearance, was an equally suitable selection. Born and educated in Quebec, he was a provincial court magistrate and a thoroughly experienced and highly respected arbitrator of labour relations disputes. He too had served on a number of commissions, most notably the one appointed by Premier Maurice Duplessis to investigate the collapse of the bridge at Three Rivers.

The remaining trustee, Charlie Millard, was the representative of organized labour. Born in St Thomas, Ontario, in 1896, Millard enlisted in the army when the First World War began. He served with distinction and rose rapidly through the ranks, becoming a sergeant major before he turned twenty. After discharge, Millard returned to Ontario and immediately became active in trade union circles. He helped to organize the United Auto Workers local in Oshawa and, as its president, led the famous 1937 recognition strike. Later Millard was chosen by the president of the Congress of Industrial Organization to take over the Steel Workers' Organizing Committee which had fallen under Communist party domination. He succeeded in rooting the Communists out and was next elected national director of the United Steel Workers, holding that post from 1942 until his resignation in 1956. At that time he was appointed director of organization for the International Confederation of Free Trade Unions, with headquarters in Brussels. He remained there until 1961, when he returned to Canada. Active in the Religion-Labour Council of Canada, a group formed to develop communication and understanding between church and union leadership, as well as in the Labour College of Canada, Millard was the CLC's choice for its representative on the Board of Maritime Trustees. [2]

At their inaugural meeting on 23 October, the trustees considered the Trusteeship Act and decided that to be consistent with its provisions they would interfere as little as possible with the operation of the maritime unions under their control. It was their view that while they owed a duty to Parliament and the public, their principal legal duty was to the members of the different maritime unions, and decisions would be made with such unions' best interests in mind. Determination of those interests, the three trustees agreed, notwithstanding the findings in the Norris Report, required careful consideration. They decided, therefore, not to make any immediate changes to the status quo. Prudence and plain good sense cautioned against precipitous moves, though they had, of course, to bring to an end the illegal SIU strike. [3]

Hal Banks was summoned to a meeting. When he arrived he was ordered to bring the walkout to an immediate end or face unnamed consequences. Banks attempted to appease the three trustees with the same answer he had earlier given MacEachen and Haythorne -- that he would consult his men, but that the decision whether or not to return to work was theirs to make. The trustees told Banks to get the men back or else. Realizing what he was up against, or deciding that it was not worth fighting over, Banks promised his co-operation. Beginning the next morning, 25 October, SIU members at different union halls along the Great Lakes system began to 'vote' in favour of returning to work. Ships began to sail immediately and by noon on 26 October the illegal walkout was completely over. The first challenge to the trusteeship had been handled deftly and with dispatch. [4]

But the successful resolution of this first crisis by the trustees did not mean that henceforth it would be smooth sailing. At the biennial convention of the Maritimes Trades Department, held in New York City, the delegates passed resolutions criticizing the Norris Report and the trusteeship, resolving with respect to the latter to complain to the United Nations and the International Labor Organization. The following week, at the annual AFL–CIO convention, Banks committed the SIU to a fight to the finish with Upper Lakes. Before it was over, he vowed, the SIU flag would be flying from the masthead of every Upper Lakes ship.[5] SIU members were soon, in fact, picketing Canadian flag ships in Chicago and other American ports. The local longshoremen respected the pickets and refused to unload the ships. Canadian authorities objected and President Kennedy asked secretary of labor Wirtz for a report. The main issue, replied Wirtz, was whether or not the administration wanted to intervene on behalf of the Canadians and a handful of their ships. He reported that he had discussions with both Meany and Paul Hall, who told him that the pickets would not be called off without a personal presidential request. Such a request would further indebt Kennedy politically to the maritime unions, which was inadvisable; he was already in their debt, and planned to approach them soon with a request that they agree to an increase in the amount of wheat shipped in Soviet, as opposed to American, bottoms. Wirtz's advice was to wait and see.[6] Stalling made some sense, particularly since the shipping season was almost over. In Canada the SIU began a legal challenge to the trusteeship.

SIU lawyer Joe Nuss appeared in the Quebec Superior Court and made an application for an injunction restraining the activities of the Board of Trustees. The application alleged that the Trusteeship Act violated provincial constitutional rights, the Canadian Bill of Rights, various international treaties, and the United Nations Declaration of Human Rights.[7] Superior Court Judge Roger Ouimet reserved his decision[8] until May 1964, when he rejected the application. This decision was unsuccessfully appealed.[9]

The court appearances necessitated by the SIU application did not delay or frustrate the work of the trustees. That work, as 1963 drew to a close, consisted of establishing actual trusteeship over the maritime unions. After setting up an office in a federal government building in Montreal, the trustees established formal links with each of the unions, took control of all their bank accounts, and retained chartered accountants to review and make recommendations about the control and investment of union funds. Trusteeship staff began a review of the welfare plan and the SIU vacation pay fund. With these projects initiated, the trustees began to educate themselves about the maritime industry. They believed this was essential to the administration of their duties. [10]

Also essential was the development of good relations with organized labour and, in particular, the CLC. Despite the CLC's support for the trusteeship, there were those in the labour movement who had deep suspicions about it. The trustees moved to allay any misgivings and confided to CLC officers that the reaffiliation of the SIU to the congress was one of their most important goals. It was a goal, as everybody knew, which was years away. In the meantime, the trustees began the task of restoring order and civility to maritime industrial relations. [11]

None of these activities seemed very significant, especially in light of the sweeping findings and recommendations of the Norris Report. But the trustees were not appointed to implement those recommendations. They were appointed according to the Trusteeship Act and, indeed, decided early on in their tenure not to look to the excesses of the past but rather to concentrate on performing their duties with a view to the future. This was something which was neither readily explained nor easily understood. A serious state of affairs had been exposed by Norris and it was only natural that there be demands for action. Views on the action required varied widely, from the implementation of some of Norris's recommendations to the wholesale adoption of his report and complete restructuring of the maritime industrial relations system. There was, however, unanimity in one area: Hal Banks had to go.

Subsection 7(2)(d) of the Trusteeship Act, also known as the Hal Banks clause, empowered the trustees to remove or suspend any officer or employee of any of the maritime unions. It was obvious that so long as the SIU chief remained on the scene, labour unrest would continue. Why then, the trustees' earliest critics asked, was the provision not used to banish Banks from the labour movement? Timing probably had a lot to do with it. Had Banks been fired immediately following proclamation of the Trusteeship Act there is no telling what might have taken place. The October march on Parliament Hill revealed that notwithstanding the excesses revealed by Norris in his report, Banks enjoyed the confidence and loyalty of a significant percentage of the membership of the SIU. However, as every newspaper reader of the day could see, it looked as if the problem of what to do with Banks was taking care of itself. [12]

The Norris Report had recommended that the government appoint special counsel to review the facts and ascertain whether any criminal charges should be laid against Banks or any of his officers. Norris obviously thought they should, and suggested a number of possible avenues of approach. [13] Two special counsel were appointed: Toronto lawyer J.J.

Robinette and Montreal lawyer Jean Martineau. Their job, justice minister Lionel Chevrier announced in the House of Commons, was to advise whether charges should be laid and, if so, what charges and against whom. [14] With the assistance of the Royal Canadian Mounted Police and other government officials, the counsel reviewed all the available evidence, including materials not adduced before the Norris Commission. The credibility and reliability of witnesses was checked and double-checked. After a thorough study, the counsel reported to the minister of justice in the fall of 1963 that there was enough evidence to support one criminal charge against Banks. That charge was conspiracy to assault, and related to the brutal beating of Captain Walsh. Not one of the many other acts of violence described by Norris both in detail and at length could be traced back to the SIU leader with the degree of certainty necessary to support a criminal conviction. [15] The special counsel had concluded that there was insufficient evidence to bring charges against Banks for the misuse of union funds. Although both Martineau and Robinette agreed that there were irregularities in the use of union money, a criminal charge of theft or embezzlement did not stand a chance of a conviction. [16]

With the special counsels' report, a warrant could have been issued for Banks's arrest at almost any time. However, a political decision was made to postpone his arrest until the end of the shipping season. Apparently the federal government, as the prime minister confided to the American ambassador, feared that arresting Banks might spark a massive disruption in shipping. [17] But sensible as the decision to delay was, when the arrest was finally made it was poorly executed. On 31 October it was announced in the House of Commons that Banks had been charged with conspiracy in the beating of Captain Walsh. The announcement made headlines and editorialists made no attempt to restrain their glee. [18] Somewhat unfairly, the warrant was not executed and, indeed, the RCMP was not ordered to arrest Banks until 5 November, five days after the public announcement was first made. [19]

Some members of parliament were disappointed to learn that Banks was only to be charged with one offence, and insisted that the government prefer additional charges against the SIU leader relating to more recent events. Banks had become something of a fixation to some Conservative party members, and in particular to their leader, John Diefenbaker. Hardly a day went by without one Tory or another demanding 'action.' In late January 1964 the government complied, and Banks and fourteen others were charged under the Criminal Code for inciting seamen, in October 1963, to desert from duty. These charges were, as it turned out, poorly advised; not one of the accused was subsequently convicted. [20]

The charge for conspiracy to assault was, however, a serious offence. If convicted, Banks faced the prospect of a lengthy jail term. After his arrest he appeared before a local magistrate to apply for bail. It was granted, although the amount of bail was less than that requested by the crown attorney. The bail terms failed to include a restriction on travel from Canada, causing some members of parliament concern. [21] Those concerns appeared to be unfounded. Banks left Canada at least once between the time of his arrest and the preliminary hearing held on 13 March 1964. At this hearing it was determined that there was enough evidence, if proved, to result in a conviction, and Banks was accordingly committed to trial in April 1964 before law and order judge Claude Wagner.

Meanwhile, the trustees determined that Banks should be removed from office before the reopening of commercial navigation. They initially decided not just to fire Banks, but to replace him, thereby avoiding the succession provisions of the SIU constitution which would have made Leonard McLaughlin president. Both the AFL–CIO and the CLC were approached for advice as a discreet search was begun for a suitable and willing replacement. The trustees came up empty-handed. [22] Organized labour was naturally reticent about providing a replacement. For political reasons, the CLC could not appear to be working hand-in-glove with the government-appointed trustees. When a final appeal produced no results, the trustees decided to act unilaterally.

A former officer of the International Brotherhood of Railway and Steamship Clerks, Charles Turner, was available. The trustees needed an experienced trade unionist and employed him to represent them in the SIU hall. When the search for a new SIU president failed, the trustees appointed Turner. At the same time, they decided that Millard would also move into the SIU Hall and act as de facto president. Turner would have the title, Millard the job. It was, it seemed, a neat solution to a difficult dilemma. [23] On 18 March Banks was dismissed.

When news of his discharge was announced in the House of Commons, members of parliament applauded and cheered. [24] Bill Mahoney of the United Steel Workers appeared to be speaking for all of organized labour when he said that it was the best news he had heard in a long time. [25] The official announcement issued by the trustees was more sober. It said that Banks's removal from office followed a long consideration of the affairs and interests of the SIU, the maritime industry, and the country. Banks was fired because he stood in the way of their doing their job. The trustees stressed that Banks's dismissal was not an act of hostility against the SIU, but was instead a move made in the interests of the rank and file. It was hoped, they added, that new leadership would emerge from the union's membership to contest a union election scheduled for the fall. From SIU headquarters, Charlie Millard issued another statement outlining the trustees' long-term plans, including readmission of the union to the CLC and continued publication of the *Canadian Sailor*, and, no doubt to allay fears that Banks's discharge was the beginning of a purge, saying that no other changes were contemplated in the SIU staff.[26]

Naturally, the decision to fire Banks did not elicit only positive reaction. The tiresome and meddling Peter McGavin of the Maritime Trades Department called the firing 'outrageous' and promised action. More to the point, SIU International president Paul Hall telegraphed the trustees that he was on his way to Montreal, and arrived within hours to pledge to Banks his all-out support.[27] Hall's promise of support gave the trustees considerable cause for concern.

By March 1964 it was clear that the Trusteeship Act was a poorly drafted piece of legislation. On the surface, the statute gave the trustees the power to 'manage and control' the maritime unions. But nowhere did the legislation define what 'manage and control' meant. This deficiency concerned the trustees from the outset, and they made a concerted effort to obtain from the government and their own counsel a legal definition of the term. It was feared that a legal argument could be advanced successfully to the effect that 'manage and control' did not permit the trustees to act at odds with the SIU's constitution. If this argument prevailed, as the trustees were inclined to believe it would, the appointment of Charles Turner as union president, as well as many other orders and directives, might be impeached.[28]

The SIU had also been studying the Trusteeship Act and had arrived at exactly the same conclusion.[29] The International SIU president could make life difficult for the trustees by attacking the Turner appointment and some of their other activities in court and insisting that the strict letter of the union's constitution be applied. But at the same time, there was probably nothing the International SIU president could do for Hal Banks: the Trusteeship Act clearly empowered the trustees to fire union officers. Hall quickly assessed the situation and decided that since Banks was a lost cause he would do what he could to protect the union.

At a private meeting with Millard held on 20 March and in negotiating sessions held throughout the rest of the month, Hall and Millard were able to cut a deal, the terms of which were announced in a joint statement given to the press on 3 April. In effect, Hall agreed not to make any waves about Banks and to end the harassment of Canadian ships on the Great Lakes. The trustees reiterated their commitment to restoring the SIU to the constitutional control of its members, and as a first step in this process they allowed the succession provisions of the SIU's constitution to take effect. Leonard McLaughlin, Banks's longtime second-in-command whom Norris had described in a most disparaging way, succeeded to the presidency. The trustees agreed that while they would continue to exercise their powers, it was their intention that the active management of the union be in the hands of the membership. It was further agreed that the close relations between the SIU of Canada and the SIU International would be maintained, that steps would be taken to unite all elements of the Canadian and American maritime industries in a co-operative effort to settle any differences on the Great Lakes, that co-operation would be sought from the central labour organizations, that all possible steps would be taken to achieve the integration of the maritime unions in Canada but only where it was in the interest of union stability, and that should either the trustees or the SIU feel that any of the above obligations had not been met, they were at liberty to consider all arrangements terminated. [30]

The final term of the agreement gave rise to considerable speculation that some secret arrangement had also been made. None had. [31] In fact, the accord was completely consistent with the trustees' announced objective: 'To do all things necessary or advisable for the return of the management and control of each of the maritime unions to duly elected and responsible officers of such unions at the earliest date consistent with the national and public interests of Canada.' With the considerable potential legal limitations to their powers the trustees, by being realistic, had actually done quite well. However, not everyone agreed. Elroy Robson of the CBRT called it peace at a terrible price, while Jack Leitch said that the deal ran contrary to Parliament's intention in establishing the trusteeship. Perhaps it had, but for the first time in years Upper Lakes ships, in the recently opened commercial navigation season, were not being molested in American ports. [32]

Although seemingly abandoned by Paul Hall, there was no chance of Banks disappearing in the shuffle. Banks's trial for conspiracy to assault Captain Walsh soon began and lasted three weeks. The prosecution, led by special counsel Jean Martineau, relied almost entirely on the eyewitness evidence of Banks's erstwhile friend and ally Richard Greaves. It had all been said before. The defence, led by a top criminal lawyer in Quebec, Joseph Cohen, hammered away at Greaves's credibility and that of John Wood and Mike Sheehan, both of whom were called to corroborate Greaves's evidence. Banks's lawyers presented a spirited defence. The evidence against their client, they said, did not stand up to the light of day. It was given by men whose actions more closely resembled those of co-conspirators than innocent bystanders. The charge was years old and had been proceeded with in questionable circumstances. Cohen argued that there was no proof to convict Banks.[33] Judge Wagner, however, believed the crown witnesses and convicted Banks. In his opinion, which even if based on suspect evidence was nevertheless undoubtedly correct, the 'beating of Captain Walsh was a manifest act of gangsterism agreed to, prepared, ordered, directed and supervised by the accused Harold Chamberlain Banks.'[34] Wagner sentenced Banks to five years' imprisonment in a federal penitentiary. Compared to the sentences of one year in jail for those actually convicted of the offence, Banks's sentence was stiff. His attorneys filed a notice of appeal. Pending hearing of that appeal there was the question of bail.

The ex-SIU president had been out on bail for some months. He had left Canada, returned for his trial, and had done nothing which would cause him to forfeit his liberty. However, he had now been convicted of a serious crime and no longer had a job. The crown argued that in these circumstances the chances of his appearing for his appeal set for the following September were not good. If bail were to be granted, the crown asked that it be in the amount of $50,000. This, Banks's lawyers said, was too much, and the chief justice of the Quebec Court of Appeal, the Honourable Mr Justice Lucien Tremblay, agreed.[35] Bail was granted in the amount of $25,000. No restrictions on the bail were asked for or ordered. All Banks had to do was appear for his appeal in September.[36]

For the most part, Banks was content to remain close to home, which for him was a spacious, well-furnished home in Pointe Claire, Quebec. At the end of May he was honoured in Buffalo for his 'outstanding service to labor,' but asked Paul Hall to pick up the award.[37] By and large, Banks was now prepared to keep out of the public eye. He stayed that way until a decision of the Supreme Court of Canada brought his name back into the headlines. The case in question had begun on 3 May 1962 at the height of the SIU–Upper Lakes dispute when lawyers acting for Upper Lakes were able to obtain an injunction from the Quebec Superior Court restraining Banks and the SIU from further picketing of Upper Lakes ships. The injunction order was appealed, but in the interim the SIU continued to picket Upper Lakes ships. Upper Lakes successfully petitioned the Quebec Court to have Banks cited for contempt and the court sentenced him to thirty days in jail. This order was upheld by the Supreme Court of Canada. The Supreme Court could not order Banks to begin serving his sentence because the contempt application had been initiated as a civil remedy. Upper Lakes, however, had that right, except that when it tried to locate Banks he could not be found.[38]

News of his disappearance quickly leaked out. But when government officials were questioned about it in Ottawa, they took the position that it had nothing to do with Banks's criminal appeal, nor with his conditions of bail.[39] Nevertheless, John Diefenbaker charged that Banks had been the coddled pet of the Liberals for years, and his charge provoked a storm of criticism.[40] The new minister of justice, the scandal-plagued Guy Favreau, was berated for 'permitting' Banks to be freed on 'only' $25,000 bail. This was silly. Favreau had nothing to do with it; the decision whether or not to grant bail was not the government's to make. It was totally within the discretion of a judge of the Quebec Court of Appeal. Where the crown had erred was in not insisting that conditions be placed on the granting of bail. Banks had been convicted of conspiracy to assault. According to the terms of the extradition treaty then in effect between Canada and the United States, this charge was not extraditable. What this meant, as was now realized, was that Banks could flee, if, in fact, he had not already done so, to the United States and not fear extradition back to Canada. This lacuna in the Canadian-American extradition treaty, which was subsequently remedied, should have been brought to the attention of Chief Justice Tremblay who, no doubt, would have ordered accordingly. It was not, and now the governing Liberals were suffering, somewhat unfairly, the results.[41]

The crown attorney handling the bail application had made a mistake, one which was in July 1964 purely academic.[42] No one knew where Banks was, but no one except Upper Lakes was entitled to know. On 17 August that changed. Banks, along with fourteen other accused, was scheduled to appear in court that day to face the criminal charges laid following the previous October's Parliament Hill demonstration. It was not really surprising that he did not show up; he had not been seen in Montreal for over a month.[43] By not appearing, Banks was now officially a fugitive from justice. Opposition members of parliament had a field day. One wag asked whether copies of Hansard should be sent to Banks so that he could be 'kept informed of the interest of this house in his whereabouts.'[44] The government continued to profess confidence that Banks would show up for his appeal, scheduled to begin on 14 September. Privately, however, the government was worried and the RCMP was asked to find Banks.[45]

The Mounties had no luck. The day set for the appeal came and went without any light being shed on the whereabouts of the former SIU leader. Favreau admitted that the government had no idea where Banks was and, more importantly, that if he was outside the country, he could probably not be brought back. It was suggested in Parliament that the Norris Report be re-examined to determine whether a new charge, and one covered by the Canadian-American extradition treaty, could be laid to bring Banks to justice, but Favreau would not make any commitments. After giving Banks one day's grace, crown attorneys, on instructions from Ottawa, moved for the dismissal of the appeal and forfeiture of the bond. On Parliament Hill, Banks's disappearance became the hottest news in town, and the subject, in the House of Commons, of almost daily debate.[46]

On 1 October the minister of justice had had enough. Red faced and stumbling over his words, Favreau charged that the Tories could have acted when they were in power. 'I am now,' he told the House of Commons, 'in a very clear position to state positively that if there has been negligence it started in 1958.'[47] He charged that on 23 February 1959 justice minister Fulton was given a full account of the conspiracy to beat Captain Walsh. This account was based largely on information supplied by Richard Greaves and was corroborated two years later by Mike Sheehan. The Tories, Favreau declared, in language which came close to blaming them for the entire disruption in shipping, had failed to take action. He claimed that the entire Norris commission was unnecessary to bring to light the evidence upon which 'the recent conviction of Banks depended.'[48] The conspiracy to assault charge could have been laid five years earlier.[49]

Visibly shaking with indignation, Diefenbaker got up to reply. For once it was not a question of which was the kettle and which was the pot. Favreau's charge was untrue. Fulton had at the time launched a thorough investigation into the case, in addition to asking the RCMP to take a look at some of the other allegations of SIU wrongdoing. After reviewing the evidence it was determined, as Favreau, Fulton's deputy minister of justice at the time, was in a position to know, that there was insufficient evidence to support a conviction. No charges were laid but, on Fulton's orders, the file was not closed. Favreau, who was not well, had failed to look at the documents carefully. If he had, he would have realized that they were a credit to the previous administration, not, as he was now suggesting, a source of embarrassment or an example of inaction.

Diefenbaker did not, of course, have access to the file and Fulton had left the House of Commons to serve as the leader of the ill-fated Progressive Conservative party of British Columbia. But the Chief knew that Favreau was wrong. He denied that his administration had failed to act and, in perhaps the single most memorable line in the whole affair, Diefenbaker charged that Banks was the 'pampered pet of Liberalism.' The House of Commons erupted into bedlam.[50]

When the war of words finished, the Tories had won. Dispassionately evaluated, the evidence indicated that Fulton had in 1958 decided that there was insufficient evidence to support a criminal charge against Hal Banks. However, he had ordered the RCMP to keep the file open. Several years later Richard Greaves, followed by Mike Sheehan, had made statements to the Mounties, who had evaluated these statements and determined that the evidence was still insufficient. Much later, at the very time that there were press and opposition demands for action, the file had again been reviewed. Special counsel had been engaged and they had opined that a criminal charge could, on the evidence they had seen, be sustained. Accordingly, the government had laid the charge. There was nothing improper in the way the Tories had handled the case. What little impropriety there was belonged to the Liberals. Announcing the arrest in the House of Commons before it was actually made was a good example of that. Favreau had no business making the charge he did. It was pure politics, it was bad politics, and it was wrong.

The worst that could be said about the handling of the matter, and this applied equally to the Grits and the Tories, was that the government had failed for years to take action in the face of increasingly documented allegations of SIU wrongdoing. Blame belonged to both parties. But the Liberals were now in office and their embarrassment was only going to increase.

After attacking Diefenbaker in debate, Favreau left the House of Commons to be interviewed for an evening television program. Predictably, he was asked whether the government had any idea where Hal Banks could be found. No, Favreau said, he did not. Within hours of making the tape a late-breaking *Toronto Star* report answered the interviewer's question. In end-of-the-world type the newspaper headline screamed, 'Star Man Finds Hal Banks.'[51] Indeed he had. *Toronto Star* reporter Robert Reguly, acting on a tip, went to New York City and in less than two hours found Banks. Reguly simply toured SIU properties and at one pier, sitting out in the open, was Banks's Cadillac, still with Quebec licence plates. Reguly soon found Banks lolling on a yacht. The story, to Favreau's consternation, caused a sensation.[52]

A newspaper reporter had been able to do in two hours what the Mounties had failed to do in weeks. The leader of the opposition now moved into high gear. As well as being the 'pampered pet of Liberalism,' Banks was also, Diefenbaker said, the 'Waltzing Matilda' of Canadian politics.[53] The government appeared incompetent and ridiculous. Like all the other scandals the Liberals faced during the Pearson years, this one would eventually go away – but not for a while. In the meantime, with Banks gone, the trustees' real work began.

12
Autonomy and Respect

The goal of the Board of Trustees was to return the maritime unions to the management and control of duly elected and responsible officers as soon as possible, consistent with the national and public interest of Canada. How that goal, imposed by the terms of the Trusteeship Act, was to be met was the subject of both dispute and debate. In brief, there were those who believed that the situation revealed by Norris in his report called for nothing less than the winding up of the SIU, with a concomitant transfer of its membership to the Canadian Maritime Union. Removing SIU president Hal Banks was only the first step in this process.[1]

The trustees, however, had quite a different view. In marked contrast to early fears that the Trusteeship Act granted the trustees draconian powers, the statute was, on closer examination, a rather mild piece of legislation. The strongest grant of power it conferred on the board was the right to exercise its discretion in accordance with the general purpose of the act to dismiss an official of one of the maritime unions. But even this power, as the recent succession of Red McLaughlin to the SIU presidency illustrated, was interpreted such that it had to be exercised in accordance with the provisions of the particular union's constitution. The other specific powers conferred by the Trusteeship Act, such as control over union finances, were more of an inconvenience than anything else.[2] With only limited specific powers, accompanied by a rather nebulous direction in the statute to 'manage and control,' there was no possible way that the trustees could have legally dismantled the SIU if they had been so inclined, which, as it happened, they were not.[3]

At their first meeting the trustees made two important decisions. The first was to look to the future, not to the past. The second was to act as trustees, in the legal sense of the word, for the members of the individual unions placed under their management and control. The second decision imposed a duty on the trustees no different from the duty earlier imposed on the trustees of the SIU welfare plan: to pursue single-mindedly the interests of the beneficiaries of the trust. The beneficiaries of the Trusteeship Act, Dryer, Lippe, and Millard reasoned, were the members of the different maritime unions. Their interests were paramount.

In the case of the SIU, the trustees were bound by law and by their interpretation of their duties to take those steps necessary to return the union to its members' control. The Trusteeship Act allowed for no other action and their fiduciary obligations demanded nothing less. The first visible step in this direction was the dismissal of Hal Banks. As long as Banks was in power, there was no way the union could be removed from his grip. The trustees also commissioned a number of independent studies and began their own review of the organization and operation of the SIU. By the time Banks was fired the results were not all in. But the results which were available indicated that the situation was not nearly as grave as Norris had described.

The union itself was, on close examination, structurally sound. Many of its officers and staff were competent union professionals, not the corrupt villains whom Norris had described in his report. The hiring hall, apart from the abuses it was subjected to under Banks's regime, was efficiently run. The SIU's constitution was as good as any and the terms of the recently established Maritime Appeal Board offered, in theory, a means of redress for union members who believed that their rights had been infringed. In short, the trustees found that the SIU was not in bad shape.

Where the SIU had gone wrong was in its leadership. Retiring Banks from office removed the most serious impediment to the establishment of a democratic tradition. Once established, that tradition would ensure, should the SIU ever fall again into the hands of evil and tyrannical men, that recourse could and would be had at fixed times at the polls.

Accordingly, the trustees decided to hold early elections. In part this decision also made a certain amount of political sense. Red McLaughlin's constitutional succession to the SIU presidency, as well as the trustees' apparent 'inaction' in reforming the SIU, had been sharply criticized in many quarters, particularly by unionists and others labouring under severe misapprehensions about what exactly the trustees could and could not do and the means they had at their disposal. An early election, followed by demonstrated responsibility and capability of the elected officers in the management of the union's affairs, would answer the trustees' critics and, at the same time, serve as an important step in the public rehabilitation of the SIU.

After some deliberation, it was decided that elections would be held in the fall of 1964. Interested parties, including the Department of Labour, urged a longer delay.[4] The trustees, however, thought that early elections would afford the rank and file an opportunity to test their political wings. A prolonged period of active politicking unhampered by any of the anti-democratic pressures of the past would, it was believed, dispel any lingering concerns or fears by the rank and file of speaking out.[5] As well, the SIU's constitution provided that the next elections should be held in the fall of 1964. The trustees were legally bound to adhere to the terms of that constitution, which also contained a reasonably detailed code of election procedures.[6]

Predictably, McLaughlin announced that he was running for president and gathered a group of candidates who, like himself, had been associated in one way or another with the previous administration. Soon enough, a number of SIU members threw their hats in the ring. By early August, Halifax business agent Stan Devine had formed a slate opposing the McLaughlin ticket. Devine later withdrew from the presidential race, deciding to campaign instead for vice-president. The void his withdrawal left was shortly filled by René Turcotte, a relatively unknown SIU member. In total, there were forty-four candidates for sixteen positions.

Voting began on 15 September 1964, supervised by an election committee composed of an SIU member and representatives of the Department of Labour, the CLC, and the Board of Trustees.[7] The procedures followed were detailed and fair.[8] Nevertheless, rumours began to circulate that the election was a sham. The most enduring was that the trustees had combined with the SIU to 'fix' the election.[9] When the trustees were informed of this rumour and certain other allegations of impropriety, they responded with alacrity. In a widely publicized press release they appealed to anyone with information about improper conduct to send it to the Election Committee. There was no response. The trustees' ready reply and demand for particulars to the rumours of wrongdoing restored what little confidence had been lost in the election procedures.[10] On 19 November, right on schedule, tabulation of the votes began at the SIU hall in Montreal. The final result was no surprise.[11]

Leonard McLaughlin beat his rival for the SIU presidency by 900 votes. A number of ballots were spoiled, a few were void, and the rest were distributed among five minor candidates for the president's office. One-time presidential contender Stan Devine lost the vice-presidency to Rod Heinekey by 141 votes, while incumbent secretary-treasurer Don Swait bested his chief opponent by almost 1500 votes. Roger Desjardins held onto the position of vice-president-organizing, beating the two other contestants for the position by more than 1000 votes. Only one opponent of the McLaughlin team was elected.[12] Conclusive though they were, the election results were somewhat disappointing to SIU members and others who had been hoping for more of a break with the past. The trustees were not disappointed; they all agreed that McLaughlin was the only candidate qualified to run the SIU, although publicly, of course, they had remained neutral.[13] One of the losers, René Turcotte, initiated a number of legal proceedings in an ultimately unsuccessful attempt to have the election set aside.[14]

In early December, following McLaughlin's election to the SIU presidency and in accordance with the arrangement earlier made with Paul Hall, Turner was removed from the SIU Hall and Millard's ongoing presence at SIU headquarters was brought to an end. In their place an officer of the trusteeship staff was appointed to act as a liaison between the trustees and the union. By holding elections the trustees had gone some way towards turning over to the members of the SIU the management and control of their union. The trustees themselves openly acknowledged the change which had taken place. No longer, Dryer said, would the trustees act independently with regard to the SIU. If it were necessary, for example, to remove an SIU officer, they would first consult the union. Failing resolution of their concerns, they would next contact the SIU International and request action. Only if both avenues of approach failed to achieve the desired results would the trustees make use of their statutory right unilaterally to remove a union officer.[15]

The SIU election was a job well done. But like the firing of Banks, it was only a step in the long-term public rehabilitation of the SIU. Much of the remaining work was bureaucratic,[16] and included the amending of the union's constitution,[17] redrafting the National Shipping Rules, and generally improving the union's administrative systems. More importantly, the trustees had to disabuse Parliament and the trade union movement of the notion that the SIU was an inherently evil institution. The 1964 election was the first step in that process. The trustees knew that establishing the SIU's credibility would take some time. In part, it would depend on the conduct of McLaughlin and the SIU. The SIU had to prove itself worthy of membership in the trade union movement. Until that was done, and until the seamen's union was back in the CLC, the trustees' work would not be finished.

With Banks gone and apparently out of reach in the United States, the trusteeship and the SIU began to fade from the public eye. An election had been held in the SIU and, for the first time, union officers had been democratically elected. It was anticipated that the 1965 shipping season would come and go without interruption. The control of the trustees over the SIU had never been great and was being reduced every day. The trusteeship over the other maritime unions was little more than a formality.

Critics of the SIU continued to charge that the trustees were doing nothing to reform the endemic problems within the SIU. What they still did not realize was that the SIU described by Norris in his report was nothing like the SIU the trustees found upon taking office and was a far distant cousin to the union now run by Red McLaughlin. The trustees had absolutely no cause for complaint about McLaughlin's leadership, or about the operation of the SIU.

From all appearances, a calm had descended both on trusteeship and upon maritime industrial relations. In some respects the calm was misleading. Trusteeship staff, while no longer occupying any significant supervisory role over SIU activities, worked with union officers on a variety of matters as part of a continuing effort to improve the status quo, and to institutionalize the changes in the union which were taking place. The trustees were also attempting to contact every man and those few women who had been blacklisted by Banks. Before he was dismissed, Banks ordered the destruction of every copy of the Do Not Ship List. Consequently, all the trustees had to work with were the incomplete copies of the list introduced as exhibits at the Norris commission. Those former SIU members the trustees succeeded in contacting were invited to apply for the reinstatement of their union membership and, if necessary, to appeal to the Maritime Appeal Board.[18]

That was the board established by Banks in the final days of the Norris commision and subsequently approved by a meeting of the general membership. Presided over by Commodore Owen Robertson, the purpose of the board was to hear the cases of SIU members dissatisfied with the union's determination of their rights. The chairman of the board was given considerable powers to make findings of fact and to redress wrongs.[19] However, very few of the arbitrarily disenfranchised seamen took advantage of its provisions. This made sense. Sailing is traditionally a high turnover industry; although some men make their careers on board ship, long-term service is exceptional. Many seamen who had been blacklisted by Banks had gone on to other things, while others denied due process in their expulsion from the union had not, the trustees learned, been expelled without cause. By the end of 1965 the appeal board had received fewer than sixty applications from union members asking to be reinstated. Of these, thirty seamen were reinstated by the appeal board as full book members, nine were placed on probation, three had their appeals denied, and fourteen applications were either not followed up by the applicants or were refused by the board because it lacked jurisdiction, as was the case, for example, where a sailor had been discharged by an employer. The board appeared to be doing an exemplary job,[20] although its reputation would not survive the departure of the maritime trustees. Nevertheless, its existence and operation certainly assisted the trustees in their efforts to convince the labour movement that the new SIU was quite unlike the old. It was much harder, however, to demonstrate this fact to Parliament, and, as a result, late in 1964 chairman Victor Dryer resigned.[21]

When Dryer agreed to serve as a trustee in the fall of 1963 he did not impose any conditions on the length or the conditions of his service. He knew that the trusteeship was required to exist by statute for at least three years and that there was then a possibility of extension. He also knew that the trusteeship was accountable to Parliament and was required to file annual reports with the House of Commons. Neither the potentially lengthy tenure nor the obligation to report annually to the House of Commons was seen as an impediment by Dryer to the performance of his duties. What was, and what primarily contributed in the fall of 1964 to his decision to resign, was the request by the House of Commons subcommittee on Industrial Relations that Dryer and other trustees appear before it and give evidence.[22]

The first of several requests that the trustees give evidence was made by New Democratic Party leader T.C. Douglas in early April 1964. Labour minister Allan MacEachen promised to give the request consideration and asked the trustees what they thought.[23] 'We are trustees for the unions,' Dryer wrote MacEachen, 'and those unions, unlike government departments or crown corporations, belong to the members and not to the government or the nation. This makes the situation facing the trustees very delicate since much of the information which we obtain as trustees belongs to those unions and not to ourselves or to anyone else.'[24] The trustees asked, should they be invited to appear, that Parliament allow them 'to discriminate between those topics into which the inquiry might be injurious to our work or improper and those which can be freely discussed.'[25] Labour minister MacEachen hastened to assure Dryer that the House of Commons understood the distinction between informtion that was properly disclosed and information the disclosure of which would interfere with the trustees' performance of their duties; nevertheless, he insisted that they appear. There was little else MacEachen could do. Parliamentary arithmetic being what it was, the minority Liberal government could not indefinitely postpone demands from both the Tories and the NDP that the trustees testify. There was no way around it, and Dryer was advised in midsummer that a formal request would be made by the House of Commons

Subcommittee on Industrial Relations. In Dryer's view, this request made the further performance of his duties impossible and, in December 1964, he returned to British Columbia and resumed his duties on the bench.[26]

René Lippe was appointed chairman. Dryer's involvement with the trusteeship was not, however, over. On 5 December, just ten days before his resignation took effect, the request from the Industrial Relations Committee arrived. The trustees were asked to appear before the committee in March 1965. Dryer was the first witness.[27] Instead of immediately taking advantage of his limited presence in Ottawa to inform themselves better about the working of the trusteeship, the committee members under chairman John Munro wasted the first part of the session in an irrelevant procedural discussion. Then the committee began to work its way through the recently released 1964 Trusteeship Annual Report, stopping occasionally to pepper Dryer with questions. By and large, the questions revealed the poor understanding that many members of parliament had about what the trustees could and could not do.[28] Moreover, some committee members were, apparently, not as interested in being informed as in exploiting the committee hearings politically. Conservative member of parliament for the Yukon, Eric Nielsen, led the fray.

Claiming, somewhat mysteriously, that there had been irregularities in the recent SIU elections, Nielsen moved for the production of all the ballots. The source of his information, Nielsen later explained, was an 'SIU man.'[29] The request was ruled out of order. Nielsen was undaunted and moved for the production of the Election Committee report, which was also ruled out of order. Implicit in both motions was an allegation of wrongdoing in the conduct of the elections.[30] That was not, chairman Munro explained, why the committee had asked Justice Dryer to attend. He was there to be asked general questions about the work of the trusteeship, not to be pilloried with innuendo. The irascible Yukon MP was reminded of the committee's terms of reference, but persisted in his line of questioning. While not exactly the type of questioning Dryer and the other trustees had feared, it came potentially close to compromising their duties as trustees.

Nevertheless, Dryer answered Nielsen's questions with both patience and respect. To the best of his ability and without breaching his duty of confidentiality to the unions under trusteeship, Dryer attempted to explain what the trustees had done and why. The questioning continued for some time until the trustees' legal counsel, Montreal lawyer Louis-Philippe de Grandpré, decided it had gone far enough. 'The trustees,' de Grandpré said, 'appeared before this committee on the understanding that the function of the committee was to inquire into the facts found and the acts performed by the trustees. The proceedings today have indicated that the committee or some members of it, consider their function to be much broader, and that the committee is in fact to investigate the conduct of the trustees. If the committee does not feel the inquiry is limited to examining the trustees and insists on examining documents and other witnesses, the trustees must conclude they are on trial. In that event they request an adjournment to enable them to consider their position, particularly with regard to the question of whether they will serve any useful purpose by continuing as trustees.'[31] De Grandpré's message could not have been more clear.

The trustees had agreed to appear before the committee but in doing so made it clear that they were the statutory trustees of the maritime unions and that this imposed upon them certain legal obligations which they could not breach. If ordered to answer questions by a committee of Parliament they had no choice but to obey. But such an order, and questions along the lines of those advanced by Nielsen, would, if pursued, leave them no choice but to resign. When de Grandpré made his remarks he was obviously not just speaking for Dryer, who had already severed his formal relationship with the trusteeship. He was speaking for the remaining two trustees, and the committee members realized immediately that they were treading in dangerous water. The last thing the opposition wanted was to be accused of meddling in the affairs of the independent trusteeship and, even worse, of precipitating the en bloc resignation of the trustees. Fortunately for everyone concerned, following de Grandpré's warning, the matter went no further as the session was about to conclude. Nielsen promised the committee members that they would 'get' Dryer as soon as possible again,[32] but, in fact, Dryer's involvement with the trusteeship was, in every respect, at an end.

Dryer had succeeded in maintaining the duty of confidentiality he believed the trustees owed to the maritime unions and their membership. At the same time, he made some important strides in disabusing the committee members of some of their more egregious assumptions. Unfortunately, he did not explain to them the secondary reasons for his decision to resign. These reasons resulted from the government's failure to adopt and implement suggestions he had made privately which, he believed, would ensure that no maritime union ever fell under the control of a dictatorial union boss, and which would also have guaranteed that shipping would never again be disrupted in the manner in which it had been in the past. The suggestions, each of which depended on the passage of legislation, were threefold: a requirement that seamen sign articles and be terminated only before a shipping master; government control of the hiring hall, or, in the alternative, joint union-employer control, thereby preventing the resurrection of the blacklist; and a provision barring officers from being members of a seamen's union. None of these suggestions, which Dryer considered essential, was warmly received by Ottawa, and their poor reception contributed to his decision to resign. [33]

Judge Lippe testified the following week before the committee and he too had some difficulty in explaining to the committee members that the trustees' fiduciary duties to the unions under trusteeship and to their officers and members prevented the release of certain information and documents. Lippe was examined at some length on the conduct of the SIU elections and read into the record an extremely detailed account of the election procedures. After Lippe's visit, the committee apparently lost interest in the trusteeship. It never again asked any of the trustees to appear and give evidence. In so far as this resulted from the testimony of Dryer and Lippe, their appearing before the committee was, in the end, all to the good.

The trusteeship was, in fact, an increasingly forgotten operation. What evidence there was indicated that McLaughlin and the other SIU officers had no intention, at least when the trustees were around, of returning to their old ways. It was hoped that by the time the trustees were ready to leave, the practice of democracy in the union would be so entrenched that the abuses of the past would be but a forgotten blot on the union's history. In the meantime, the trusteeship had at least one more year to run. There was still a lot to do; in particular, the way had to be paved for the union's readmission to the CLC. That, to some extent, depended on the representative of organized labour on the trusteeship – Charlie Millard.

After spending the better part of a year hanging around the SIU hall, Millard had reached the conclusion that the trusteeship had served its purpose and it was now time for Parliament to bring it to an end. Even more so than the other two trustees, Millard came quickly to believe that the SIU was not nearly as bad as some, like Norris, had made out. Of all the trustees, Millard had the most hands-on contact with the SIU, although his assessment of the Norris Report was somewhat questionable, considering he never read it. [34] However, as a very experienced trade unionist, his views on labour matters merited consideration.

These particular views were given their first public expression in November 1964, just after the SIU elections, when Millard publicly confessed that the trustees found that 'the so-called crisis was not nearly so deep-seated nor as dangerous as it had been claimed or portrayed.' [35] The next month he wrote privately to the Executive Committee of the CLC and advised it that a union-run trusteeship would now be both appropriate and successful.[36] Millard was unable to convince the CLC, nor was he successful in gaining the support of the other trustees, including Dryer prior to his resignation. Unable to mobilize support for his views privately, he decided to write his own annual report.

The Trusteeship Act required the trustees to submit an annual report to Parliament. It did not, however, contemplate independent or minority reports, which is exactly what Millard in late 1964 and early 1965 began to write. What made it noteworthy was Millard's most important recommendation: that the trusteeship be brought to a speedy end.[37] 'Canada,' Millard wrote, 'has experienced the greatest lake shipping season on record. It has been accomplished without harassment, without jurisdictional warfare, without stoppages and has produced a healthier climate of international understanding.'[38] In his view, this was proof of the positive changes which had been brought about. Some problems remained, and some improvements could still be made, but that was always the case. Now was the time, Millard wrote, to hand over the remaining reigns of power to the SIU and its members. 'It is not possible to develop a full measure of responsibility under continuing authority. Since we learn by doing, it is equally obvious that democracy cannot be built undemocratically.'[39]

It took a lot of courage for Millard to come out and say what he thought. He had been appointed at the request of the CLC to represent organized labour's interests in the trusteeship. In law he was, of course, bound only by his obligations under the Trusteeship Act. However, in the circumstances which then existed, Millard's public expression of his thoughts was impolitic. The CLC and some of its affiliates, in particular the CBRT, had waged a public campaign against Banks and the SIU, culminating in the CLC's unprecedented request to the government to appoint an industrial inquiry commission. That had been followed by more than one hundred days of hearings and the highly embarrassing public airing of organized labour's dirty laundry. Now Millard was saying in public that the situation was not nearly as serious as the CLC had claimed or as grave as Norris had described. There was some truth to this, as all three trustees unanimously agreed. It was not, however, the full story and Millard's account was, in the circumstances, overly optimistic. After having served the labour movement for decades, Millard became an outcast.

Millard should have continued his private lobbying a little while longer, ensuring that at the end of the trusteeship's minimum term, 31 December 1966, it was not extended by government proclamation. His public pronouncements ended his effectiveness as organized labour's representative on the Board of Trustees. While he formally remained a trustee until the end, his active involvement with the maritime unions was over. The trusteeship itself continued. In early 1965 Joseph MacKenzie, the CLC director of organizing, was appointed to the board.[40] He was in every sense of the word a replacement for Millard, in whom the CLC had lost all confidence. MacKenzie's appointment was crucial to the success of the trusteeship and the accomplishment of its most major goal: the readmission of the SIU to the CLC.

From all appearances that was years away. At the April 1964 CLC convention the issue of the readmission of the SIU to the congress was brought up for discussion. The discussion was brief. It was decided that the SIU would not be readmitted unless and until its entire leadership changed. William Dodge declared that the Executive Council would never accept into the CLC a union 'that has as officers the kind of people who are now officers of that organization.'[41] When Dodge made this statement, Banks had been dismissed but the old guard remained. It did not appear that the leadership of the SIU was likely to change significantly. What had to change, then, was the opinion of the CLC about that leadership. In promoting that change, MacKenzie, whose views were respected as much as Millard's were now ignored, played an indispensable role, and one which lasted for quite some time. The CLC's view would not change overnight; it was something which had to be handled slowly and diplomatically. But the rehabilitation of the SIU and its leaders was not the only thing standing in the way of the readmission of that seamen's union to the congress. A method had to be devised of settling Canadian labour disputes in Canada, whether they involved national or international unions. It was undeniable that one of the main causes of the SIU affair was the CLC's inability to resolve and enforce jurisdictional disputes effectively, such as the one which brought the SIU, NAME, and the CBRT into conflict. Not only did a formal adjudicative mechanism have to be established, but for it to be effective the AFL–CIO had to agree to respect it.[42]

The first step in that direction had been taken in November 1963 when CLC vice-president Joe Morris addressed the delegates to the fifth annual AFL–CIO convention in New York City. 'It would be less than honest of me,' Morris said, 'to ignore the fact that there have been disagreements recently between the labour movements of Canada and the United States.'[43] Morris then gave the delegates some of the background to the dispute. 'You should be aware,' he told them, 'that during the last few years there has been the development of national feeling in Canada and a growing desire for greater national self-determination within the family of free nations. The dispute relating to the maritime union situation has focused sharp attention on these sentiments of nationalism and self-determination.'[44] The CLC shared these sentiments as much as anyone else. It was not a question of the CLC rejecting international unions, or of it deprecating its association with the AFL–CIO; it was instead an assertion of the right to determine for itself questions and issues relating to national affairs. 'To do less,' Morris concluded, 'would be to surrender our sovereignty.'[45]

Morris had made a declaration of independence. It was one which had been made in the past on countless occasions to little effect by his predecessors, most recently at the CCL–TLC merger convention.[46] Now it was time to give the brave words some bite. The first step in doing so was in establishing a dispute-resolving mechanism which would ensure that labour problems were decided in Canada by Canadians. This was done, with the AFL–CIO's apparent approval, at the CLC's fifth constitutional convention. The CLC's constitution was amended to provide for a compulsory mediation and arbitration process. Modelled after the procedure used by the AFL–CIO to settle its own jurisdictional and other disputes, the amendment empowered the CLC president to establish procedural rules for handling complaints. If voluntary settlement failed, recourse was to be had to an impartial umpire. Penalties in the form of sanctions were provided for non-compliance with the umpire's decision.[47]

Passage of this constitutional amendment was an important and long overdue step in the assertion of the Canadian labour movement of its right to make decisions for itself. It was certainly welcomed by the trustees, who realized that it was a prerequisite to the readmission of the SIU to the CLC. Without a formal and enforceable dispute-settling mechanism, history could easily repeat itself. It was not, however, the *sine qua non* to SIU acceptance. That would have been too easy and, besides, it was too soon. Nevertheless, it was a positive development.

A related development was the SIU's own decision in August 1964 to separate formally the licensed and unlicensed divisions of the union. Creation of the SIU-Licensed Division, followed by the raid on NAME, had been one of the main causes of the dispute and was the proximate cause of the SIU's expulsion from the congress. Many engineers had never reconciled themselves to being in the same union with the unlicensed crew; and, in fact, they had only ended up there because of Banks's dream of one union representing all maritime workers. The formation of the new union, known as the Canadian Marine Officers' Union, received the overwhelming approval of the marine engineers when it was put to them in a properly supervised vote.[48] Although the leadership of the new union was drawn almost exclusively from the old SIU-Licensed Division, it was formally, if not entirely in practice, independent of the SIU.

The establishment of this union, the creation of a made-in-Canada jurisdictional dispute-solving mechanism, and the continued efforts of Joseph MacKenzie all contributed to a growing acceptance by organized labour of the SIU. The trustees' efforts also assisted in this process. Their refining the SIU administrative machinery, such as the operation of the welfare plan, made the union a more effective organization. Membership meetings were regularly held and, as far as anyone could tell, the union's members no longer feared speaking out. The Do Not Ship List was a thing of the past. Indeed, the operation of the union's hiring hall was, according to the trustees, exemplary.[49] After registering at the hiring hall, a man was dispatched on a rotation basis subject to the union's shipping rules and to the two-tiered system of membership. This system had been retained with the union members' consent. Although strongly criticized by Norris in his report and by others as a system designed solely to inflate the workforce and thereby enrich the union's coffers, the membership of the union largely approved of it, acting as it did to discourage casual labour. Full-book members were, accordingly, given absolute preference when it came time to ship out. They were followed by probationers and then by applicants.[50]

As far as the trustees knew, this system did not cause any complaints. On the contrary, the efficiency of the system, the trustees said, accounted for the success the SIU enjoyed in securing and maintaining the loyalty of its members. It also explained, in part, why the members of the union were willing to overlook some of their leaders' misconduct.[51] That too, apparently, was a thing of the past. The eradication of the blacklist was accompanied by set procedures to be employed should the union decide to disenfranchise one of its members. Independent review of these procedures was available at the Maritime Appeal Board.[52] All the evidence indicated that the SIU had been completely reformed. Administratively, the operation of the union had always been reasonably efficient. Now both its operation and its practices compared favourably with those of any other union in Canada. As there was no way of telling whether that situation would change after the trustees were no longer around, it was believed essential that the SIU be brought back into the CLC fold.

After MacKenzie was appointed to the trusteeship in 1965, the CLC showed signs of softening on the question of when the SIU might be readmitted. In 1965 at the CLC annual convention, the Executive Committee asked delegates to give it the authority to affiliate the SIU if it was satisfied that the union met the criteria for membership set out in the congress constitution. This request evoked heated debate, but the request was approved by a large majority.[53] Later in the year the CLC issued a policy statement expressing the hope 'that on, or perhaps before the expiry of the three-year term established by the trusteeship legislation, conditions will be such that the trusteeship will be terminated.'[54] At the CLC's 1966 convention, the Executive Committee was given the power to affiliate the SIU on whatever terms it thought best.[55]

It was widely expected that the tempo of the SIU–CLC discussions would now accelerate. The CLC had been given a carte blanche by its affiliates and, for its part, the SIU was extremely anxious to return to the CLC before the mandatory term of the trusteeship was allowed to expire. The SIU leadership believed that the sooner it was reaffiliated with the congress the less likely it was that the government would extend the trusteeship by proclamation. However, 1966 came and went without the CLC extending an invitation of membership. As expected, the government extended the term of the trusteeship by one year.[56]

Except for the readmission of the SIU to the CLC, the work of the trusteeship was all but over. Initially, the trustees had had some hope of seeing the maritime unions putting aside their differences and combining for the common good. Over the course of the trusteeship some steps in that direction had been taken. For example, in Vancouver the SIU and Local 400 of the CBRT, both of which represented unlicensed seamen, worked together in negotiating collective agreements with the employers' organization. This was impossible on the Great Lakes. In the first place, some of the different employers individually negotiated their collective agreements, while the participation of others in the Association of Lake Carriers was purely pro forma. Feelings were still intense; there was no way that Jack Leitch was going to sit down at the bargaining table with the SIU unless he had to.

Leitch in fact had come out of the affair quite nicely, if relatively impoverished. The Canadian Maritime Union represented his unlicensed crews, and the Canadian Merchant Service Guild his mates and engineers. Although it once went on strike, the Canadian Maritime Union was not much of a union.[57] It only succeeded in organizing the crews on a few ships other than those owned or controlled by Upper Lakes and today it represents the employees of only one company: Upper Lakes Shipping. It failed to grow as originally anticipated and could not survive financially on its own. After a few rocky years in which it cast about for an affiliation, it ended up as a local of the CBRT. Mike Sheehan, Banks's former associate and the first president of the Canadian Maritime Union, was voted out of office.[58] Sheehan did not just hang up his seaboots and go away; he fought this decision and his fight took him on more than one occasion to the trustees' offices (and in the end, to the Supreme Court of Canada), but there was little the trustees could do for him.[59]

At the end of 1967 the government decided not to extend the trusteeship again. The year had been uneventful. Even a thirty-seven-day legal strike by the SIU against the members of the Association of Lake Carriers had failed to ripple the Great Lakes waters. The trustees believed that the Trusteeship Act should be allowed to expire. Although the SIU had not, by December 1967, been readmitted into the CLC, there was every expectation that early in the new year the CLC would invite the SIU and the Canadian Marine Officers' Union to apply for affiliation. This expectation proved correct. In January 1968, following a conference with SIU officers, the Congress Executive Committee voted to recommend the affiliation of the SIU and Canadian Marine Officers' Union. The affiliation was not without price. 'As a condition of reaffiliation of the SIU and the affiliation of the Canadian Marine Officers' Union,' acting CLC president Donald MacDonald said, 'the international and Canadian officers have signed an undertaking which states that they will abide fully by the constitution and principles and policies of the CLC. They recognize that no affiliate of the Congress has exclusive jurisdiction in this field. They have also made a commitment that no former member or former officer of the Canadian affiliate will exercise influence over its policies and actions.'[60] It was also agreed, among other things, that the SIU would continue to make available to its members a public board of appeal and that an SIU–CLC Liaison Committee would be established, the purpose of which, it was widely assumed, was to keep the SIU on the straight and narrow.

It appeared that the rehabilitation of the SIU was complete. The trustees certainly thought so. In their final annual report the trustees advised Parliament that the undemocratic procedures which had once been the hallmark of the SIU were a thing of the past. The rights of Canadian seamen were protected in law and practice.[61] The trustees could not, of course, guarantee the future, but they were satisfied that with the foundations that had been laid there was no reason the SIU, the other maritime unions, and the shipping companies could not 'write for themselves a brighter chapter in the history of Maritime Labour Relations in Canada.'[62]

The promise of these words showed some prospect of being met. Approximately one year after the trusteeship ended, SIU members returned to the polls in another general election. The campaign was a lively one, with incumbent president Red Mclaughlin and challenger Rod Heinekey, the SIU's man on the west coast, waging the closest contest.

McLaughlin won by 700 votes. Unlike the previous election, this one was not contested in court. The only blemish on what would have otherwise been a model campaign was the small number of SIU members eligible to vote. According to the SIU constitution which had been redrafted during the trusteeship and approved by the members in a supervised vote,[63] only SIU members with sixty days sea-time were eligible to vote. The thirty-seven-day Great Lakes strike cut almost in half the number of union members who were constitutionally entitled to cast their ballots.[64]

Nevertheless, what was important was that the election was a fair one, and no one suggested it was not. In 1971 SIU members again returned to the polls and McLaughlin, in a bitter campaign, beat presidential challenger William Glasgow by forty-one votes. The defeated candidate did not accept the results with equanimity. In fact, he alleged that the voting had been fixed and initiated legal proceedings to have the election set aside. In the end, McLaughlin's presidency was confirmed. Nevertheless, the allegations raised in the legal challenge were disquieting.[65] It was also worrisome, and somewhat difficult to explain, that soon after he was victorious at the polls McLaughlin began to withdraw from active union activities. His second-in-command, executive vice-president Roman Gralewicz, appeared to be in charge. McLaughlin, it was said, was spending his time in Ottawa lobbying on behalf of the union. As it turned out, he must have also done a good job of lobbying on behalf of himself. Soon after his 1971 re-election, at the suggestion of CLC president Donald MacDonald, McLaughlin was assisted by the government of Canada in obtaining a position at the International Labor Organization in Geneva. He has retained it ever since. His successor to the SIU presidency was none other than Roman Gralewicz.

Gralewicz had played a small role in the SIU cast during the Banks years. He sailed between 1948 and 1952, when he joined the union staff. In the mid-1950s he left the union for a brief stint in private industry, but the call of the sea, or least of the SIU union hall, beckoned, and by 1958 he had returned to the union. Described by some as 'ruggedly handsome,' Gralewicz was more than six feet tall and weighed over 200 pounds. Physically, he was not dissimilar to Hal Banks, and was the exact opposite of the bookish and relatively diminutive Red McLaughlin. In appearance, Gralewicz was a man a sailor could respect.[66]

His leadership, as it turned out, was an entirely different matter. Soon after McLaughlin's active involvement with the union ended, allegations began to arise that, earlier appearances to the contrary, the SIU had not changed. A number of members who claimed to have been beaten up for attempting to exercise their union rights founded the 'Seamen's Reform

Committee,' its purpose being to bring the union back on track. It made submissions to the SIU–CLC liaison committee about the violence, but as was the case a decade earlier, almost none of the allegations of violence could be traced back to the SIU. By and large, the CLC pronounced itself satisfied with the way Gralewicz ran SIU affairs.[67]

The 'Seamen's Reform Committee' soon faded away. It had not been the first such committee in the history of the Canadian SIU, and would not be the last. With increasing regularity, allegations about racketeering, violence and intimidation, fixed elections, political bribes, blacklists, and every other impropriety imaginable have been made against the union and its officers. How much there is to them – and all too many ring true – is a question for future historians to answer.

13
Extradition

The conclusion of the trusteeship and formal return of the SIU to its members' control brought considerable relief to the government of Canada. Canadian governments, both provincial and federal, prefer organized labour to regulate its own affairs and will interfere only if necessary. It had taken the closing of the St Lawrence Seaway, following the repeated requests of the CLC, to convince the minister of labour to appoint the Norris Commission. Similarly, trusteeship legislation was only passed and proclaimed after every conceivable effort was made to find an alternative. The trusteeship had its critics, and there were those who maintained that the SIU had not changed, but the expiry of the Trusteeship Act on 31 December 1967 officially concluded the government's involvement in the activities of the SIU. The federal government now longed to wash its hands of the affair and could have done so had the opposition allowed the one major piece of unfinished business to fade away. That was bringing Hal Banks back to Canada to face justice.

Extradition between Canada and the United States is governed by the 1842 Webster-Ashburton Treaty, which has over the years been modified by a number of supplementary conventions. In general, to succeed in an extradition application four prerequisites must be met. The demanding state must prove in court that the act charged was committed within its jurisdiction, the act charged is a crime within its jurisdiction, the act charged is a crime in the other state's jurisdiction, and the act is listed in the extradition treaty. [1] Extradition will be granted provided it meets these criteria, with two exceptions. The first is that no person is to be surrendered for a political crime; the second is that a person who is surrendered may not be tried or imprisoned for any offence committed before the extradition other than that for which he was surrendered, until he has had an opportunity to return to the surrendering state.

In Canada, the administration of criminal justice is generally exercised by the provinces. Accordingly, provincial authorities usually initiate extradition applications. The formal request for surrender is, however, made through diplomatic channels by the Canadian government. The process requires a considerable degree of intergovernmental co-operation.

As those opposition members of parliament knew who demanded that Banks be returned to Canada so that justice would be 'vindicated,' the ex-SIU president had fled Canada after being convicted of a crime not listed in the Canadian–American extradition treaty.[2] If conspiracy to assault had been a listed offence, his extradition would have been straightforward. It was not, and to bring Banks back to Canada, a new charge that met the criteria in the extradition treaty would have to be laid. It was essential that Banks be convicted under the new charge; if he were not, the government would be faced with the embarrassing situation of having to escort Banks to the border and, notwithstanding the conviction for conspiracy to assault, set him free.

Accordingly, for the second time since Norris delivered his report, special counsel were retained to review the evidence and determine if there were sufficient grounds to lay another charge.[3] Nevertheless, the opposition Tories hammered away at the government for its 'inaction.' Whether they really wanted Banks back or whether they were just trying to embarrass the government is irrelevant. The repeated public attacks and demand for action put pressure on the federal government, which therefore continued, although without enthusiasm, to see if there was anything it could do.[4]

Some two-and-a-half years after Banks fled, the solicitor general of Canada, L.T Pennell, gave a progress report to the House of Commons. Discussions had taken place, Pennell said, with officials in Quebec City and at Queen's Park. The Ottawa–Quebec City discussions were over; they had terminated after it was decided that the 'facts did not warrant any further proceedings being taken.'[5] However, the discussions with the attorney general of Ontario were continuing.

Six days later, Ontario attorney general Arthur Wishart acknowledged that he had been consulted about the Banks matter. Wishart said that if the RCMP laid a charge, the province of Ontario would, as was customary, seek Banks's extradition.[6] On 15 December Pennell announced, again in the House of Commons, that the RCMP believed there was sufficient cause to place the evidence it had been accumulating before the crown.[7] It appeared that the government counsel and RCMP investigators had found enough hard evidence against Banks to support a criminal charge and, equally important, one that fell within the ambit of Canada's extradition agreement with the United States.

Having made these announcements in the House of Commons, it was expected that the government would now proceed quickly against Banks. In fact, nothing more was heard about the matter until the following April, when Justice minister Pierre Trudeau announced in the House of Commons that the matter had been placed in the hands of another lawyer, local provincial assistant crown attorney John Cassels. Cassels, Trudeau said, was 'consulting with superiors.'[8]

Publicly, it may have appeared that the government's 'stonewalling' was continuing. In fact, it was not. In late August a number of people assembled in the chambers of Ottawa justice of the peace Livius A. Sherwood, who, on the basis of information and testimony given by RCMP corporal J. Borsa, issued a warrant for Banks's arrest. The charge was perjury, which satisfied all of the preconditions for extradition between Canada and the United States. It was alleged that Banks had perjured himself before the Norris Commission when he denied under oath any complicity in the beating of Captain Walsh. It was Banks's conviction for that offence which had precipitated his flight from Canada. The charge was highly questionable, as all of the facts pertaining to it had been in the crown's possession for years. Furthermore, the charge was laid in the middle of an SIU strike, that union's first legal strike in years. Although likely coincidental, the timing of the charge left the government open to the accusation that it was interfering in collective bargaining.

It had never been understood in many quarters, following the release of the Norris Report, why Banks had not been charged with numerous crimes. When Pennell first indicated that discussions between Ontario and Ottawa were continuing there was some expectation that, finally, Banks was going to be hauled in to answer for his conduct. A charge of perjury for evidence given before an Industrial Inquiry Commission relating to an incident for which Banks had been subsequently convicted somehow fell short of what many believed the situation required. Toronto *Telegram* columnist Frank Tumpane asked why, if the Department of Justice had a perjury case against Banks, it did not initiate it while Banks was still in Canada and under the jurisdiction of the court. The *Montreal Star* wondered aloud why the case was proceeding and hinted, rather darkly, that 'political pressure' was involved.[9] For his part, the attorney general of Ontario explained that 'the reason why he wished to bring this man back was in the course of the administration of justice, to have him answer for what was perjury in a trial in a series of events affecting our whole life in this country.'[10]

Having decided to lay the charge, the government had to pursue it. Corporal Borsa flew to New York and, along with Manhattan lawyer Richard Kuh, appeared on 29 August 1967 before United States extradition commissioner Salvatore Abruzzo. Commissioner Abruzzo ordered the United States marshal to arrest Banks, who upon being taken into custody asked, 'Do you have to do this to me?'[11] Unfortunately for Banks, they did. He was arraigned on 30 August and his application for bail refused. On 1 September the ambassador of Canada to the United States, A.E. Ritchie, delivered a note to the American secretary of state formally requesting that Banks be extradited to Canada.[12]

Following two requests for adjournment by Abraham H. Brodsky, the attorney representing Hal Banks, the case came to trial in late September. A transcript of the proceedings is no longer available. However, the issues of law and fact were canvassed by lawyers for both sides in detailed legal briefs which they submitted following the conclusion of the hearing. Brodsky submitted his brief first.[13]

With one major exception, Brodsky's arguments were nonsense – novel certainly, inspired perhaps, but almost wholly devoid of legal merit.[14] Brodsky's first proposition was that the articles of extradition relied on by Canada in making its request could not apply because Canada was not a contracting party to the initial Webster-Ashburton extradition agreement. This startling claim, if indeed it was made seriously, was based on a complete and profound misunderstanding of the development of dominion status. It failed to realize that part and parcel of this development was a devolution to the Crown in Right of Canada of pre-existing treaties and other similar arrangements. Not only that, but as a little research would have revealed, American courts consistently gave effect to properly made Canadian extradition requests and, more importantly, the United States government had unequivocally recognized the 1842 treaty and subsequent conventions as continuing the extradition obligations between Canada and the United States.[15]

In an alternative submission, Brodsky argued that assuming that Canada had the right to request the surrender of an individual, this right was not delegable to the province of Ontario. Even conceding, for the sake of argument, that Brodsky's understanding of Canadian constitutional law was correct, the facts of this case revealed a significant federal role in the request for Banks's extradition. Brodsky's third line of argument was even further removed from the facts and the law applicable to the case. He stated that Banks could not have committed perjury because the Norris inquiry was not a judicial proceeding. 'Judge Norris,' the American attorney said, 'was nothing more than a private individual with no authority to hold hearings or to take testimony.'[16] The novelty of this point did not come close to making up for its obvious deficiencies.

Brodsky next argued that the application should fail because the crime charged was not a crime in both Canada and the United States. Perjury was one of the listed crimes, so what Brodsky had to do to make his argument prevail was convince Commissioner Abruzzo that had Banks falsely testified in a similar proceeding in the United States a perjury charge would not lie. It was, like all the preceding arguments, a difficult one to make. If his case had been based on it or any of the others alone, it would surely have failed. However, Brodsky had one wild card up his sleeve.

Article II of the 1889 Blaine-Pauncefote Convention excluded from extradition offences of a political character: 'A fugitive criminal shall not be surrendered if the offence in respect of which his surrender is demanded be one of a political character, or if he proves that the requisition for his surrender has in fact been made with a view to try or punish him for an offence of a political character.' As University of New Brunswick law professor and future Supreme Court of Canada justice Gerard La Forest noted in his authoritative text on extraditions to and from Canada, determining whether an offence fell within this definition is no easy matter. [17]

Every case in which Article II is pleaded must be decided on its own facts. If the facts do not of themselves reveal that the accused is being sought for a political purpose, the burden of proof shifts to the accused, who must then lead affirmative evidence to prove that the prosecution is politically motivated. Vague accusations that one is wanted for political purposes, the case law unanimously agreed, is insufficient to bar an extradition application. [18] Accordingly, in this case the burden fell squarely on Banks.

The offence of perjury with which Banks was charged did not arise out of a demonstrably political activity such as, for example, a demonstration. Neither Banks nor his counsel was privy to the discussions and decisions on Parliament Hill and elsewhere which had led to his being charged and could not, therefore, easily prove that these events were motivated by concerns other than for the prosecution of criminal justice. However, there was evidence of a political interest in Banks which his attorney, Brodsky, could lead on his behalf. That interest was the out-of-the-ordinary concern about Banks and his affairs by members of parliament. In general, those charged with the prosecution of a case refuse to comment on it until a decision has been reached and any possibility of appeal is either exhausted or abandoned. This general reluctance to engage in public debate on a matter that is or may become before the courts makes considerable sense where there is any possibility that public discussion or debate may prejudice an accused's right to a fair trial. There was certainly that possibility in the Banks case and there was, as Brodsky pointed out, the added element that the widespread parliamentary discussion of Banks's case had transformed the prosecution into one motivated by political purposes.

'The Conservatives,' Brodsky said, 'charge the Liberals with "molly coddling" or "shielding" Mr. Banks. The Liberals to avoid political embarrassment, must show the lie to their opposition's charge by ... a ... crusade to "get Banks," and thereby purge the stain upon their political escutcheon. Banks, called by the Leader of the Opposition, Diefenbaker, "the pampered pet of Liberalism" and "the Waltzing Matilda of Canadian politics" has in fact become the hot potato of Canadian politics.'[19] A stack of Hansards which Brodsky unsuccessfully sought to introduce into evidence proved, Brodsky claimed, that the Canadian extradition application was the result of pernicious political machinations.[20]

The reply of the Province of Ontario to this point was brief. There was not, Kuh claimed, even a scintilla of proof to support the charge that the perjury prosecution was politically based. Unsworn statements made in Canada's Parliament were incapable of demonstrating that a prosecution was political. The Hansards were the stuff that fugitives' dreams were made of, not the evidence necessary to prove that a prosecution was motivated by political considerations.[21]

Despite Kuh's reply, it is hard to imagine what could be more illustrative of a political interest in the prosecution of a crime than extracts from Hansard. What other 'proof' could an individual adduce that the government's decision to charge him was based on political, and therefore improper, purpose? The most an accused who wishes to raise Article II of the Blaine-Pauncefote Convention can do is lead what evidence is available and suggest the inferences which should be drawn. In this case there were inferences suggested by the limited available evidence. Banks had been a public figure of great ill-repute in Canada, his name and misdeeds had been bandied about in Parliament and the press for years, and now, in the midst of a legal strike by the SIU of Canada, he was being sought on a charge which could have been prosecuted years earlier. Whether these facts were sufficient to raise a strong inference that he was being sought for political reasons was a question for the extradition commissioner to decide. But there was no denying that the issue, and Brodsky's argument on this point, was serious and legitimate.

Before concluding his submissions, Brodsky raised one final point. He argued that no extradition orders should be made because Banks had been denied the protection of the Fifth Amendment to the American Constitution: the protection against self-incrimination. Unlike the Fifth Amendment which entitles an accused to refuse to answer a question on the grounds that his answer may incriminate him, the Canada Evidence Act

requires a witness to answer all questions put to him. In return, the wit
ness is entitled to claim the protection of a provision of the act which pro
vides that any answers given (although not evidence derived from those
answers) are not admissible against the accused in a subsequent pro
ceeding. Unlike the real protection afforded a witness by the Fifth
Amendment, that provided by the Canada Evidence Act is largely
illusory.

Given this situation, Brodsky argued, when Banks was testifying at the
Norris commission he was on the horns of a trilemma: to admit awareness
of the facts and circumstances of the Walsh beating would have been to
incriminate himself completely and virtually invite prosecution for this
crime; to deny everything would hazard prosecution for perjury; or to
refuse to answer would ensure his being cited for contempt of court.
Faced with these three choices, Banks denied everything. This, Brodsky
argued, was wrong. Banks should have been able to claim the protection
of the Fifth Amendment. [22]

The fatal flaw in this argument was, obviously, that American citizens
do not enjoy the protection of their constitution away from home. The
fact that Canadian law provided less protection to a witness than
American law was perhaps a cause of regret. It was not by any means a
sufficient reason to vitiate obligations created under treaty and the prac
tice of decades. [23] With the exception of Brodsky's penultimate point, his
arguments made little sense. As Counsel Kuh aptly quoted, they were 'full
of sound and fury, signifying nothing.' [24] Having established the four pre
requisites to an extradition request, Kuh suggested that an extradition
order should be automatic.

After receiving Kuh's brief on 23 October 1967, Commissioner Abruzzo
retired to consider his decision. Less than two weeks later he ordered that
Banks be certified for extradition. Relying heavily on Kuh's written argu
ment, Abruzzo rejected all the submissions made on Banks's behalf. In
particular, he found that there was no legal proof or testimony to substan
tiate Banks's claim that the prosecution was politically motivated. [2]
Banks, who was still in jail, faced two options. He could appeal Abruzzo's
decision through the courts or he could appeal directly to the secretary of
state, Dean Rusk. Under American law, the secretary of state sits as the
final court of appeal in extradition matters. In exercising this duty he is
free to examine questions of fact and law and to consider the impact of
extradition on foreign relations. An immediate appeal to secretary of state
Dean Rusk was the option Banks chose.

To prepare and present his case Banks retained two well-connected
counsel: Abram Chayes, the former senior legal adviser at the Depart-

ment of State, and Myer Feldman, a former White House aide. After notice of appeal was served and before any argument was heard, Rusk began to receive a number of interesting, informed, and persuasive submissions from individuals with varying degrees of interest in the case. The first, probably at Rusk's request, came from the secretary of labor, Willard Wirtz. Describing the events involving Banks as 'sordid,' 'ugly,' and a chronicle of awkwardness,' Wirtz advised Rusk that the situation on the Great Lakes was quiescent and gave every promise of remaining so, except that the extradition of Banks would threaten that promise. The secretary of labour did not care about the ex-SIU president personally: 'Banks as a particular person, presents no case for special consideration.' But Wirtz did care about the principle involved in extraditing a man to face a stale charge and, perhaps more importantly, the havoc that extradition could wreak on the calm Great Lakes waters.[26]

Rusk was also lobbied by American organized labour. The day after Christmas, George Meany wrote and urged Rusk not to allow the extradition. Meany told Rusk that he had followed Banks's career for years, beginning with his involvement in Canadian trade union affairs which came about in response to a request by the Canadian and American governments for American trade union assistance in dealing with a serious problem of Communist subversion in the Canadian maritime industry.'[27] The AFL–CIO president advised the secretary of state that neither justice nor equity would be served by Banks's return to Canada.

Banks was, Meany explained, a product of the waterfront environment. In his career, he had rendered substantial constructive service to the labour movement and to seamen. Meany advised Rusk that at the time of his arrest Banks was employed by the Harry Lundeberg School of Seamanship, a school which, the AFL–CIO president hastened to point out, was providing a national service. 'This enterprise is engaged in training young men of all races, most of whom are drawn from underprivileged and deprived backgrounds, to equip them as seamen and to give them an opportunity in a meaningful and rewarding seagoing career. The function of this undertaking,' he added in a point sure to be appreciated by Rusk, 'in filling the manpower needs of the Merchant Marine necessitated by the present Viet Nam conflict is also worthy of mention.'[28] In light of all of these circumstances, Meany urged Rusk not to allow Banks's extradition to proceed.

This was a view to which Rusk and a number of his advisers were becoming increasingly sympathetic. Rusk, of course, needed a lot more information before he could make any decision, and an opportunity arose to obtain the Canadian position at a prearranged dinner meeting with

Prime Minister Pearson in late December. Department of State legal adviser Leonard C. Meeker prepared a number of questions for Rusk to ask should Banks's extradition be brought up for discussion. Meeker's proposed questions reveal a concern with what was at the bottom of Canada's extradition request.[29]

First, Meeker suggested that Rusk ask why Banks was not tried for perjury in 1964 since all the evidence bearing on a perjury charge was available at that time. Second, was it normal practice under Canadian law to try a defendant after a substantial passage of time for a crime he could have been tried for at the time of an earlier prosecution based essentially on the same facts? Third, were there any political considerations in Canada which led to the extradition request? Fourth and finally, did Canada, in light of the previous discussion, wish to maintain that request? As is clear, these questions went straight to the heart of Banks's claim that he was being sought for political, not criminal, purposes. If these questions were indeed asked, and what little evidence is available suggests that they were not, it is hard to imagine what Pearson could have said on Canada's behalf.[30]

Following his meeting with the Canadian prime minister, Rusk asked Kuh and Banks's new lawyers to prepare written arguments for his consideration in advance of a to-be-scheduled hearing.[31] Chayes spared Rusk the fantastic legal arguments cited by his predecessor. Instead, in a two-pronged attack, the brief went directly to the points most likely to persuade in an appeal of this kind. The first prong began with a resurrection of the cruel trilemma theory. Chayes reviewed the applicable principles and made an eloquent and stirring plea for the rights of the individual. The crux of this part of the argument was that Canada should not be allowed to do what was constitutionally impossible in the United States: that is, force an individual to testify against himself. 'Mr. Banks,' the brief said, 'should not be surrendered so that Canada can do what no United States authority would be permitted to do. Such an exercise of federal power would be, if not an outright violation of the constitution, a serious infringement of our deep-seated sense of justice and at odds with basic notions of extradition law.'[32]

This was the same argument Brodsky had made earlier and which Commissioner Abruzzo had, without a moment's notice, rejected. As it was without authority in law, the success or failure of the extradition appeal depended on the second prong of Chayes's argument. That argument was that the extradition request was politically motivated. This argument stood a greater chance of success before the secretary of state than before an extradition commissioner, advancing as it did political considerations.

For the benefit of the secretary of state and by way of general introduction, the brief noted that Hal Banks had been a figure of some public interest since his arrival in Canada. The disruption in shipping, the Norris Commission, the trustees' decision to fire him, his trial, and subsequent flight from Canada had, Chayes wrote, intensified that interest. In an appendix attached to his brief, Chayes noted that Banks's name had been brought up in the House of Commons at least thirty times between 1964 and 1968. Drawing from Hansard reports, Chayes formulated seven points which he suggested indicated that the decision to charge and extradite Banks was politically based.

First, Chayes noted, even before Banks failed to surrender in accordance with the terms of his bail, the Tories challenged the handling of the prosecution against him on the ground that the crime for which he was tried was not extraditable and that his bond was insufficient in its amount and inadequate in its provisions. Second, the Tories charged that the handling of the Banks case evinced favouritism and special solicitude towards him by the governing Liberal party. Third, after the date of Banks's appeal and non-appearance, the opposition intensified its charges of special treatment and adduced as an explanation the fact that Banks and the SIU had made campaign contributions to the Liberal party and its candidates. Fourth, the opposition repeatedly demanded that since Banks had been convicted of a non-extraditable crime, new charges should be brought against him so that he could be extradited. These demands were often linked with a repetition of the charge that the government was protecting Banks because of his contributions to the Liberal party. Fifth, the government at first contended that Banks's activities had been investigated by special counsel and that these counsel found that the evidence would only sustain the conspiracy charge on which he was actually tried. Later, as the pressure from the Tories mounted, the government agreed to undertake a further investigation to see whether evidence to support charges of extraditable crimes could be developed. This probably was the most damning point. Sixth, in late 1966 and early 1967 the insistence of the opposition grew. At almost every question period, questions were put to the government as to the development of the new charges. The government responded regularly that consultations were proceeding with provincial law enforcement authorities, but still no charges were brought. Seventh, and finally, when the perjury charge was laid, the SIU was out on strike. There was every reason, Chayes suggested, to believe that the incidents outlined in these seven points were connected.

These seven points were also, Chayes added, compelling evidence that the perjury charge was part and parcel of a long and continuing campaign to 'get Banks.'[33] The campaign was brought by a government under political pressure to prove that it was not indebted to Banks. The facts and the inferences to be drawn from them, Chayes suggested, proved that the perjury charge was laid not to vindicate justice but to relieve the Liberal government of political embarrassment. As such, the extradition request was a cloak for political action and should be denied under Article II of the Blaine-Pauncefote Convention. [34]

Two weeks after Chayes submitted his brief he was notified that a meeting with the secretary of state was set for 16 February 1968. Both Chayes and Kuh were to be given fifteen minutes to make oral argument before Rusk. At the beginning of February, Kuh submitted a long brief in favour of extradition which basically restated the legal arguments he had advanced in the first instance. Where, however, the second brief differed from the first was that Kuh now faced head-on the allegation that political machinations were behind the perjury charge and extradition application. [35]

It would have been senseless to deny the range and scope of the parliamentary interest in Banks. Instead, Kuh attempted to trivialize it. Hansard merely revealed, he suggested, the political opportunism and political fencing common in any democracy. Hal Banks was a figure of national interest and attention with a generally conceded record of criminal conduct. Kuh argued that a little notoriety should not be enough to transform a criminal offender into a political one. Accordingly, he requested that the secretary of state exercise his discretion in favour of extradition. [36]

Faced with two conflicting briefs, Rusk asked Meeker for advice, and he submitted a carefully drafted and thoughtful legal memorandum. [37] It noted that there had never been an occasion in which a court of the secretary of state had denied extradition solely on the ground that rights as extensive as those under the United States constitution had not been or would not be accorded in a foreign jurisdiction. Furthermore, Meeker noted that Article II, strictly read, could not be relied upon by Banks on the facts of this case. That article did not, Meeker said, encompass the motivation of the demanding country. 'While motivation might be relevant where there is a question whether the fugitive will be given a fair trial, this is not an issue in Banks' case.'[38] Despite his earlier unease about Canada's extradition request, as evidenced in the list of questions he prepared for the Rusk-Pearson meeting, Meeker recommended that the extradition order be given effect. [39]

The day before the hearing was set to take place, the Canadian ambassador to the United States delivered a note to the Department of State. The government of Canada, the note said, was anxious to clear up some misconceptions, in particular that the return of Hal Banks was being sought in order to prosecute and punish him for an offence of a political character. 'While his conduct in Canada may have become, to some extent, a political issue, it certainly does not flow from this that the offence with which he stands charged is of a political character.'[40] The note pointed out that there were no other instances in which the secretary of state had refused extradition after it had been ordered by a United States commissioner. The government of Canada, the note concluded, wished to emphasize its concern that nothing be done 'which could alter for the future the long established practice on the part of both governments whereby fugitives from justice in the United States and Canada found extraditable by judicial processes are surrendered up for extradition.'[41]

The next day, 16 February, seven lawyers, a number of advisers, and the secretary of state gathered in Rusk's inner office to discuss Canada's extradition request. The proceeding took less than an hour and Rusk asked questions and heard brief argument. A little less than one month later, Rusk released his decision. He had decided not to allow the extradition: Because the charge of perjury in this case arises directly out of a denial of guilt of a non-extraditable offence, I have concluded that it would not be compatible with the overall design and purpose of the extradition treaty, which is limited and not universal in its coverage of offences, to agree to extradition on the facts of this case.'[42] On 15 March Banks was set free.

Rusk did not, however, make this decision on legal grounds alone. As was his right, he considered the political and foreign policy ramifications of agreeing to the request. American organized labour had made clear its view that extradition should not be granted. At the time the AFL–CIO was one of President Lyndon Johnson's strongest supporters in the American government's prosecution of the war in Vietnam. Much less to the point but nevertheless influential was, Rusk claimed, the fact that a member of the Canadian cabinet contacted a member of the American cabinet with the information that the government of Canada did not really want Banks back but was making the request because it had become an inflammatory issue in Parliament.[43]

If this were true, and it was denied by both Prime Minister Pearson and Paul Martin, the secretary of state for external affairs, one would have expected the government of Canada to accept the decision 'with regret.' However, as soon as the decision was publicly announced, the government said that it had instructed Ambassador Ritchie to request Rusk to reconsider his decision or to consent to its adjudication by an international tribunal.[44] The Department of State believed it could defend its decision successfully before an international tribunal but did not relish the prospect. On 25 March 1968 Rusk wrote Ritchie and informed him that after further reflection his decision remained the same. Ritchie wa also advised that the American government did not wish to refer the mat ter to an international tribunal or to arbitration because, by and large the present system was working well. For a time this ended the matter.[4]

It did not, however, end interest in the case. The *Toronto Star* sug gested that 'the fix' was in for Banks via counsel Chayes and Feldman and because of pressure from George Meany and Paul Hall, who were busy swinging organized labour behind the administration's Vietnam policies The *Globe and Mail* elaborated on this theme when it published an edito rial cartoon depicting Rusk as a middle-aged hippie carrying a placard reading 'Hell no Banks Won't Go' and burning a Canada–United State extradition card.[46] Amusing as the *Globe*'s cartoon was, it too suggested that there was a political element to Rusk's decision. This, as Meany's 2(December 1967 letter to Rusk makes clear, was absolutely correct. There was also nothing wrong with it; Rusk was duty-bound to consider the for eign policy implications of his decision. There was an excellent possibility that had he upheld Commissioner Abruzzo's decision, the foreign policy interests of the American government could be prejudiced. While there was nothing wrong with Rusk considering the foreign policy implication of his decision, a *Wall Street Journal* story which broke on 19 July 196? suggested, in fact, that serious political wrongdoing had taken place.

It was reported that days after Rusk made his decision, cheques from the SIU International began to trickle in to various Democratic party cam paign offices. The SIU International contribution came in two equal packets of ten cheques each. To avoid limit restrictions, each of the cheques was made out for $5000. Half of the money, $50,000, was ear marked for Vice-President Hubert Humphrey's election campaign, the rest to groups which had been working for President Johnson' re-election.[47]

Rusk denied any connection between the donation and his decision and the facts indicate that he knew nothing about it. While Democratic party fundraisers may have misled Paul Hall into believing that only a sizeable donation would set Banks free, there is not one iota of evidence to suggest that Rusk was involved with the solicitation of the donation.[4] Needless to say, the *Wall Street Journal* story brought Banks back into the news. It also gave a little-known Republican senator from Arizona, Paul Fannin, the opportunity to further his political ambitions. Alleging that there were 'improprieties' in the case, he charged that the Democratic administration in Washington was 'protecting' Banks. This charge, and some other statements Fannin subsequently made, fuelled speculation in

Canada that the change of government in the United States following the November 1968 elections would result in the reopening of the Banks case.[49]

In Canada there was also a new cast of players in office. Pearson was gone and had been replaced by Pierre Trudeau. The Tories had also switched leaders, but John Diefenbaker, who had remained in the House of Commons, gave no sign of relinquishing his commanding role. Indignant and self-righteous as only Diefenbaker could be, he continued to make demands that all possible steps be taken to obtain Banks's return. Other members of his caucus, however, felt differently and privately informed United States embassy officials that their party was not really interested in reopening the Banks case.[50] 'Thus,' the embassy reported to Washington, 'when Diefenbaker raised the question of extradition on January 30 – as he can be expected to do again, it was for the purpose of needling and embarrassing the Government and is not to be taken seriously.'[51]

American authorities may have come to the same conclusion about Senator Fannin. He too was a man with a mission. Sure that an investigation would reveal all sorts of evidence about Democratic party wrongdoing down at Foggy Bottom, Fannin wrote secretary of state William Rogers in early May 1969. Following an incomplete, partially incorrect, and entirely superficial account of the events leading up to Rusk's decision not to extradite Banks, Fannin asked Rogers to 'initiate an investigation into the Banks matter to ascertain the basis upon which this decision was made, particularly in light of the events which transpired subsequent to the Secretary's decision.'[52] Fannin was obviously attempting to embarrass Rusk.

Nevertheless, having received a request, Rogers asked legal adviser Meeker to look into it. Meeker advised Rogers in April 1969 that there were precedents for reconsideration of extradition decisions where extradition had been refused by a court on grounds such as insufficient evidence.[53] However, Meeker could not find a single case where an incoming secretary of state reversed the decision of his predecessor. In fact, it was not at all clear that the secretary of state had the right to do so, but even if he did possess that power he could not exercise it until he received a new extradition certificate from another extradition commissioner. The chances of Canada obtaining such a certificate were, in Meeker's opinion, very slim. Should Canada initiate another extradition application, there was an excellent likelihood that Banks would be able to advance certain legal arguments, claiming protection against double jeopardy, and obtain a court order setting the Canadian application aside. Nevertheless, the

decision whether or not to proceed with the application was the government of Canada's to make.[54]

The Canadian government was no doubt aware when it asked Washington in May 1969 whether there was any way it could reopen the case
that it could not be prevented from initiating an extradition application
but that such an application stood little chance of success. At the same
time, Ottawa asked Rogers to give it an advance decision should any
extradition order be appealed to his office. This was a preposterous request. The rights and liberties of an individual were at stake and it was
wrong to ask someone who would more than likely end up making a decision about those rights to decide the case in advance, without affording
the individual concerned an opportunity to make representations.[55]

Rogers had no trouble reaching a decision, particularly after Meeker
also advised him that reports from Canada indicated the government of
Canada did not really want Banks back. Therefore, Rogers rejected the
request for an advance ruling and Canada was told that it could take its
chances in court.[56] Although this decision was clearly communicated to
Canadian authorities in December 1969, the Canadian embassy in Washington again requested an advance ruling from the secretary of state
should he receive an extradition certificate on Hal Banks. Washington
had, by now, had enough, and replied summarily that its position had not
changed.[57]

Once again the Americans had made clear that Canada could, if it
wished, initiate an extradition application in the courts but that the secretary of state would not provide it with any advance decisions. American
authorities could not have made their position any more clear. It was time
to go to court or to let the matter drop. Instead, the government of Canada for the third time asked Rogers to hold a pre-hearing hearing. Realizing, belatedly, that one of the secretary of state's reasons for rejecting the
two earlier requests was that they did not contemplate allowing Banks the
opportunity to make any representations, the government in its new
diplomatic note said that it would have no objection whatsoever to Banks
being present or represented by counsel if such a hearing is possible.'[58] It
was not. For the third time, Canada was told that the secretary of state
would not hold an administrative hearing of the nature proposed by
Canada and would not decide in advance what it would do if the Banks
case was again certified by an extradition commissioner. At last, Canadian authorities got the message. Questionable in its conception, the
government of Canada finally abandoned its attempt to obtain the extradition of Hal Chamberlain Banks.[59]

Conclusion

Long before the Canadian government abandoned its efforts to bring the former leader of the SIU of Canada back to face justice, Banks's career in organized labour had come to an end. His career with the SIU was also over. Banks returned to California and for the remainder of his life operated a small pilot ship, *The Malabar*, out of the San Francisco marina. He died on 24 September 1985 at the age of seventy-six.

Banks's unquenchable thirst for power and members' dues to fund his opulent lifestyle caused him to forfeit a position in the Canadian labour movement which he would have otherwise long enjoyed. Had he kept his activities hidden from public view, neither the CLC nor the Canadian government would have taken action against him. Only when his conduct threatened the legitimacy of the labour movement on the one hand, and created a reign of terror on the other, did the CLC and the government of Canada finally act. Until then, both the government and the labour movement not only tolerated Banks, but on far too many occasions encouraged and approved of his activities.

The circumstances surrounding Banks's arrival in Canada had a lot to do with this acceptance. Following the Second World War the CSU, which had always been under Communist party control, became increasingly the instrument of Communist party policy. The *Islandside* affair, in which the CSU refused to supply men from its hiring hall to work a ship transporting arms to be used in the fight against the Communist party of China, and the Sullivan revelations were just two of a number of incidents which convinced the shipping companies, elements in organized labour, and the government that the ongoing activities of the CSU seriously threatened the established order.

The response of some of the shipping companies was simple enough. They refused to deal with the CSU, the industrial relations system notwithstanding. Their cynical disregard for Canadian law proved, in the end, to be to their advantage as no action was, or under the existing legislation reasonably could have been, taken against them. The shipping companies could not, however, have acted alone. Without direct government intervention, the deep-sea shipping companies, represented by the Shipping Federation of Canada, and their Great Lakes counterparts, in particular, Canada Steamship Lines and the Misener organization, could not have withstood the monolithic opposition of organized labour to their union-busting efforts. There was no such opposition.

Long smouldering in the background was the unsuccessful attempt of the American Federation of Labor to obtain the expulsion of the CSU from the TLC. On numerous occasions in the past, the AFL had succeeded in forcing the TLC to conform to international policy. From time to time, Canadian trade union leaders had resisted this American interference, but because of the numerically strong presence of international unions in the Canadian trade union movement, the TLC had never been able to assert unqualified jurisdiction over all matters related to Canadian labour affairs. In 1948 the long-awaited declaration of Canadian labour independence was made over the issue of the CSU.

Some years earlier, Percy Bengough, the president of the TLC, had dealt firmly and effectively with AFL demands to expel the CSU and admit the SIU in its place. Pat Sullivan's position as number two man at the TLC undoubtedly influenced Bengough and was responsible, in part, for the TLC's uncharacteristic defence of its small national affiliate. However, even in light of Sullivan's revelations and independent evidence of untoward Communist party manipulation of the CSU, Bengough continued to support the union under the rubric of defending the right of Canadians to exercise jurisdiction over their own affairs. The attempt almost tore the TLC apart and was doomed to failure.

What Bengough should have done was assert Canadian trade union autonomy by placing the national CSU under trusteeship. By so doing he could have illustrated that Canadians were not only masters of their own house, but wise and competent ones as well. Trusteeship would have given Canadian seamen, for the first time ever, a real opportunity to chart their future course democratically. Instead, Bengough did nothing and thousands of Canadian seamen suffered as a result. With little to lose, the Communist leaders of the CSU launched the union on a disastrous world-wide strike. When it was over, so was the CSU. Gone, for a time, was the opportunity to prove Canadian labour independence by action instead of words.

The SIU was quickly admitted into affiliation by the TLC. Within short order it had become one of the strongest unions in Canada and also one of the most disreputable. Both the TLC and the government of Canada were well informed about some of the more questionable internal SIU practices. There was, perhaps, insufficient evidence to support criminal charges against Banks or anyone else. What there was, however, was more than enough evidence to merit – indeed demand – a closer inspection of goings-on within the seamen's union. Nevertheless, year after year, both organized labour and the government failed to act.

Cabinet minutes and other documents make clear that the government felt indebted to Banks for the service he performed in ousting from the Canadian waterfront the Communist-dominated CSU. Banks's entry and continued presence in Canada, his appointment as a Canadian representative to an international conference in Geneva, the friendship and public support of successive ministers of labour are among the more noteworthy examples of governmental blessings of Banks and the SIU. However, to explain governmental support for Banks as a result of continuing gratitude for his campaign against the CSU is somewhat incomplete. There must have been more to it than that.

The easy answer is that the government dared not act. The expensive mirrors in the Drummond Street apartment were long rumoured to conceal hidden cameras which recorded cabinet minister cavorting. Was Banks blackmailing politicians? This is a facile charge to make, but it is one, at present, which is totally devoid of proof. Even the fact that Banks sought to build and entrench a relationship with the governing Liberal party falls short of convincingly explaining the longstanding failure of the government and the Department of Labour to take action against the SIU. To be sure, the SIU contributed to Liberal candidates in federal and provincial election campaigns and SIU members assisted in electioneering. But what of it? Many unions and union members regularly contribute and work on behalf of the New Democratic Party. Banks's Liberal party support was never, in any event, of such significance to indebt anyone to either Banks or the SIU.

The only credible explanation for the government's years of failure to act decisively to bring Banks and the SIU into line is that the government, already reluctant to interfere in the activities of private organizations such as trade unions, lacked the moral and political integrity the situation so urgently required. Junior officials in the Department of Labour cried out for action, but their demands, in the face of increasing evidence of SIU impropriety, were ignored. Even the change of government following

John Diefenbaker's election to power only marginally altered official attitudes towards SIU malfeasance. It was, in the end, up to organized labour to do what needed to be done.

In fact, from the very beginning, it was up to the TLC and then the CLC, in circumstances which ironically parallel those that existed in regard to the CSU, to take action against its affiliate to ensure that organized labour in Canada was both strong and free. Bengough followed by Claude Jodoin did nothing. After the CSU debacle, Bengough was powerless as he knew that taking action against Banks and the SIU would split and destroy the TLC. For his part, Jodoin was determined to entrench the legitimacy of organized labour in Canadian society and he feared the consequences of exposing a renegade in organized labour's midst. To make matters worse, Jodoin was politically indebted to Banks and far too often displayed what must be charitably described as a startling lack of judgment. Provided that the SIU did not give him any public reason to act, Jodoin, like the government, preferred to let matters be.

In these circumstances, Banks's rule could have continued indefinitely. His consolidation of power over the SIU was complete. Only a foolhardy few attempted to challenge his rule, and they were dealt with as brutally as they were efficiently. Had Banks been prepared to rest on his laurels, the combined cowardice of government and labour would have ensured the continued and unhampered operation of his organization. Banks, however, was fuelled by great ambition: control over everything that floats. His plan revealed genius.

If Banks and the SIU controlled the collective bargaining rights of every Canadian seaman, mate, and engineer, and of the employees of the St Lawrence Seaway Authority, he and the union would control Canada's inland water transportation systems. The shipping companies and even the government would be hard pressed to resist SIU bargaining demands. Strike-breaking in the maritime industry would be a thing of the past. It was a grand ambition and, like the bargaining tactics Banks used to divide and conquer the Great Lakes shipping companies, it had great promise of success. Had Banks been a different kind of man, it might have worked.

It would have required that the SIU organize or persuade the mates and engineers to join in, and stay in, for the common good with the SIU. The SIU would also have had to run and win an organizing campaign among the Seaway workers. In short, for the plan to succeed, Banks and the SIU would have had to conduct themselves according to the book and in so doing gain the support of Canadian organized labour. However, Banks and the SIU did not organize workers; they organized companies. Canadian seamen under the SIU had never had an opportunity to select their trade union democratically: indeed, in all the years of Banks's reign, they never had any real chance to elect their union officers democratically. The SIU's pattern of organization perhaps stood it in good stead in the early days when it was locked in battle with the CSU, but those days were over.

Banks, by the exercise of some force and considerable cunning, assisted by the shipping companies and a government that looked the other way as the Industrial Relations Disputes Investigation Act was violated right and left, was able to bring the engineers under the SIU flag. Although it was the filing of raiding charges at the CLC relating to these events that ultimately resulted in the Congress suspending and then expelling the SIU, it was Banks's campaign for control over the bargaining rights of all Canadian seamen and the St Lawrence Seaway Authority workers that spelled his downfall.

It was that campaign that brought Banks and the SIU into conflict with the CBRT. Canada's largest national union, the CBRT was led by William Smith and Elroy Robson, men who refused to sacrifice principle to expediency. They insisted that the CLC stand up and do what was right. In the early days Smith and Robson had to fight alone. Soon enough they were joined by another man of like mind who refused, unlike all his contemporaries, to capitulate to Banks's quest for power. That man was Jack Leitch, the president of Upper Lakes Shipping. Together the CBRT and Upper Lakes were able to challenge the SIU in a way it had never been challenged before. It was the most unusual and important labour-management alliance in Canadian history.

Banks had no intention of allowing either the CBRT or Upper Lakes to stand in his way and responded in the only way he knew: with violence. This violence spilled over into the United States as the SIU International embraced its Canadian affiliates' campaign and enlisted the support of other AFL–CIO unions in the SIU's struggle against Upper Lakes and the CBRT. For the second time in a decade Canadian organized labour had to decide whether or not to fight a battle for autonomy over a seamen's union. This time, of course, the battle was differently drawn. Instead of supporting a national union in the face of an attempt by the AFL to displace and replace it with an international union, the Congress had to decide whether to take action against an international union in support of a national union and thereby upset the uneasy balance between national and international unions in the Canadian trade union movement.

That the CLC decided, in the end, to do what was right is a matter of record. It had little choice. Once the National Association of Marine

Engineers filed raiding charges against the SIU and once those charges were upheld, the Congress had no alternative, Jodoin's efforts notwithstanding, but to take action against Banks and the SIU. The waterfront warfare between the SIU and the CBRT and Upper Lakes subsequently focused further attention on Banks and his union as the dark underside of the SIU came increasingly into public view. Organized labour and the government may have known for years what was going on at the SIU's Montreal headquarters, but the public certainly did not, and as the facts began to leak out people were shocked.

It was also disturbing for many Canadians, at a time of growing nationalism, to see the way Canadian ships, manned with Canadian crews, certified by the Labour Relations Board, were treated in the United States. It was, in a word, disgraceful. American unions, in an effort to enforce the will of the AFL–CIO over the CLC, were waging a campaign of economic and other warfare against legitimate Canadian organizations. George Meany, Paul Hall, and a host of other American labour leaders made clear, in promoting American internationalism, that Canadian sovereignty meant nothing. That Banks was himself an American only exacerbated the situation, which was intolerable.

Still the government refused to take action against the SIU, and the CBRT was left with no choice but to bring matters to a head. The boycott of SIU ships at the Welland Canal was the result, leading finally to the appointment of an industrial inquiry commission. With hindsight it is clear that the practices and procedures adopted by that commission gave the SIU an opportunity to frustrate and unnecessarily prolong the inquiry. When it was over and the report was in, it contained very few surprises. Of all the recommendations, trusteeship was the important one.

The government had no intention of implementing the specific trusteeship suggested by Norris in his report; that recommendation was far too severe to be seriously considered. In fact, the government did not want to implement any trusteeship recommendation at all. What it wanted was to have organized labour do what it should have done years earlier: clean its own house. Following the release of the Norris Report, the government spared no effort to assist the CLC in coming to terms with the AFL–CIO over a private union-run trusteeship. This effort failed because the leaders of the AFL–CIO, as well as the United States secretary of labour, Willard Wirtz, could not understand that any private trusteeship that did not provide for Canadian control would be unacceptable to the CLC and the people of Canada. In the end, the government was left with no choice but to legislate a trusteeship. If Canadian autonomy over Canadian affairs could not be voluntarily recognized, then it would be imposed by law. That the

CLC was later able to obtain AFL–CIO recognition of CLC autonomy and jurisdiction over all Canadian labour matters, including those relating to the international unions operating in Canada, was in no short measure the result of this breakdown in negotiations and the trusteeship legislation of the government of Canada.

The trustees worked long and hard to effect the public rehabilitation of the SIU. Banks was fired and, after his conviction for conspiracy to assault, he fled the country. Fair elections were held and, soon enough, the union was readmitted into the CLC. It was hoped that democracy had been entrenched in the union and that, as a CLC affiliate, any problems and internal abuses would be remedied quickly as a result of the vigilance of the congress. In theory, this made some sense. In practice, as history may show, democracy does not appear to have become a mainstay of the SIU, and the CLC pays no closer attention to the SIU today than in the heyday of Banks's reign.

It would be wrong to blame the trustees for not bringing about a comlete reformation of the SIU. They were obliged to act as trustees for the members of that union and were circumscribed by the narrow powers of the Trusteeship Act in what little they could actually do. More than anyone else, chairman Victor Dryer realized that this was the case, and that is why he decided to resign. Dryer asked the government, among other things, to take over the operation of the union-controlled hiring hall and thereby ensure that it never again be subjected to abuse. He also asked the government to take what legislative steps were necessary to ensure that engineers and ordinary seamen were prohibited from being members of the same union. Both requests were rejected; and the failure to implement these recommendations may, in part, be responsible for some of the problems that exist in the maritime industry today.

But this, too, would be overly simplistic, for the problems faced by seamen during the CSU years, during Banks's time in power, and today require a more detailed solution than the regulation of union hiring halls and of jurisdictional disputes over union representation. Any solution must first and foremost address the problem of how seamen are best to participate in the government of their industrial lives. Unlike workers in many industries, their workplace is not stationary, these workers have little ongoing contact with each other, and their union leadership quickly becomes entrenched. Add to that union control over the hiring process and a seasonal, high-turnover workforce, and abuses of what should be fundamental rights are almost guaranteed to result.

The solution is not greater vigilance by the CLC over Canadian maritime unions, indeed over any unions, for the CLC, as is the case with the government, has proved itself both philosophically and practically un-suited to that task. Rather, the solution must come in the form of legisla-tion upon which all seamen, indeed all workers, can rely in the exercise of certain fundamental rights. The right to participate in regular, sched-uled, and secret elections, the right of equal access to campaign funds and the instruments of electioneering such as the union newspaper, the right to fully participate in union meetings and conventions: all of these and other rights must be provided for by law and enforced by an institution such as a labour board which is unhampered by political or other con-siderations. Paradoxically, unions, which are formed out of a democratic impulse in industrial life, sometimes become organizations led by tyrants and riddled with corruption. This is not to say that the union movement today is rife with the undemocratic abuses characteristic of the Banks administration. If anything, the opposite is true; the trade union move-ment in Canada is dedicated to democratic goals. Legislative reform can give that dedication a legal bite. The rule of law, as the saga of Pat Sullivan, Hal Banks, and seamen's unions in Canada reveals, must exist for justice to prevail.

Notes

Preface

1 Richard Neilsen Papers, Hal Banks to 'My Darling,' 27 April 1949

Chapter 1: The Canadian Shipping Industry and the Birth of a Union

1 This section is adapted from the *Second Report of the Canadian Maritime Commission*, 'Review of Canadian Maritime History' (Ottawa 1949), 11–29
2 Ibid., 11
3 Ibid., 13
4 F.J. Bullock, *Ships and the Seaway* (Toronto 1959), 79–81. See also George Musk, *Canadian Pacific: The Story of the Famous Shipping Line* (Toronto 1981).
5 *Second Report of the Canadian Maritime Commission*, 13
6 Ibid.
7 Ibid.
8 Bullock, *Ships and the Seaway*, 61
9 *Second Report of the Canadian Maritime Commission*, 13–14
10 Ibid., 13–15
11 Ibid., 16–17
12 Ibid., 17
13 Later, Wartime Shipbuilding Limited
14 The Department of Munitions and Supply was responsible for building naval and other military ships.
15 *Second Report of the Canadian Maritime Commission*, 17–19
16 See, generally, the St Lawrence Seaway Authority fact sheets: 'The Welland Section of the St Lawrence Seaway,' July 1981, and 'The Montreal–Lake Ontario Section of the Seaway,' Oct. 1975.
17 Bullock, *Ships and the Seaway*, 3
18 H.A. Logan, *Trade Unions in Canada* (Toronto 1948), 286

19 Properly described, the St Lawrence Seaway is the system of channels and locks between Montreal and Lake Ontario. The name is often used to refer to the St Lawrence and Great Lakes waterway system which officially opened in 1959.

20 Carleton Mabee, *The Seaway Story* (New York 1961), 259

21 The deepening of the Upper Lakes channels and locks continued until 1962.

22 M.C. Urquhart and K.A.H. Buckley, eds., *Historical Statistics of Canada* (Ottawa 1983), T97–106

23 Jacques Lesstrang, *The Saga of the Great Lakes Fleet–North America's Freshwater Merchant Marine* (Seattle 1977), 68

24 J.B. Dempsey, 'Canada Steamship Lines Ltd: World's Largest Inland Water Transportation Company,' *Inland Seas* 15 (1959): 4–14

25 Wally Macht, *The First 50 Years: A History of Upper Lakes Shipping Ltd.* (Toronto 1981). See also *Loyal She Remains: A Pictorial History of Ontario* (Toronto 1984), 614–15, 622–3.

26 University of Toronto Archives, Kaplan Files, J.A. Chricton, 'The Shipping Federation of Canada 75th Anniversary'

27 Dominion Marine Association, *Annual Report* 1978, iii

28 See Macht, *The First 50 Years*, 45.

29 PAC, J.L. Cohen Papers, MG 30, A94, vol. 18, file 2790C, 'Our Case before the Board,' special supplement to the *Searchlight*, official organ of the CSU, May 1940

30 Mabee, *The Seaway Story*, 31

31 'Our Case before the Board,' 8

32 Ibid., 9

33 A.W. Currie, *Economics of Canadian Transportation* (Toronto 1954), 587. The situation was not much better for the officers and mates. See PAC, Department of Labour Papers [DOL], RG 27, vol. 161, file 612-01-43, H.N. McMaster to W.A. Gordon, 31 Jan. 1933.

34 Frank Fraser, 'Sailors Are Human Beings Too,' *Canadian Forum* 20 (1940): 183

35 'Our Case before the Board,' 2

36 J.A. (Pat) Sullivan, *Red Sails on the Great Lakes* (Toronto 1955), 10; *Labour Gazette*, 1949, 721.

37 See the Canada Shipping Act, RSC 1927, c 186, RSC 1934, c 44, and RSC 1952, c 29.

38 Canada Shipping Act, RSC 1952, c 29, section 229

39 Imprisonment for desertion was abolished in 1915.

40 Laurel Sefton McDowell, 'The Formation of the Canadian Industrial Relations System during World War Two,' *Labour/Le Travailleur* 3 (1978): 179. See also F.R. Anton, *The Role of Government in the Settlement of Industrial Disputes in Canada* (Don Mills 1962), 69–80.

41 Ibid.

42 See Logan, *Trade Unions*, 287. See also the document entitled 'History' in the Houtman Papers.

43 *Canadian Marine News* (1937): 12; PAC, Cohen Papers, vol. 19, file 801-6
44 But see DOL, file 612-01-43, J.A. Sullivan to N.M. Rogers, 27 March 1936.
45 Joanne Miko, 'The Rise and Fall of the Canadian Seamen's Union, 1936–1951,' MA thesis, University of Guelph, 1974. See also Charles Mac-Donald, 'Betrayal: The History of the Canadian Seamen's Union,' unpublished manuscript, Labour Canada Library, Ottawa 1980, 26.
46 Ibid.
47 Cohen Papers, vol. 19, file 2801-4, Affidavit of J.A.P. Sullivan, 30 Dec. 1940
48 The following section is derived substantially from Irving Abella, *The Canadian Labour Movement: 1902–1960* (Ottawa 1975).
49 Ibid., 3–4
50 Kathleen M. Seaver, 'The Demise of the Canadian Seamen's Union,' senior year thesis, Carleton University, 1978, 6
51 Logan, *Trade Unions*, 287
52 Ibid., 288. See also MacDonald, 'Betrayal,' 13.
53 Tim Buck, *Thirty Years* (Toronto 1975), 119; also Salsberg interview, 7 July 1982
54 Abella, *Canadian Labour Movement*, 16
55 Ibid., 17
56 Salsberg interview
57 Logan, *Trade Unions*, 288
58 Ibid.
59 Sullivan, *Red Sails*, 14–17
60 See Logan, *Trade Unions*, 288; Sullivan, *Red Sails*, 17; and MacDonald, 'Betrayal,' 27.
61 Abella, *Canadian Labour Movement*, 17
62 Sullivan, *Red Sails*, 20–1
63 Miko, 'Rise and Fall,' 14; see also Sullivan, *Red Sails*, 19–20.
64 Sullivan, *Red Sails*, 20
65 Ibid., 21
66 Charles P. Larrowe, *Maritime Labor Relations on the Great Lakes* (East Lansing, Mich. 1959); Walter Galenson, *The CIO Challenge to the AFL* (Cambridge, Mass. 1960); Bernard Raskin, *On a True Course: The Story of the National Maritime Union* (Washington, DC 1967)
67 Miko (15) states that the union application was made on 12 September 1936. Sullivan indicates, however, that an application was not made, formally at least, until the following year; *Red Sails*, 28–9, 34–5.
68 Sullivan, *Red Sails*, 27; Miko, 'Rise and Fall,' 21–2
69 There were probably never many more than the 300 dues-paying members reported by Sullivan in 1946, notwithstanding the Communist party's efforts. See Sullivan, *Red Sails*, 24, 30.
70 Logan, *Trade Unions*, 289
71 Sullivan, *Red Sails*, 31–4
72 Ibid., 36–7: see also 'Our Case before the Board.'

73 MacDonald, 'Betrayal,' 47
74 Sullivan, *Red Sales*, 34–7
75 Ibid.
76 MacDonald, 'Betrayal,' 56
77 Miko, 'Rise and Fall,' 25
78 Sullivan, *Red Sails*, 46
79 MacDonald, 'Betrayal,' 67
80 This is the way the CSU certainly described itself. See 'Our Case before the Board,' 4.
81 Fraser, 'Sailors,' 182
82 MacDonald, 'Betrayal,' 26
83 Ibid.
84 Fraser, 'Sailors,' 182
85 Sullivan, *Red Sails*, 47–52; *Labour Gazette*, 1938, 736
86 *Labour Gazette*, 1938, 737. For a detailed account of events see PAC, RG 27, vol. 144, file 611-04-20.
87 'Our Case before the Board,' 4
88 Fraser, 'Sailors,' 183
89 'Our Case before the Board,' 4
90 Sullivan, *Red Sails*, 57
91 Houtman interview
92 See Appendix A, 'The Hiring Hall,' extract from Hearing of Industrial Commission as to Shipping in the Great Lakes and St Lawrence River System, 13 March 1963, published by the Canadian Labour Congress, Ottawa.
93 Logan, *Trade Unions*, 365
94 Ivan Avakumovic, *The Communist Part in Canada: A History* (Toronto 1975), 147

Chapter 2: The War Years, 1939–45

1 Cohen Papers, vol. 19, file 2801, Address by J.A. Sullivan
2 Avakumovic, *Communist Party in Canada*, 140, 149
3 *Canada's Party of Socialism: History of the Communist Party of Canada, 1921–1976* (Toronto 1982), 140
4 Sue Calhoun, *The Lockeport Lockout* (Halifax 1983). Much of the following section is derived from this booklet.
5 Donald MacDonald interview
6 Calhoun, *Lockeport Lockout*, 8–10
7 Ibid., 15–18
8 See *Annual Report of the Royal Canadian Mounted Police* (Ottawa 1940) 14.
9 Calhoun, *Lockeport Lockout*, 15–8
10 RCMP, *Annual Report*, 1940, 14
11 Calhoun, *Lockeport Lockout*, 20
12 RCMP, *Annual Report*, 1940, 14; Calhoun, *Lockeport Lockout*, 20–1
13 Calhoun, *Lockeport Lockout*, 20

14 *Labour Gazette*, 1940, 14
15 'Our Case before the Board,' 15ff
16 Cohen Papers, vol. 48, file 8, I.E. Flint, 'Collective Bargaining and the Great Lakes,' undated
17 Fraser, 'Sailors,' 185
18 *Labour Gazette*, 1940, 443. See also RCMP Papers, report dated 20-4-40, note 26.
19 *Labour Gazette*, 1940, 443. See also RCMP, *Annual Report*, 1941, 12.
20 Ibid.
21 Fraser, 'Sailors,' 184
22 Flint, 'Collective Bargaining,' 33–4; Fraser, 'Sailors,' 184
23 MacDonald, 'Betrayal,' 117
24 Flint, 'Collective Bargaining,' 35
25 *Labour Gazette*, 1941, 541; Flint, 'Collective Bargaining,' 35; *Globe and Mail*, 12 April 1941
26 This and the following information comes from RCMP Papers in my possession obtained under the Access to Information Act. Many of these papers have been censored, and none has any file indications; thus, identification of individual documents is difficult. See report dated 26 Feb. 1940 and Kusch to Perlson, 22 April 1940.
27 See City of Vancouver Archives, BC Shipping Federation Papers, vol. 53, file 8, Reports–Personal Seamen.
28 RCMP Papers, Report of H.A. Gagnon, 20 April 1940
29 See, for example, the report dated 5 April 1940.
30 Ibid.
31 *Re Sullivan* [1941] OR 417, *Ex Parte Sullivan* [1942] 2 DLR 799 (CA)
32 'In the matter of the Defence of Canada Regulations and in the matter of J.A. Sullivan,' transcript of evidence, 16–17 Oct. 1941. See also Cohen Papers, vol. 19, file 2801-3, J.L. Cohen to Canadian Seamen's Union, 28 Oct. 1941; affidavit of J.A. Sullivan, 30 Dec. 1940.
33 See, for example, Cohen Papers, vol. 20, file 2807, 'Regulation 21,' address by J.L. Cohen, 1 Nov. 1940.
34 Ibid. See also Flint, 'Collective Bargaining,' 37; 'In the matter of the Defence of Canada Regulations and in the matter of J.A. Sullivan.'
35 Ibid.
36 House of Commons, *Debates*, 27 Feb. 1941, 1073 (hereafter *Debates*)
37 *Debates*, 14 May 1941, 2810-11
38 Cohen Papers, vol. 19, file 2801-1, Moore to Cohen, 6 Aug. 1940. See also ibid., file 2801-2, Letter to Delegates to the 56th TLC Convention from Dewar Ferguson; and Woodsworth to Mrs J. Penner, 29 July 1940, cited by Desmond Morton in a review of *Dangerous Patriots: Canada's Unknown Prisoners of War* (Vancouver 1982) in *Labour/Le Travail* 14 (1984): 232.
39 Sullivan, *Red Sails*, 71–91. See also RCMP report dated 24 July 1940 in which the reaction of the CSU membership to the internments is described.
40 *Canada's Party of Socialism*, 9, 140–1; Cohen Papers, vol. 20, file 2806, Sul-

livan to Director of Inmate Operations, 1 July 1941; Sullivan, *Red Sails*, 92
41 MacDonald, 'Betrayal,' 137
42 See Sullivan, *Red Sails*, 96; also MacDonald, 'Betrayal,' 152, and *Labour Gazette*, 1942, 1943, 1944, and 1945, where only one strike involving seamen is reported.
43 David Lewis, *The Good Fight* (Toronto 1981), 218
44 Sullivan, *Red Sails*, 95–108
45 Ibid., 116–17. See Gad Horowitz, *Canadian Labour in Politics* (Toronto 1968), 182
46 John Stanton, *Life and Death of the Canadian Seamen's Union* (Toronto 1978), 26
47 Ibid., 56; MacDonald, 'Betrayal,' 164–7; Currie, *Economics of Canadian Transportation*, 618; Canadian Maritime Commission, Report No 1, 9, and Report No 2, 20
48 *Debates*, 16 July 1943, 4938
49 MacDonald, 'Betrayal,' 167 and 221
50 See, for example, Privy Council Order 14/3550 of 14 May 1941.
51 Lionel Chevrier, *Canada's Merchant Seamen* (Ottawa 1945), 6–11
52 James E. Dorsey, *The Canada Labour Relations Board: Federal Law and Practice* (Toronto 1983), 17–18
53 A summary of these orders can be found in Laurel Sefton MacDowell, ' "Remember Kirkland Lake": The History and Effects of the Kirkland Lake Gold Miners Strike 1941–42,' Ph D thesis, University of Toronto, 1982, Appendix A, 429–30.
54 MacDonald, 'Betrayal,' 177
55 Sullivan, *Red Sails*, 123–4
56 'We Stand for Unity,' CSU publication, June 1944
57 PAC, CLC Papers, MG 28 I 103, vol. 6, file SIU-1944-45, Lundeberg to all Trades and Labor Councils in Canada affiliated with the AFL, 11 Aug. 1944. See also the 1944 AFL Resolution in the same file.
58 CLC Papers, vol. 6, file SIU-1944–45, Bengough to Green, 18 July 1945. See also ibid., Gervin to Green, 18 July 1945.
59 Ibid., Bengough to Gervin, 22 Nov. 1944
60 Ibid.
61 See ibid., Bengough to Green, 18 July 1945
62 Ibid., and Executive Council of TLC to Lundeberg, 4 Sept. 1945

Chapter 3: The Great Lakes Strike of 1946

1 'Seamen Successful,' *TLC Journal* 25 (1946): 15
2 Sullivan, *Red Sails*, 187
3 MacDonald, 'Betrayal,' 240
4 Arthur MacNamara, letter to the Ottawa *Citizen*, 21 July 1949. Davis's real name was Popovitch.
5 Sullivan, *Red Sails*, 129

6 'Seamen Successful, 15; Seaver, 'Demise of the C.S.U.,' 17; MacDonald, 'Betrayal,' 247
7 See *Globe and Mail*, 10 April 1946.
8 There were over 1200 casualties among merchant seamen, more than 600 of which were fatal. See *Debates*, 27 April 1947, 2612. Slogan from Seaver, 'Demise of the C.S.U.,' 12
9 See *Debates*, 16 April 1946; Logan, *Trade Unions*, 291; MacDonald, 'Betrayal,' 248; and RCMP Papers, report dated 28 March 1946, which spoke of the impending strike.
10 *Globe and Mail*, 13 April 1946
11 Ibid., 15 April 1946
12 Ibid., 29 April 1946
13 Ibid., 25 May 1946; MacDonald, 'Betrayal,' 252–3; Seaver, 'Demise of the C.S.U.,' 17–18; and Stanton, *Life and Death*, 85ff
14 See *Globe and Mail* throughout May and June, for example, 28 May 1946. See also *Debates*, 7 June 1946, 2270; 10 June 1946, 2322; and Miko, 'Rise and Fall,' 104–5.
15 *Debates*, 17 June 1946, 2569
16 See CLC Papers, vol. 6, file CSU 1946–50; MacDonald, 'Betrayal,' 258; and Seaver, 'Demise of the C.S.U.,' 19.
17 *Debates*, 9 June 1946, 2154
18 *Debates*, 11 June 1946, 2369–70
19 MacDonald, 'Betrayal,' 259
20 Ibid.; see also *Debates*, 19 June 1946, 2632–3.
21 *Globe and Mail*, 11 June 1946
22 Brand interview; *Debates*, 21 June 1946, 2700–1
23 See *Debates*, 21 June 1946, 2700–1.
24 *Globe and Mail*, 26 June 1946
25 *Labour Gazette*, 1946, 279 and 981. See also 'Seamen Successful.'
26 Department of National Defence, Eric Brand Papers, vol. II, 81/145, Brand Diary, 3. The abuse of the act probably backfired because the public realized for the first time how its provisions were being used. The government, moreover, set up a Senate Committee to consider amendments to the act. See Cohen Papers, vol. 10, Representations by the CSU to the Senate Committee, 19 April 1948.
27 Brand Diary, 3
28 Ibid.
29 Ibid.
30 Ibid., 7
31 Ibid., 6–7
32 Ibid., 6–20
33 Flint, 'Collective Bargaining,' 39
34 Brand Papers, 'Some Remarks on the Engagement and Employment of Seamen'
35 Ibid.

36 Ibid.
37 Brand Diary, 11. Brand was not going to take the chance of another
   seamen's srike and he devised a secret contingency plan to have the Royal
   Canadian Navy man certain ships to transport vital cargoes should shipping
   once again grind to a halt. Brand interview. See also Seaver, 'Demise of the
   C.S.U.,' 22.
38 Brand Diary, 11 and 14, somewhat to the contrary
39 *Labour Gazette*, 1947, 1274–5
40 Brand Diary, 12
41 MacDonald, 'Betrayal,' 278

Chapter 4: Communist Revelations and Repercussions

1 See Sullivan, *Red Sails*, 171–89; Seaver, 'Demise of the C.S.U.,' 25; Stanton,
   Life and Death, 96–8: Miko, 'Rise and Fall,' 114; and Salsberg interview.
2 PAC, DOL, vol. 3524, file 3-26-10-4 pt 15, 5, McManus to Mitchell, 27 July
   1948
3 DOL, vol. 3532, file 10, Reoch to King, 1948
4 George Donovan letter, DOL, vol. 3523, file 10
5 DOL, vol. 3524, file 3-26-10-4 pt 15, 6, McManus to Mitchell, 27 July 1948
6 'CSU and Great Lakes Shipping Companies Reach Agreement,' *TLC Journal*
   26 (1947): 40
7 PAC, Frank and Libbey Park Papers, MG 31 K 9, vol. 10, Brockington-
   McNish Report
8 See Flint, 'Collective Bargaining,' 42; Stanton, *Life and Death*, 99 and 103.
9 *Debates*, 25 June 1948, 5861
10 MacDonald, 'Betrayal,' 327
11 Seaver, 'Demise of the C.S.U.,' 32
12 Ibid., 35
13 Ibid., 37
14 Brockington-McNish Report
15 Ibid., 6
16 *Globe and Mail*, 11 June 1948
17 Ibid., 16 June 1948
18 *Labour Gazette*, 1948, 573, 581. See also RCMP, *Annual Report*, 1949, 24,
   and MacDonald, 'Betrayal,' 350.
19 DOL, vol. 3524, file 3-26-10-4 pt 15, 2, McManus to Mitchell, 27 July 1948
20 For parallel developments in the United States see Raskin, *On a True
   Course*, 54–61.
21 MacDonald, 'Betrayal,' 337
22 See 'Canadian Sailors Shun China Bound Arms Ship,' *Daily Worker*, 1 Feb.
   1948; Seaver, 'The Demise of the C.S.U.,' 29; and MacDonald, 'Betrayal,'
   345.
23 Jack Williams, *The Story of Unions in Canada* (Toronto 1975), 179
24 DOL, vol. 3498, file 1-10T 100-1 pt 3, 23–4, see, Submission to the Executive

Council of the American Federation of Labor by the Associated Representatives of International Unions in Canada, 7 Feb. 1949
25 See *The Canadian Seamen's Union and You* (undated CSU publication)
26 Department of Labour, Ottawa, Department of Labour Papers, SIU, vol. 1,
file 1-10-'s'-284-HJ, R. Trepanier to M.M. Maclean, 30 Aug. 1948; Fraser
Isbester, 'Draft History of the Department of Labour,' 17. This draft history
was made available to me by the Department of Labour with the condition
that I indicate in the notes that it was a draft, unrevised work written by a
terminally ill man. See also *Labour Gazette*, 1948, 1082, and 'Excerpts of
the Minutes of the Meetings of the Trades and Labor Congress of Canada
September 10–11, 1948,' cited in Gerald S. Swartz, 'Hal Banks: The Rise
and Fall of the Maritime Trade Union Leader in Canada,' MA thesis, University of Illinois, 1969, 129
27 See note 24.
28 Swartz, 'Hal Banks,' 130–1
29 DOL, vol. 3498, file 1-10T 100-1 pt 2, 'Appeal to the 63rd Annual Convention of the Trades and Labor Congress of Canada'
30 See, generally, note 24.
31 'An Informed Membership Will Strengthen Democracy and Defeat Domination,' *TLC Journal* 28 (1949): 11
32 Ibid.; *Labour Gazette*, 1949, 1369–70
33 See note 24.
34 The representatives were George Meaney, AFL secretary-treasurer; William
Hutcheson, Carpenters Union; and George Harrison, international president
of the Brotherhood of Railway and Steamship Clerks
35 See note 24; and 'Minutes of the Specially Summoned Meeting of the Executive Council of the Trades and Labour Congress February 14–17, 1949,'
cited in Swartz, 'Hal Banks,' 133–4
36 'Statement by the Executive Council of the American Federation of Labor
February 8, 1949,' cited in Swartz, 'Hal Banks,' 134–6
37 Ibid., 136
38 See note 31; and, generally, 'Statement issued by the Executive Council of
the Trades and Labor Congress Ottawa February 22, 1949,' cited in ibid.,
137–9.
39 Swartz, 'Hal Banks', 137–9
40 Ibid.
41 *Montreal Gazette*, 18 Oct. 1948; Stuart Jamieson, *Industrial Relations in
Canada* (Ithaca, NY 1957), 50. At its 1948 convention CCL president Mosher
warned the Communist-led United Electrical Workers to change their tune
or they would be thrown out. They did not, and they were expelled.

Chapter 5: The Demise of the CSU

1 Canadian Maritime Commission Report No 2; see also J.W.F. Spence,
Report of the Royal Commission on the Coasting Trade (Ottawa 1957), 55

2 James A. MacKinnon, 'Canadian Shipping and the War,' *TLC Journal* 24 (1945): 16

3 MacDonald, 'Betrayal,' 181

4 Cohen Papers, vol. 42, file 3138, 'Submission of the CSU to the Government of Canada,' 30 May 1944; ibid., 'A National Shipping Policy for Canada,' Sept. 1945

5 'Submission of the CSU to the Government of Canada,' 9

6 'A National Shipping Policy for Canada'

7 *Report of the Royal Commission on the Coasting Trade*, 17; Canadian Maritime Commission Report No 1, 5–8

8 MacDonald, 'Betrayal,' 275

9 Canadian Maritime Commission Report No 2, 32, 34

10 Ibid. Univeristy of Toronto–York University Joint Program in Transportation – Marine Transportation Policy Project, Field Report No 84, May 1978, 25

11 MacDonald, 'Betrayal,' 329; Miko, 'Rise and Fall,' 121

12 *Debates*, 15 April 1949, 2335. See also Seaver, 'Demise of the C.S.U.,' 54.

13 *Labour Gazette*, 1949, 719; see also DOL, vol. 3526, file 3-26-10-4, 'In the Matter of the Industrial Relations Disputes Investigation Act and A Dispute between Various Deep Sea Dry Cargo Shipping Companies and the Canadian Seamen's Union.'

14 RCMP Papers, Report from Cpl N.O. Jones, 3 March 1949

15 DOL, vol. 3525, file 3-26-10-4 pt 19, 1, T.G. McManus to Humphrey Mitchell, 20 April 1949

16 'Executive Council Statement on the CSU Strike,' *TLC Journal* 28 (1949): 13

17 *Labour Gazette*, 1949, 719

18 'Report of an Industrial Inquiry Commission concerning matters relating to the disruption of shipping on the Great Lakes, the St Lawrence River system and connecting waters (pursuant to section 56 of the Industrial Relations Disputes Investigation Act),' July 1946 (hereinafter referred to as the Norris Report), 48–9; Seaver, 'Demise of the C.S.U.,' 59

19 *Debates*, 5 April 1949, 2335

20 See PAC, RG 2, 16, vol. 16, Cabinet Conclusions, 20 and 31 March 1949.

21 See *Ottawa Journal*, 18 and 19 April 1949; *Montreal Gazette*, 18 and 19 April 1949; RCMP Papers, Report dates 8 April 1949; MacDonald, 'Betrayal,' 446; see also RCMP Report dated 8 May 1949.

22 *Ottawa Citizen*, 12 April 1949

23 However, see RCMP reports dated 23 and 25 April 1949.

24 *Labour Gazette*, 1949, 720; *Debates*, 5 April 1949, 2335–6. See also Public Record Office, CAB 130/46 4690, 2–3, 'Notes on the Unofficial Dockers Strike in Sympathy with the CSU.'

25 Doucette interview

26 Gloria Montero, *We Stood Together* (Toronto 1979), 148; MacDonald, 'Betrayal,' 445–82; PRO CAB 130/46 4690, 3, Gen. 291 / 1st Meeting, Strike of Canadian Seamen Minutes of Meeting, 25 May 1949; K. Jeffery and P. Hennessy, *States of Emergency* (London 1983), 198–202

27 'Where Is the Seamen's Strike?' *TLC Journal* 28 (1949): 7. See also P. Conroy to A.T. Lanceford, 4 July 1949, in Swartz, 'Hal Banks,' appendix, and John Harkin exposé, *Montreal Gazette*, 28 May, 19 and 20 July 1949.
28 International Transportworkers' Federation Resolution, 17 May 1949. Copy in author's files.
29 MacDonald, 'Betrayal,' 457; Seaver, 'Demise of the C.S.U.,' 91; Philip Taft, *The Structure and Government of Labour Unions* (Cambridge, Mass. 1954), 209
30 'Executive Council Statement on the CSU Suspension,' *TLC Journal* 28 (1949): 13–14
31 Hennesey, *States of Emergency*, 203–7. See also PRO CAB 130/146 4690, Minutes of Ministers on Strike, 4 July 1949.
32 Minutes of Ministers on Strike, 4 July 1949
33 Hennesey, *States of Emergency*, 205–6
34 Ibid., 207–8
35 'The CSU and You,' 20–1; *Labour Gazette*, 1949, 877; Minutes of Ministers on Strike, 4 July 1949. See *Review of the British Dock Strikes, 1949* (London 1949), 26; DOL, vol. 22, file 3-26-10-4, Memorandum Re CSU, 28 June 1949; Hennesey, *States of Emergency*, 207–8; and *Montreal Gazette*, 13 and 14 July 1949.
36 *Montreal Gazette*, 25 July 1949
37 *Debates*, 5 April 1949, 2335
38 Department of Labour Papers, SIU, vol. 1, 'Memorandum Concerning the Practices of the Seafarers' International Union of North America in Organizing Canadian Seamen,' unsigned, undated, 4
39 Ibid., 8–9
40 For a history of Upper Lakes see Macht, *The First 50 Years*.
41 Houtman interviews
42 Houtman Papers, file 1947–1949, Memorandum, 1 April 1949
43 Montero, *We Stood Together*, 153
44 'The CSU and You,' 30. The CSU's resignation letter called on the TLC to 'stand as a bulwark against reaction and for a progressive Canada.'
45 *Labour Gazette*, 1949, 1355
46 *Monteal Gazette*, 21 Sept. 1949
47 'Executive Council Statement on C.S.U. Suspension'
48 MacDonald, 'Betrayal,' 504
49 *Montreal Gazette*, 6 March 1950
50 See Houtman Papers, file 1950–1951, Memorandum Re Conversation with McManus.
51 See ibid., Memorandum Re Meeting of 28 February 1950.
52 See note 38.
53 Ibid., 15
54 Ibid., 14
55 Ibid., 15
56 Houtman Papers, file 1951–1952, Memorandum of Understanding between

Upper Lakes Shipping and SIU, September 1950
57 A copy of the resolution has been deposited at the University of Toronto Archives.
58 *Review of the British Dock Strikes*, 3
59 *Montreal Gazette*, 17 Dec. 1949
60 See *CSU v. CLRB and Branch Lines Ltd.* [1951] 2 DLR 356. See also H.D. Woods and S. Ostry, *Labour Policy and Labour Economics in Canada* (Toronto 1962), 105–7, and A.R. Carrothers, *Collective Bargaining Law in Canada* (Toronto 1965), 30.
61 See Swartz, 'Hal Banks,' 164.
62 PAC, CLC Papers, vol. 7, file CSU, Bengough to B.A. McClellan, 26 Jan. 1951
63 T.G. McManus, 'The Reds are Ready to Wage War inside Canada' *Maclean's*, 15 Nov. 1950, 7, 61; and 'Death of Union,' *Maclean's*, 1 Dec. 1950, 18–19, 58; 'Lessons of the McManus Case,' published in *National Affairs Monthly*, a Communist party organ cited in Stanton, *Life and Death*, 166–7
64 See Norris Report, 51.

Chapter 6: The SIU and Consolidation of Power

1 Transcript of the Industrial Inquiry Commission concerning matters relating to the disruption of shipping on the Great Lakes, St Lawrence river system, and connecting waters (hereinafter referred to as Transcript of Evidence), vol. 30, 15 Oct. 1962, 4848–9; Richard Nielsen, 'Hal Banks and His High Class Friends,' *Globe and Mail Magazine*, 5 Dec. 1970, 7–11; Leitch interview; Sydney Katz, 'Should We Kick Hal Banks Out of Canada?' *Maclean's*, 15 Feb. 1955, 11–13, 42–8. See also FBI Papers, Freedom of Information Act request 266191.
2 Todd interview
3 See Katz, 'Should We Kick Hal Banks Out of Canada?' for Banks's detailed explanation of all the charges.
4 Nielsen papers, Hal Banks to 'My Darling,' 27 April 1949
5 Department of Labour Papers, SIU, vol. 1, file 1-10-'s'-284, H.J. Walker to A. MacNamara, 7 March 1949, and V.I.M. to MacNamara, 16 March 1949
6 *Union Busting: New Model. The Case against the Coast Guard Screening Program*, pamphlet published by the International Longshoremen's and Warehousemen's Union, Oct. 1951
7 See RG 12, vol. 2831, Minutes from the meeting of 15 or 16 Sept. 1950; Reginald Whitaker, 'Origins of the Canadian Internal Security System, 1946–1952,' *Canadian Historical Review* 65 (1984): 170–1.
8 See RG 12, vol. 2831; for example, G.R. Donovan to H.V. Anderson, 11 Sept. 1950.
9 PC 1939, 22 March 1951
10 Application for Citizenship – Reasons for Decision, Harold Chamberlain Banks, No. 164805, 10 April 1958, 9. This citizenship application is also reproduced in the Norris Report, schedule 32, 475–90. The RCMP were aware

of the list as early as December 1949. See RCMP Report dated 10 Dec. 1949 from Sgt D.E. Hughes.

11 Fraser Isbester, 'Draft history.' The RCMP, for its part, later maintained that at no time did it supply the SIU with information concerning seamen. See RCMP Papers, To the D.C.I. from the D.S.I., 7 Feb. 1967, file H58HQ-1070-Q-7.

12 Department of Labour Papers, SIU, vol. 1, Bernard Wilson to M.M. Maclean, 17 Oct. 1950

13 Ibid., Maclean to MacNamara, 30 Aug. 1951

14 Ibid. See, for example, F.J. Ainsborough to Maclean, 20 Oct. 1950; Maclean to Wilson, 26 Oct. 1950; Wilson to Maclean, 28 Oct. 1950; G.R. Carroll to Maclean, 14 Nov. 1950; Maclean to Brown, 16 Nov. 1950.

15 Ibid., Maclean to McDougall, 8 Dec. 1950

16 Ibid., Milton Gregg to MacNamara, 20 April 1951

17 See RG 12, vol. 2831, Minutes of the Security Panel meeting, 9 Oct. 1953.

18 Ibid. See also Memorandum of 9 Oct. 1953.

19 Todd interview

20 Ibid.; see also *Proceedings of the SIUNA Biennial Convention*, 26–30 March 1951, Whitcomb Hotel, San Francisco, 'Report of the Canadian District Administrator,' 94–9.

21 Ibid., 98

22 Katz, 'Should We Kick Hal Banks Out of Canada?' 9; see also 'Court of Canadian Citizenship, Decision April 10th, 1958 re Hal C. Banks,' reproduced in Norris Report, vol. II, 483.

23 Katz, 'Should We Kick Hal Banks Out of Canada?' 9

24 FBI Papers, Freedom of Information Act request F25-52482

25 Todd interview

26 Ibid. See Norris Report, 'Unfair Trials,' 236–45.

27 Department of Labour Papers, SIU, vol. II, 'Appeal to the Executive Committee of the SIUNA. See also ibid., Bengough to MacNamara, 1 Oct. 1952, and PAC, CBRT Papers, MG 28, I 215, vol. 76, 'Special Supplement,' Todd Charges.

28 Norris Report, 244. Incredibly, the Department of Labour considered the trial a positive development. See Department of Labour Papers, SIU, vol. II, M.M. Maclean to MacNamara, 18 Oct. 1952.

29 See *Proceedings of the SIUNA Sixth Biennial Convention*, 23–7 March 1953, California; 'Report of Vice-Presidents Hall and Weisberger re Todd,' 127–8, and 'Report of Vice-President Hal Banks – Administrator Canadian District,' 87–91, from which the following section is largely derived.

30 Ibid., 90

31 Department of Labour Papers, SIU, vol. 1, 'Comparison of Certain Agreements of SIU with Agreements Previously in Effect,' 2 April 1951; SIU, vol. II, MacNamara to Gregg, 12 Dec. 1951. See also ibid., MacNamara to Gregg, 3 March 1952.

32 *Labour Gazette*, 1953, 1597; see also *Proceedings of the SIUNA Sixth Biennial Convention*, 87.

33 See, for example, Peter Stursberg, *Lester Pearson and the Dream of Unity* (Toronto 1978) 231.

34 *Harold C. Banks v. The Globe and Mail Limited and Oakley Dalgleish* [1961] SCR 474. See Canadian Maritime Commission Reports, 9–13; *Proceedings, SIU – Ninth Biennial Convention*, Sheraton–Mount Royal Hotel, Montreal, 25–9 May 1959.

35 *Labour Gazette*, 1951, 1339; 1955, 394

36 CBRT Papers, vol. 82, file SIU – NAME, Hal C. Banks to All Officials, 23 March 1955

37 Ibid.

38 The other two takeovers were of the Canadian Seamen's Association and the Association of Government Seafarers Yard and Ward Employees. See *Debates* 21 July 1955, 6539; 'Report of the Canadian District,' *Proceedings SIUNA Seventh Biennial Convention*, 23 May 1955, 37–9

39 See Isbester, 'Draft history,' 32, 59; and Department of Labour Papers, SIU, vol. III, Beaston to Maclean, 7 July 1953, Maclean to Banks, 8 July 1953, Maclean to Beaston, 9 July 1953; vol. I, M.M. Maclean to MacNamara, 30 Aug. 1951; CLC Papers, file SIU 1951–2, Hal Banks to L.C. Audette, 12 May 1952.

40 See *Debates*, 12 April 1954, 3978; 11 Feb. 1955, 1065–6. RCMP Papers, director criminal investigations to the commissioner, 23 Nov. and 1 Dec. 1964; George B. McClellan, commissioner RCMP, to minister of justice Guy Favreau, 11 Dec. 1964

41 Letter from Dominique Graham to William Kaplan, 30 July 1982

42 *Debates*, 22 Feb. 1954, 2301–2. See also PAC, RG 2, 16 (unprocessed), Cabinet Conclusions for the meeting on 25 Feb. 1954; CLC Papers, vol. 6, file SIU 1952–7.

43 *Debates*, 22 Feb. 1954, 2347

44 Cabinet Conclusions (unprocessed), 25 Feb. 1954

45 Ibid., 30 June 1954. See also letter from Walter Harris to Kaplan, 16 April 1982; Katz, 'Should We Kick Hal Banks Out of Canada?' 78; *Debates*, 9 June 1954, 5702; and Hal Banks citizenship application, extracted in Norris Report, schedule 32, 475–90.

46 CLC Papers, file SIU, 1952–7, vol. 6

47 *Debates*, 23 Feb. 1954, 2347

48 Ibid.

49 See generally *Proceedings SIUNA Seventh Biennial Convention*.

50 Minutes of the TLC Executive Council, 9 Sept. 1950, in Swartz, 'Hal Banks,' 141

51 See, for example, Department of Labour Papers, SIU, vol. II, Bengough to MacNamara, 1 Oct. 1952.

52 Ibid.

53 See John Bunker, 'SIU Builds National Reputation as a Union,' *Seafarers' Log*, July 1981, 22–3; *Proceedings SIUNA Seventh Biennial Convention*, 4.

54 *Proceedings SIUNA Seventh Biennial Convention*, 6

55 See Department of Labour Papers, SIU, vol. II, letter dated 20 April 1951 from MacNamara.

56 The founding members of the Association of Lake Carriers were Canada Steamship Lines, the Misener companies, Paterson and Sons, and Upper Lakes.
57 *Proceedings SIUNA Seventh Biennial Convention*, 57
58 Canada Steamship Lines [CSL] Papers, Montreal, Leitch to Misener, 25 Jan. 1954, copy to T.R. McLagan
59 Ibid., Leitch to McLagan, 21 Oct. 1954
60 Norris Report, 210–27; in particular, 211 and 223
61 CSL Papers, Leitch to McLagan, 21 Oct. 1954
62 Ibid., McLagan to Leitch, 27 Oct. 1954
63 *Labour Gazette*, 1956, 713; see also *Debates*, 8 May 1956, 3669.
64 *Debates*, 8 May 1956, 3670
65 *Labour Gazette*, 1956, 627
66 Goldenberg interview. The following section is derived almost entirely from this interview.
67 *Labour Gazette*, 1956, 633
68 Ibid., and 627

Chapter 7: Domination and Discontent

1 Richard Greaves Papers, *Address by the President*, Thirty-Third Meeting of the NAME National Council, King Edward Hotel, Toronto, 16–18 Feb. 1959, 1
2 CBRT Papers, vol. 82, file SIU-NAME, *Proceedings Fourth Convention of the NAME Great Lakes and Eastern District*
3 *Globe and Mail*, 16 July 1957; and see, generally, note 1.
4 See generally note 1.
5 Greaves interview.
6 See CLC Papers for numerous telegrams from the Eastern District of NAME, and CBRT Papers, vol. 81, file SIU-NAME, for a copy of a NAME resolution passed on 15 November 1956 calling on the CLC to cancel the SIU's affiliation. Isbester, 'Draft history,' 34, note 65; and *Globe and Mail*, 11 Feb. 1957
7 Norris Report, 52
8 Ibid.; Greaves interview
9 See note 1.
10 Ibid.; and see Norris Report, 52; *Globe and Mail*, 16 July 1957; CBRT papers, vol. 82, file SIU-NAME, open letter from James Patterson, 8 Aug. 1957; Greaves Papers, NAME National Executive Council Meeting, 24 Aug. 1957, and *Name v. McGough and Sterling*, Quebec Superior Court, 31 Dec. 1957.
11 Minutes of the Thirty-Second Meeting of the National Council of NAME, 14–15 June 1958; see also *R. v. Hal Banks*, No. 15987, Court of Sessions of the Peace, Montreal, 1 May 1964, Judgement of Claude Wagner.
12 Wagner Judgement, 24

13 Ibid., 25
14 Ibid., 19
15 Ibid., 10
16 Smith interview
17 Smith interview; Robson interviews. See CBRT Papers, vol. 82, file SIU-NAME 1956–9, Robson to Harry Plummer, 7 Feb. 1957.
18 Ibid.
19 Ibid.
20 Banks Citizenship Application, Norris Report, 475–90
21 CBRT Papers, vol. 82, file SIU-NAME 1956–9, Robson to Harry Plummer, 9 Feb. 1957; Robson interviews
22 Paul Phillips, *No Power Greater: A Century of Labour in British Columbia* (Vancouver 1967), 127, 144; MacDonald, 'Betrayal,' 528–30; Robson interviews
23 *Globe and Mail*, 11 and 25 Sept. 1959
24 Ibid., 25 Sept. 1959; see also *Seamen's Voice* 1 (Oct. 1959), issued by the CBRT; CBRT Papers, vol. 76.
25 *Globe and Mail*, 29 Sept. and 3 Oct. 1959
26 *Labour Gazette*, 1958, 838
27 Greaves interview. See also George Musk, *Canadian Pacific: The Story of the Famous Shipping Line* (Toronto 1981), 83.
28 Greaves interview
29 Greaves Papers, Greaves to John Wood, 1 Aug. 1958
30 *Labour Legislation of the Past Decade* (Ottawa 1961), 74
31 Greaves interview
32 Ibid.
33 *Banks v. NAME* 16 DLR (2d) 304 (BCCA). See also CBRT Papers, vol. 82, file SIU-NAME, Greaves to Claude Jodoin, 27 Oct. 1958.
34 Greaves Papers, Greaves to John Wood, 1 Aug. 1958; *Labour Gazette*, 1958, 838
35 Greaves Papers, Greaves to John Wood, 1 Aug. 1958
36 Norris Report, 53; schedule 25, 423–32, decision of the Canadian Labour Relations Board dated 23 Aug. 1961, *SIU et al.*
37 Ibid.
38 Norris Report, 58
39 CBRT Papers, vol. 82, file SIU-NAME 1956–9, Greaves to Jodoin, 9 Nov. 1958
40 *Proceedings of the Thirty-Third Meeting of NAME*. See also CBRT Papers, vol. 72, file SIU-NAME, 'Confidential Memo'; *Globe and Mail*, 16 Dec. 1958.
41 Norris Report, 54–5; Isbester, 'Draft history,' 37
42 Norris Report, 54
43 *Globe and Mail*, 13 Feb. 1959
44 Ibid.
45 Ibid., 1 April 1959, and undated articles in *Globe and Mail* research files
46 Norris Report, 58
47 Ibid., 56–7; see also *Globe and Mail*, 30 Sept. 1960.
48 Norris Report, 56–7

49 Starr interview
50 Ibid.; Norris Report, 57
51 Norris Report, 423–30
52 David Hunter, 'The History of the CSU and the SIU,' unpublished paper, Osgodde Hall Law School, 1976, 42
53 Norris Report, 57–60, 423–30; Greaves interview
54 *Globe and Mail*, 15 June 1961
55 Ibid.; see also John Brewin, 'Fear and Dishonesty Rule the SIU,' *Canadian Labour* 6 (July-Aug. 1961): 27
56 Norris Report, 423–30
57 Ibid., 62

Chapter 8: The SIU at Bay

1 'Congress Suspends Seafarers,' *Canadian Labour* 4 (June 1959): 66
2 See *Proceedings SIUNA Ninth Biennial Convention*, 19–20; *Labour Gazette*, 1959, 576; *Proceedings SIUNA Tenth Biennial Convention*, San Juan, Puerto Rico, 13–18 March 1961, 113.
3 *Proceedings SIUNA Tenth Biennial Convention*, 113; *Globe and Mail*, 19 June 1959, 27 and 28 April 1960
4 Ibid.
5 Norris Report, 6–9, and schedules 6, 7, 8, 9, 10, 11, and 12, 389–401; see *Canadian Labour* 4 (1959): 5–6.
6 CBRT Papers, vol. 47 file Canal Employees SIU-CBRT
7 Swartz, 'Hal Banks,' 96; CBRT Papers, vol. 47, file Canal Employees SIU-CBRT, Robson to A. Brisson, 3 July 1959
8 Smith and Robson interviews; *Globe and Mail*, 15 June 1961
9 Isbester, 'Draft history,' 36; Starr interview
10 Fulton interview
11 Ibid.; see RCMP Papers, file no 58 HQ 1070-Q-7, A.J. Carroll Report, 23 Feb. 1959.
12 RCMP Papers, E. Davie Fulton to C.H. Nicholson, 10 Nov. 1958; Carroll Report; Nicholson to Fulton, 23 Feb. 1959
13 The RCMP Papers made available to me have been deposited without restriction at the archives of the University of Toronto.
14 Carroll Report, 4
15 Ibid., 23
16 RCMP Papers, Nicholson to Fulton, 23 Feb. 1959
17 See also RCMP Papers, W.R.J. to Fulton, Memorandum for the minister of justice, 15 July 1959.
18 See SIUNA Canadian District Secret File Reference no. 58HQ 1070-Q-7, C.W. Harrison to Fulton, 18 May 1961; report by A.J. Carroll, 8 June 1961.
19 Macht, *The First 50 Years*, 14; see also Houtman Papers, 'History.'
20 'History of the Dispute between the SIU and the Norris Grain Co. Ltd., et al.,' 11 April 1962, mimeographed document issued by the SIU

21 Ibid., 3
22 Isbester, 'Draft history,' 37–8
23 Macht, *The First Fifty Years*, 57
24 'History of the Dispute between the SIU and the Norris Grain Co. Ltd., et al.,' 5
25 Ibid.; Norris Report, 76
26 Hartford interview
27 Houtman Papers, Tom Houtman to Leitch, 18 July 1960
28 Robson interviews
29 Ibid.
30 Marc Zwelling, *The Strikebreakers* (Toronto 1977), 91–2
31 Houtman interviews; see CBRT Papers, vol. 82, file Seamen Island Shipping, Leitch to all employees, 25 July 1961
32 Norris Report, 77; Macht, *The First Fifty Years*, 13–15
33 Houtman and Sheehan interviews
34 Isbester, 'Draft history,' 39, and Norris Report, 85
35 *Globe and Mail*, 16 Aug. 1961
36 CBRT Papers, vol. 82, file Island Shipping, Jodoin to Meany, 19 Sept. 1961
37 See Document prepared by George Haythorne for Arnold Heeney, co-chairman of the IJC in November 1964. Furnished to author courtesy of George Haythorne
38 *Labour Gazette*, 1962, 131
39 Smith and Robson interviews
40 Dodge interview; see also CLC Papers, file 16, Summary of Extracts from Department of Organization Reports and Minutes of Executive Committee and Council Meetings; CBRT Papers, vol. 76, Minutes of the National Executive Board Meeting, 14–18 Nov. 1961; CLC Papers, file 37, Donald MacDonald to Jodoin and Dodge, 11 Aug. 1961
41 Norris Report, 83
42 Houtman Papers file 1961–2, Memorandum dated 16 Oct. 1961
43 Norris Report, 78
44 See Rene Lippe to Kaplan, 24 Sept. 1984, 'History of the Dispute,' 9–11; Norris Report, 78–9; Swartz, 'Hal Banks,' 103; Isbester, 'Draft history,' 42–3. In late April 1961 a meeting took place in Ottawa; present were Jodoin, Dodge, Maurice Wright, Jack Geller, Jack Leitch, H.H. Cater, and G. Bertrand of the Department of External Affairs, and George Haythorne and Bernard Wilson of the Department of Labour.
45 Norris Report, 79, see also SIU published document, Montreal, undated, *The Strange Conspiracy to Destroy the Standards and Security of Canadian Workers*.
46 Isbester, 'Draft history,' 42–3
47 Norris Report, 85
48 Swartz, 'Hal Banks,' 106
49 Norris Report, 83
50 Ibid.; Swartz, 'Hal Banks,' 107

51 Norris Report, Schedule 13, 402–4; Jodoin to Diefenbaker, 23 May 1962; see also *Canadian Labour*, 21 June 1962.
52 Norris Report, 404; Dodge interview
53 CLC Papers, MG 28, I 103, file 37, 791563, Fulton to Jodoin, 30 May 1962
54 Ibid. Jodoin to Meany, 1 June 1962, and Meany to Jodoin, 3 Aug. 1962
55 Ibid., Joseph P. Molony to Jodoin, 5 June 1962
56 Ibid., Jodoin to Wright, 13 June 1962; Norris Report, Schedule 17, 409–10, H.C. Green to Jodoin, 28 June 1962
57 See Norris Report, Schedule 52, 600–10.
58 Ibid., Schedule 14, 405–6, Jodoin to Fulton, 26 June 1962
59 Ibid., Schedule 16, 408, Robson to Diefenbaker, 20 June 1962
60 *Extract from Hearing of the Industrial Commission as to Shipping in the Great Lakes and St. Lawrence River System – Submission to the Norris Commission*, 13 March 1963, 4
61 CBRT Papers, vol. 76, R.J. Rankin to F.D. Nicoll, 27 June 1962; St Lawrence Seaway, *Annual Report*, 1962, 5
62 See Norris Report, 10–29.
63 See CLC Papers, file 37, CLC press release, 6 July 1962.
64 The government of the United States also agreed to appoint a commission and named Judge Samuel Rosenman as chaiman. See Rosenman Report; Norris Report, 30–1.

Chapter 9: The Norris Commission

1 Norris Report, Schedule 2, Privy Council Order 1962–1031
2 Norris Report, Schedule 1, 319–20
3 PAC, RG 36/29, Norris Commission, Transcript of Evidence, vol. 1, 7 Aug. 1962, 7
4 Ibid., 7, 28
5 Ibid., vol. 2, 14 Aug. 1962, 52
6 Ibid., 138
7 Ibid.
8 Ibid., 141
9 See *Ottawa Citizen*, 3 Aug. 1968.
10 Transcript of Evidence, vol. 3, 15 Aug. 1962, 314
11 *CLC Great Lakes Union Inquiry – Bulletin No 1*, 10 Sept. 1962. See also 'Testimony of Violence in Great Lakes Probe,' *Canadian Labour* 7 (1962); 43.
12 See Transcript of Evidence, vols. 16, 17 and 18; 'Former SIU Members Tell of Reform Attempts,' *Canadian Labour* 7 (1962): 45; *CLC Great Lakes Union Inquiry Bulletin No 3*, 1 Oct. 1962.
13 Ibid.
14 *Canadian Labour*, Dec. 1962, 42
15 *Maritime Register*, Oct.–Nov. 1962, 3
16 Norris Report, 288

17 Ibid.; Transcript of Evidence, vol. 36, 26 Oct. 1962
18 Transcript of Evidence, vol, 45, 9 Nov. 1962
19 Ibid., vols. 45 and 46, 13 Nov. 1962, 6961. See G.G. McLeod to Kaplan, 21 Sept. 1982; Couture and Nuss interviews.
20 G.G. McLeod to Kaplan, 21 Sept. 1982; Couture and Nuss interviews
21 Transcript of Evidence, vol. 46, 13 Nov. 1962, 6961
22 Ibid., vol. 49, 19 Nov. 1962, 7239ff
23 Ibid., 7239–49
24 Ibid.
25 Ibid.
26 Ibid., 7250, 7251
27 *CLC Great Lakes Inquiry Bulletin No 6*, 24 Dec. 1962; Norris Report, ix
28 Ibid.
29 See Transcript of Evidence, vol. 72, 7 Jan. 1963, 10, 580–1.
30 For average salaries and expenses see Norris Report, 99, 106–13. For comparable CBRT expenses see CBRT Papers, file Norris Commission Inquiry – Salaries and Expenses, 1958–1962.
31 'Banks Testimony about Expenses,' *Canadian Labour* 8 (1963): 25
32 Ibid.
33 Transcript of Evidence, vol. 73, 8 Jan. 1963. See also *CLC Bulletin No 7*, 29 Jan. 1963, and *Globe and Mail*, 7 and 8 Jan. 1963.
34 Transcript of Evidence, vol. 73, 8 Jan. 1963, 10, 789
35 *Globe and Mail*, 8 Jan. 1963
36 Transcript of Evidence, vol. 78, 15 Jan. 1963; vol. 76, 11 Jan. 1963, 11, 330–1
37 Ibid., vol. 80, 17 Jan. 1963, 12, 115
38 Ibid., vol. 81, 18 Jan. 1963, 12, 282; *Globe and Mail*, 18 and 19 Jan. 1963
39 Transcript of Evidence, vol. 81, 18 Jan. 1963, 12, 281; *Globe and Mail*, 21 Jan. 1963
40 See generally, Transcript of Evidence, vol. 82, 21 Jan. 1963, and *Globe and Mail*, 22 Jan. 1963.
41 Transcript of Evidence, vol. 82, 21 Jan. 1963, 12, 362; vol. 83, 22 Jan. 1963, 12, 547
42 Ibid., vol. 84, 23 Jan. 1963, 12, 687–8
43 See generally, ibid., vol. 85, 24 Jan. 1963.
44 Ibid., vol. 84, 23 Jan. 1963, 12, 701–2. Robson in turn began calling Nuss, 'Ness.'
45 Ibid., vol. 85, 24 Jan. 1963, 12, 734; *Globe and Mail*, 25 Jan. 1963
46 Transcript of Evidence, vol. 86, 25 Jan. 1963
47 The CLC had, as we have seen, been advised by both seamen and Department of Labour officials in very certain terms about the rampant wrongdoing within the SIU.
48 Transcript of Evidence, vol. 86, 25 Jan. 1963, 12, 925
49 Ibid., 12, 927
50 Ibid., 12, 929

51 Ibid., 12, 935–6
52 Transcript of Evidence, vol. 91, 1 Feb. 1963, 13, 710; *Globe and Mail*, 2 Feb. 1963
53 Transcript of Evidence, vol. 104, 11 March 1963, 15, 627
54 Ibid., vol. 98, 14 Feb. 1963, 14, 780
55 Ibid., 14, 784–5
56 In contrast, only one of the ten witnesses the CLC asked to be called was actually called. See *Globe and Mail*, 12 March 1963.
57 Transcript of Evidence, vol. 104, 11 March 1963, 15, 736
58 Ibid., 15, 742–67
59 Ibid., 15, 756
60 Ibid., 15, 758. See also *Globe and Mail*, 12 March 1963.
61 Ibid.; see also Transcript of Evidence, vol. 105, 12 March 1963; *Globe and Mail*, 13 March 1963
62 Transcript of Evidence, vol. 105, 12 March 1963
63 Ibid., 15, 833–6
64 Some of the questions which Nuss was never able to pursue at the Norris Inquiry were subsequently raised in Zwelling, *The Strikebreakers*.
65 See Norris Report, Schedule 52, 600–10.
66 See, generally, *Extract from Hearing of Industrial Inquiry Commission as to Shipping in the Great Lakes and St. Lawrence River System*.
67 Ibid., 5
68 Ibid.; see also Norris Report, Schedule 44, 535–73.
69 Ibid., 9
70 Ibid., 32
71 Ibid.
72 Ibid., 33
73 Ibid., 34–5
74 Ibid., 35. This view was certainly shared by the CBRT. See CBRT Papers, vol. 71, Memorandum of CBRT, undated, by Harry Crowe.
75 See note 66.

Chapter 10: The Norris Report

1 *Globe and Mail*, 18 April 1963
2 See, for example, *Globe and Mail*, articles throughout April and May.
3 See CLC Papers, file 37, CLC release, 23 April 1963, and Pearson to Jodoin, 23 April 1963.
4 *Globe and Mail*, 10 May 1963; *Debates*, 1 Aug. 1963, 2880–1; George Hay-thorne, 'Talk to Collective Bargaining Seminar – Littauer Centre, Harvard University,' 19 Feb. 1964, supplied to author courtesy of George Haythorne
5 See generally the Haythorne talk referred to in note 4.
6 Ibid.
7 *Globe and Mail*, 12 May 1963
8 Ibid.

9 See Norris Report, Schedule 1, 319–20.
10 Norris Report, 106. See also R.A. O'Shea, 'The Norris Report: Review and Reflection,' *Faculty of Law Review* 22 (1964): 41–59; Peter Gzowski, 'Hal Banks – Waterfront Warlord,' *Maclean's*, 18 May 1963; and document prepared and distributed by Upper Lakes Shipping on editorial reaction to the Norris Report.
11 Norris Report, 296–9
12 Ibid., 304–6
13 See Shea, 'The Norris Report,' for a detailed analysis of these issues, 47–8.
14 '*Statement of SIU of Canada in Respect to the Norris Commission Report,*' undated, mimeographed, 1; *Statement of the Seafarers' International Union Relative to the Report of the Industrial Inquiry Commission on the Disruption of Shipping*, published by the SIU of Canada, Sept. 1963; CBRT Papers, vol. 71, MTD Release of Executive Board Meeting, 10–11 Sept. 1963; Arthur Kruger, 'The Norris Report,' *Canadian Forum*, Oct. 1963
15 David Kwavnick, *Organized Labour and Pressure Politics: The Canadian Labour Congress 1956–1968* (Montreal and London 1972), 155–6. See also 'Trusteeship and the Maritime Unions,' *Canadian Labour* 8 (1963): 5–7; CBRT Papers, vol. 71, CBRT press release, 16 July 1963; Ken Lefolii, 'The Best New Reason for Living in Canada: We Can Still Beat Thugs Like Hal Banks,' *Maclean's*, editorial, 10 Aug. 1963, 4.
16 *Debates*, 22 July 1963, 2451
17 Ibid., 18 July 1963, 2327
18 Ibid., 1 Aug. 1963, 2880–1
19 James M. Minifie, *Open at the Top* (Toronto 1964), 131. See also Swartz, 'Hal Banks,' 115.
20 CLC Papers, F-37-2, Meany to Jodoin, 10 Sept. 1963
21 Ibid., Pearson to Jodoin, 9 Sept. 1963. See also John F. Kennedy Papers, William Tyler to secretary of state, 6 Sept. 1963, 'Briefing Paper for Visit of Canadian External Affairs Minister Paul Martin,' 7 Sept. 1963; Minifie, *Open at the Top*, 131.
22 George Haythorne to Kaplan, 12 July 1982
23 CLC Papers, F-37-3, 'Summary of Report on Efforts to Establish a Private Trusteeship,' 17 Oct. 1963
24 CBRT Papers, vol. 71, CBRT policy statement, 22 Sept. 1963
25 *Globe and Mail*, 24 Sept. 1963
26 See CLC Papers, F-37-2, Jodoin to Meaney, 27 Sept. 1963; Swartz, 'Hal Banks,' 112.
27 Haythorne talk, 9; see also Donald MacDonald, 'Trusteeship and Maritime Unions,' *Canadian Labour* 8 (1963): 5–7.
28 CLC Papers, F-37-2, Minutes, meeting, 28 Sept. 1963, Boston Hilton Hotel
29 Haythorne talk, 9; CLC Papers, F-37-2
30 CLC Papers, F-37-3, 'Summary of Report on Efforts to Establish a Private Trusteeship,' 17 Oct. 1963
31 Ibid., Smith to Jodoin, 3 Oct. 1963; Jodoin to Smith, 4 Oct. 1963

32 'Summary of Report on Efforts to Establish a Private Trusteeship'; Haythorne talk, 13; *Debates*, 9 Oct. 1963, 3370; CBRT Papers, vol. 71, Kent
   Rowley to MacEachen, 2 Oct. 1963
33 CBRT Papers, vol. 17, AFL-CIO release, 10 Oct. 1963; see also Swartz, 'Hal
   Banks,' 115.
34 US Information Service, 10 Oct. 1963, cited in Swartz, 'Hal Banks,' 173
35 *Debates*, 11 Oct. 1963, 3441, and 14 Oct. 1963, 3525; S.M. Girard, *Canada
   in World Affairs*, XII: *1963–5* (Toronto 1979), 52; *New York Times*, 17 Oct.
   1963; see also *Globe and Mail*, 14 Oct. 1963.
36 Haythorne talk, 10; Girard, *Canada in World Affairs*, 52; *Debates*, 11 Oct.
   1963, 3459
37 See *Debates*, 11 Oct. 1963, 3505.
38 *Globe and Mail*, 18 Oct. 1963
39 Chapter 17, R.S.C.
40 See the act.
41 *Debates*, 21 Oct. 1963, 3836; MacDonald, 'Trusteeship and the Maritime
   Unions,' 7
42 Haythorne talk
43 *Globe and Mail*, 29 May 1963
44 Girard, *Canada in World Affairs*, 53
45 *Globe and Mail*, 19 Oct. 1963
46 Ibid.
47 Ibid., 22 Oct. 1963
48 *Labour Gazette*, 1963, 1090
49 See *Debates*, 22 Oct. 1963

Chapter 11: Trusteeship

1 *Debates*, 23 Oct. 1963, 3900; *Labour Gazette*, 1963, 1090; *Globe and Mail*,
  26 Oct. 1963
2 *Labour Gazette*, 1963, 1090, The Religion-Labour Council undertook during
  the 1964 shipping season a survey of seamen. See David Summers to Kaplan,
  2 June 1982. The Department of Labour undertook a not unrelated study in
  1967: 'Survey of Hours of Work in Great Lakes Shipping,' prepared by the
  Economics and Research Branch.
3 Dryer and Lippe interviews; *Globe and Mail*, 25 Oct. 1963; *Labour
  Gazette*, 1963, 1090
4 Report of the Board of Trustees of the Maritime Transportation Unions as of
  December 31, 1963. Government of Canada Sessional Papers, 26th Parliament 101. All the trustees' annual reports have the 31 December year end
  but will be cited for examble, as 1965 Trustees' Annual Report. See also
  Globe and Mail, 25 Oct. 1963.
5 *Globe and Mail* 13, 14 and 19 Nov. 1963; Girard, *Canada in World Affairs*,
  57

6 John F. Kennedy Papers, National Security Files, country series, 'Canada – General 1963,' box 19, Memorandum for the President: Re the Canadian Maritime Situation November 5, 1963; see also Minifie, *Open at the Top*, 132.
7 *Globe and Mail*, 12 Nov. 1963
8 Ibid., 12 Nov. 1963
9 *Debates*, 22 Nov. 1963, 5065; see also *Globe and Mail*, 17 May 1964 and 1965 Trustees' Annual Report, 47.
10 1963 Trustees' Annual Report, 5–9
11 See Trustees' Directive Number Two.
12 Trustees' 1963 Annual Report, 10
13 Norris Report, 311
14 *Debates*, 22 July 1963
15 Ibid.; see also RCMP Papers, George B. McClellan to L.T Pennell, 27 Jan. 1966.
16 Robinette interview; *Debates* 20 Nov. 1963, 4950, and 23 Nov. 1964, 10411
17 See John F. Kennedy Papers, Butterworth to secretary of state, 15 Nov. 1963; see also *Debates*, 5 Nov. 1963, 4389–90
18 *Debates*, 31 Oct. 1963; *Toronto Star*, editorial, 1 Nov. 1963
19 *Debates*, 6 Nov. 1963, 4449–50
20 Ibid., 31 Oct. 1963, 4215; *Globe and Mail*, 31 Jan. 1964; see also *Montreal Gazette*, 23 Feb. 1965; *Globe and Mail*, 6 July 1966 and 30 Jan. 1967; and *Debates*, 6 Nov. 1968, 2472–3.
21 *Debates*, 15 Nov. 1963, 4781; 11 Dec. 1963, 5703
22 1964 Trustees' Annual Report, 5
23 Ibid., 7; letter from Mr Justice Victor Dryer to William Kaplan, 11 May 1983
24 *Globe and Mail*, 19 March 1964
25 Ibid.; see also letter dated 20 April, Appendix C to 1964 Annual Report.
26 See 'Trustees Fire Banks,' *Canadian Labour* 9 (1964): 41. See also Comminiqué of the Board of Trustees, 18 March 1964, and Dryer testimony before the House of Commons Industrial Relations Committee, 34.
27 *Globe and Mail*, 19 and 20 March 1964; 1964 Trustees' Annual Report, 8
28 *Debates*, 11 Dec. 1963, 5700; see also University of Toronto Archives, Dryer Papers, Dryer to Haythorne, 4 Feb. 1964; S. Samuels (Department of Justice) to Haythorne, 20 Feb. 1964, copy to Dryer; Dryer to Haythorne, 3 March 1964: Dryer to Haythorne, 20 March 1964; L.P. de Grandpré to Dryer, 13 April 1964 (two letters of that date); Dryer to de Grandpré, 14 April 1964; Dryer to Haythorne, 29 April 1964.
29 The SIU's American attorney advised H. Alan Hope, then executive assistant to the Board of Trustees, 'that he realized that our Act gave us very little power beyond the power to remove an officer.' See Victor Dryer Papers, 1964 Draft Annual Report.
30 Trustees' 1964 Annual Report, 8. See also Millard-Hall, Joint Statement, 3 April 1964, Sessional Papers, 101 Session No 84b, 26th Parliament.

31 Dryer, Lippe, and Howard interviews
32 *Globe and Mail*, 6, 7, and 9 April 1964
33 Ibid., 2 May 1964
34 Wagner judgment, 56
35 *Globe and Mail*, 2 May 1964
36 *Debates*, 28 July 1964, 6084–5
37 *Globe and Mail*, 25 May 1964; see also 'Sentence Banks,' *Canadian Labour* 9 (1964): 28.
38 Ibid.; *Globe and Mail*, 30 June 1964; see also *Upper Lakes Shipping v. Banks* 50 DLR (2d) 734.
39 *Debates*, 28 July 1964, 6085
40 Ibid., 27 July 1964, 6024; see also John Diefenbaker, *One Canada*, vol. 2 (Toronto 1977), 215–18.
41 The gap was filled when the treaty was renegotiated in 1971. See C.V. Cole, director, Legal Advisory Division, Department of External Affairs, to Kaplan, 5 July 1983, and *Debates*, 4 Sept. 1967, 7691.
42 *Debates*, 28 July 1964, 6085; 4 Sept. 1964, 7688–91; 7 Oct. 1964, 892
43 *Globe and Mail*, 18–20 Aug. 1964
44 *Debates*, 18 Aug. 1964, 6948
45 Ibid., 7 Oct. 1964, 8839
46 Ibid., 14 Sept. 1964, 7960–1; 1 Oct. 1964, 8620–1
47 *Toronto Star*, 2 Oct. 1964; *Debates*, 1 Oct. 1964, 8620, 2 Oct. 1964, 8667–9
48 Ibid.
49 Ibid.
50 Ibid.; Fulton interview
51 *Toronto Star*, 1 Oct. 1964
52 See W.R. Cunningham to Kaplan, 28 April 1982; Reguly interview.
53 *Debates*, 2 Oct. 1964; see also *Globe and Mail*, 2 Oct. 1964.

Chapter 12: Autonomy and Respect

1 Todd, Greaves, and Sheehan interviews
2 Todd interview; see also 1964 Trustees' Annual Report, 25.
3 See PAC, Margot Thomson Papers, MG 31, 1328, vol. 2, Millard to Margot Thompson, 6 Feb. 1964; Gordon G. Cushing to MacEachen and Haythorne, 9 Oct. 1964, confidential report, furnished to Kaplan courtesy of George Haythorne, 7, hereinafter referred to as the Cushing memorandum.
4 See Haythorne to Kaplan, 22 Aug. 1983.
5 See Cushing memorandum; Dryer to MacEachen, 8 Sept. 1964, Appendix A to 1964 Trustees' Annual Report.
6 See *House of Commons Standing Committee on Industrial Relations Minutes of Proceedings and Evidence 1964–1965*, 16 March 1965, 36.
7 Ibid.
8 Ibid., 54–5; see also Board of Trustees of Maritime Transportation Unions

Communiqué, 9 Sept. 1965, and Lippe's testimony before the same standing committee on 2 March 1965, 98–100.

9 Cushing memorandum, 5

10 Board of Trustees Communiqué, 26 Sept. 1964; see also Trustees' 1964 Annual Report, 10.

11 Board of Trustees of the Maritime Transportation Unions Communiqué, 20 Nov. 1964

12 *Globe and Mail*, 3 Dec. 1964

13 Cushing memorandum, 5–6. However, see Appendix B to 1964 Annual Report.

14 *Minutes of Proceedings and Evidence of the House of Commons Committee on Industrial Relations 1964, 1965*, 2 March 1965, 96; 'Legal Decisions Affecting Labour,' *Labour Gazette*, 1968, 105–6

15 1964 Trustees' Annual Report, 7; *Globe and Mail*, 27 Nov. 1964; *Minutes of Proceedings*, 16 March 1965, 25

16 See 'A Supplementary Maritime Unions Trustee Report for the Period January 1, 1964 to December 31, 1964, dated February 12, 1965,' *Debates*, 14 April 1964, 2159–60.

17 1964 Trustees' Annual Report, 16. See A.W.R. Carrothers to Kaplan 12 May 1982.

18 See *Debates*, 26 May 1964, 3580; see also Sessional Papers 101, 26th Parliament, no 84.

19 See *Canadian Who's Who* (Toronto 1984), 1017; Norris Report, Schedule 45, 5746; and 1964 Trustees' Annual Report, 13.

20 1964 Trustee's Annual Report, 13

21 Dryer was also influenced in his decision by a disagreeable incident involving John Wood, the former head of the SIU Licensed Division. See William Miller to Board of Trustees, 21 April 1964, Sessional Papers 101, 26th Parliament; Charles Turner to John Wood, 6 May 1964, Sessional Papers 101, 26th Parliament; Howard Papers, Haythorne to Dryer, 1 June 1964, Dryer to Haythorne, 4 June 1964, Haythorne to Dryer, 9 June 1964, and Dryer to Haythorne, 12 June 1964; Victor Dryer Papers, Dryer to MacEachen, 28 Aug. 1964; see also Cushing memorandum; *Debates*, 4 Sept. 1964, 7674; and Haythorne to Kaplan, 22 Aug. 1984. Dryer also did not think that the Department of Labour was giving him the co-operation he requested. See, for example, Dryer Papers, Dryer to Haythorne, 5 Feb. 1964, Haythorne to Dryer, 22 April 1964, and Dryer to Haythorne, 29 April 1964.

22 Dryer interview; letter from Dryer to Kaplan, 19 July 1983, 2

23 *Debates*, 7 April 1964, 1847; 9 April 1964, 1947; see also *Debates*, 30 April 1964, 2761.

24 *Debates*, 12 Aug. 1964, Appendix A, 6750–1, copy of letter from Dryer to MacEachen, 31 July 1964

25 Ibid. See Cushing memorandum, 6; *Debates*, 1964, Appendix A, 6750–1, copy of letter from MacEachen to Dryer, 7 Aug. 1964.

26 See 1964 Trustees' Annual Report, 34; *Labour Gazette*, 1964, 214.

27 See Dryer to Kaplan, 19 July 1983, 8.

28 *Minutes of Proceedings*, 20–3

29 Ibid., 15, 46
30 It is perhaps noteworthy that René Turcotte, the defeated SIU presidential
   aspirant, launched his court suit to have the SIU election set aside approximately two weeks after Dryer's appearance and Nielsen's questions in the
   House.
31 *Minutes of Proceedings*, 69
32 Ibid., 73
33 See Dryer Papers, Dryer to MacEachen, 30 July 1964; Dryer and Howard
   interviews.
34 See *Debates*, 4 Sept. 1964, 7685.
35 See typed excerpts from text used by C.H. Millard at the 22 Nov. 1964
   educational meeting at the Oshawa UAW hall. Margot Thompson Papers, file
   C.H. Millard
36 CLC Papers, file 37-3, C.H. Millard to executive members of the CLC,
   'Private Memorandum Re Trusteeship,' 18 Nov. 1964; see also letter from
   René Lippe, 2 Feb. 1965, which is attached to this document.
37 'A Supplementary Maritime Union Trustee Report for the Period ending
   January 1, 1964 to December 31, 1964,' submitted by C.H. Millard, 12 Feb.
   1965.
38 Ibid., 1
39 Ibid., 5
40 See *Labour Gazette*, 1965, 214; Board of Trustees Communiqué, undated;
   and MacKenzie interview.
41 *Labour Gazette*, 1964, 465
42 If the international unions could 'appeal' CLC jurisdictional decision to the
   International Headquarters and to the AFL–CIO, any effectiveness would be
   lost.
43 'Canadian Autonomy,' text of address by CLC executive vice-president Morris, fraternal delegate to the fifth convention of the AFL–CIO, New York City,
   15 Nov. 1963; *Canadian Labour* 8 (1963): 13
44 Ibid., 13–14
45 Ibid., 14
46 Ibid.
47 *Labour Gazette*, 1964, 465–6
48 See *Labour Gazette*, 1964, 770, and *Labour Gazette*, 1965, 100; 1965
   Trustees' Annual Report, 10.
49 See 1966 Trustees' Annual Report, 16.
50 Ibid.
51 Ibid.
52 Ibid.
53 *Labour Gazette*, 1965, 282
54 Ibid., 317–18
55 Ibid., 29 April 1966
56 *Debates*, 16 Jan. 1967, 11807; see also *Labour Gazette*, 1967, 773; 1966
   Trustees' Annual Report, 50; and *Globe and Mail*, 30 Dec. 1966.

57 See 'Mike Sheehan and Upper Lakes Shipping and CBRT & GW, June 14, 1979,' Canada Labour Relations Board, file 745–36.
58 His loss of the Canadian Maritime Union presidency and subsequent expulsion from that union spurred litigation which did not end until the late 1970s. See the CLC Papers and the Michael Sheehan Papers.
59 See *Sheehan and Upper Lakes Shipping et al.*, [1976] Can. LRBR 187; *Sheehan and Upper Lakes Shipping et al.*, 77 CLLC 14, 827; *Sheehan v. Upper Lakes Shipping et al.*, [1979] 1 Can. LRBR 531; *Sheehan et al.*, [1979] SCR 902; *CBRT et al.*, [1979] 3 Can. LRBR 7; *Sheehan et al.*, [1980] 2 Can. LRBR 278.
60 *Canadian Labour* (March 1968): 41; see also *Labour Gazette* 1968, 201.
61 1967 Trustees' Annual Report
62 Ibid., 2
63 *Globe and Mail*, 11 Jan. 1966; see René Lippe to Kaplan, 27 July 1982.
64 'SIU Re-elects McLaughlin,' *Canadian Labour*, Jan. 1969, 38
65 *Globe and Mail*, 8 Dec. 1971
66 Barry Conn Hughes, 'You Talk to Working Men – Be on Their Level – So "Shotgun" Gralewicz Swears a Lot,' *Canadian Magazine*, 27 Oct. 1973, 2–7
67 Ibid., 7

Chapter 13: Extradition

1 See generally Gerald La Forest, *Extradition To and From Canada* (New Orleans 1961).
2 This had, at the time, caused the governing Liberal party considerable embarrassment.
3 *Globe and Mail*, 5 July 1966
4 See Department of State Papers, 'Schedule of References to Prosecution of Harold C. Banks in House of Commons from 1964 to Date,' Exhibit C to memorandum prepared by Abram Chayes for the secretary of state
5 *Debates*, 3 Nov. 1966, 9474
6 *Globe and Mail*, 9 Nov. 1966
7 *Debates*, 15 Dec. 1966, 11151
8 Ibid., 24 April 1967, 15231
9 Toronto *Telegram*, 1 Sept. 1967; *Montreal Star*, editorial, 1 Sept. 1967
10 *Ontario Debates*, 14 March 1968, 769. See Arthur Wishart to Kaplan, 14 July 1982.
11 *Globe and Mail*, 30, 31 Aug. 1967
12 Department of State Papers, Embassy of Canada to the United States secretary of state, 1 Sept. 1967
13 Ibid., 'In the Matter of the Extradition of Hal Chamberlain Banks, a Fugitive from the Justice of the Dominion of Canada, Brief for Hal C. Banks,' 9 Oct. 1967
14 See the brief-submitted by Kuh in reply, ibid., 'In the Matter of the Extradi-

tion of Hal Chamberlain Banks, Brief in Support of the Application,' 23 Oct. 1967

15 See Kuh brief, 21–5.

16 Brodsky brief, 39–40

17 La Forest, *Extradition To and From Canada*

18 Ibid., 46–7

19 Brodsky brief, 68–9

20 Ibid., 68

21 Kuh brief, 53. See also *Debates*, 25 Sept. 1967, 2433.

22 Brodsky brief, 84

23 Kuh brief, 59

24 No doubt he also thought that they were a tale told by an idiot too.

25 Kuh Papers, Abruzzo opinion, 3 Nov. 1967, 7, furnished to author courtesy of Richard H. Kuh.

26 L.B. Johnson Library, Austin Texas, L.B. Johnson Papers, Department of Labor, microfilm reel A8, 'Memorandum to the Secretary of State from the Secretary of Labor,' 20 Dec. 1967

27 State Department Papers, Meany to Rusk, 26 Dec. 1967

28 Ibid., 2

29 See ibid., Meeker to Rusk, 27 Dec. 1967.

30 Ibid.

31 See ibid., 'In the Matter of the Request for the Extradition of Hal Chamberlain Banks before the Hon. Dean Rusk, Submission on Behalf of Mr. Banks,' 8 Jan. 1963.

32 Chayes brief, 30

33 Ibid., 42

34 Ibid.

35 Frederick Smith Jr, assistant legal adviser, to Chayes, 25 Jan. 1968. See also 'In the Matter of Hal C. Banks, a Fugitive from the Justice of the Dominion of Canada, Submission on Behalf of the Dominion of Canada, February 6, 1968.' Kuh delivered a supplementary brief on 27 Feb. 1968.

36 Kuh brief; 'In the Matter of Hal C. Banks, a Fugitive from the Justice of the Dominion of Canada, Submission on Behalf of the Dominion of Canada, February 6, 1968,' 42–5

37 Department of State Papers, 'Memorandum for the Secretary of State,' 13 Feb. 1968; see also Leonard Meeker to Kaplan, 4 April 1983.

38 *Memorandum*, 13 Feb. 1968

39 While Meeker was drafting his legal memorandum, an official in the Department of Labor approached him and attempted to persuade him to consider the political and other consequences of extradition. Meeker rejected the request. Rusk subsequently asked his political adviser, Nicholas de B. Katzenbach, to draft a decision paper.

40 Department of State Papers, A.E. Ritchie to Rusk, 15 Feb. 1968, note no 57

41 Ibid.

42 Department of State Papers, Rusk to Ritchie, 13 March 1968

43 Dean Rusk to Kaplan, 19 May 1982; see also Paul Martin to Kaplan, undated 1982; L.B. Pearson, *Mike* III: *1957–1968* (Toronto 1975), 151.

44 See *Debates*, 14 March 1968, 7610; see also Department of State Papers, Ritchie to Rusk, note no. 93, 14 March 1963, Herbert Reis to Meeker, 15 March 1968, and a memorandum probably prepared by Meeker entitled 'International Adjudication in the Banks Extradition Case' 19 March 1968.

45 See State Department Papers, Rusk to Ritchie, 20 and 25 March 1968.

46 *La Presse* also published an editorial cartoon showing Banks with a pair of handcuffs dangling from one wrist and with his other arm around US President Johnson. The caption read, 'One Banks is worth 16,000 draft-dodgers hiding in Canada.' See, generally, State Department Papers, American embassy, Ottawa, to Department of State, 4 April 1968, Millard to Rusk, 27 March 1968. Then a private consultant in Toronto, Millard wrote Rusk an unsolicited letter 'thanking him' for his decision. See also *Ontario Debates*, 14 March 1968, 769; 19 March 1968, 926.

47 Jerry Landauer, 'A Friend in Court,' *Wall Street Journal*, 19 July 1968

48 Rusk to Kaplan, 19 May 1982; see also Myer Feldman to Kaplan, 26 July 1982.

49 See *Financial Post*, 16 Nov. 1968; State Department Papers, American embassy, Ottawa, to Department of State, Nov. 1968.

50 State Department Papers, American embassy, Ottawa, to State Department, 8 Feb. 1968

51 Ibid.

52 See ibid., Fannin to Rogers, 5 May 1969.

53 See State Department Papers, Meeker to Rogers, memorandum for the secretary of state, 9 April 1969.

54 See ibid., and Meeker to Rogers, 13 June 1969.

55 Ibid.

56 Ibid.; memorandum of conversation between Keith Henry, Canadian embassy, and H. Rowan Gaither, Department of State, 17 Sept. 1969.

57 See ibid., note no 395, 19 Dec. 1969, Canadian embassy to the Department of State, Department of State document, 6 Jan. 1970.

58 Ibid., note no 68 from Canadian embassy to the Department of State, 1 March 1970, reply is document dated 20 March 1970, Department of State to Canadian embassy

59 Ibid.

Select Bibliography

Published Books and Articles

Abella, Irving. *Nationalism, Communism, and Canadian Labour*. Toronto 1973
- *The Canadian Labour Movement, 1902–1960*. Ottawa 1975
Anton, F.R. *The Role of Government in the Settlement of Industrial Disputes in Canada*. Don Mills, Ont. 1975
Avakumovic, Ivan. *The Communist Party in Canada*. Toronto 1975
Banks Testimony about Expenses.' *Canadian Labour* 8 (1963): 25
Buck, Tim. *Thirty Years*. Toronto 1975
Calhoun, Sue. *The Lockeport Lockout*. Halifax 1983
Canadian Autonomy.' *Canadian Labour* 8 (1963): 13–14
Canadian Seamen's Union. *The Canadian Seamen's Union and You*. Undated
- 'Our Case before the Board.' Special supplement to *The Searchlight*, 1940
- *We Stand for Unity*. June 1944
Canadian Who's Who. Toronto 1984
Carrothers, A.R. *Collective Bargaining Law in Canada*. Toronto 1965
Chevrier, Lionel, *Canada's Merchant Seamen*. Ottawa 1945
Communist Party of Canada. *Canada's Party of Socialism: History of the Communist Party of Canada 1921–1976*. Toronto 1982
Crispo, John. *International Unionism*. Toronto 1967
- *The Canadian Industrial Relations System*. Toronto 1978
Currie, A.W. *Economics of Canadian Transportation*. Toronto 1954
Dempsey, John B. 'Canada Steamship Lines Ltd.: World's Largest Inland Water Transportation Company.' *Inland Seas* 15 (1959): 4–14
Diefenbaker, John, G. *One Canada*, vol. 2. Toronto 1977
Dorsey, James E. *The Canadian Labour Relations Board: Federal Law and Practice*. Toronto 1983
Executive Council Statement on the Canadian Seamen's Union Suspension.' *TLC Journal* 28 (1949): 13–14
Former SIU Members Tell of Reform Attempts.' *Canadian Labour* 7 (1962): 45
Fraser, Frank. 'Sailors Are Human Beings Too.' *Canadian Forum* 20 (1940): 182–5

Galenson, Walter. *The CIO Challenge to the AFL*. Cambridge, Mass. 1960

Girard, S.M. *Canada in World Affairs*, XII: *1963–65*. Toronto 1979

Gzowski, Peter, 'Hal Banks – Waterfront Warlord.' *Maclean's*, 18 May 1963

Horowitz, Gad. *Canadian Labour in Politics*. Toronto 1968

Hughes, Barry Conn. 'You Talk to Working Men – Be on Their Level – So "Shotgun" Gralewicz Swears a Lot.' *Canadian Magazine*, 27 Oct. 1973, 23

International Longshoremen's and Warehousemen's Union. *Union Busting: New Model. The Case against the Coast Guard Screening Program*. Oct. 1951

Jamieson, Stuart. *Industrial Relations in Canada*. Ithaca, NY 1957

Jeffery, K., and P. Hennessy. *States of Emergency*. London 1983

Katz, Sidney. 'Should We Kick Hal Banks Out of Canada?' *Maclean's*, 15 Feb. 1955, 11–13 and 42–8

Kruger, Arthur. 'The Norris Report.' *Canadian Forum* 43 (1963): 147–50

Kwavnick, David. *Organized Labour and Pressure Politics: The Canadian Labour Congress 1956–1968*. Montreal and London 1972

Larrowe, Charles P. *Maritime Labour Relations on the Great Lakes*. East Lansing, Mich. 1959

Lefolii, Ken. 'The Best New Reason for Living in Canada: We Can Still Beat Thugs Like Hal Banks.' *Maclean's*, 10 Aug. 1963

Lesstrang, Jacques. *The Saga of the Great Lakes Fleet – North America's Freshwater Merchant Marine*. Seattle, Wash. 1977

Lewis, David. *The Good Fight*. Toronto 1981

Lipton, Charles. *The Trade Union Movement of Canada*. 4th ed. Toronto 1978

Logan, H.A. *Trade Unions in Canada*. Toronto 1968

Loyal She Remains: A Pictorial History of Ontario. Toronto 1984

MacDowell, Laurel Sefton. 'The Formation of the Canadian Industrial Relations System during World War Two.' *Labour/Le Travailleur* 3 (1978): 175–96

Macht, Wally. *The First 50 Years: A History of Upper Lakes Shipping Ltd*. Toronto 1981

MacKinnon, James, A. 'Canadian Shipping and the War.' *TLC Journal* 24 (1945): 15–17

McManus, T.G. 'The Reds Are Ready to Wage War inside Canada.' *Maclean's* 15 Nov. 1950, 7 and 61

– 'Death of a Union.' *Maclean's*, 1 Dec. 1959, 18–19 and 58

McPherson, John, C. *Government Imposed Trusteeship of Trade Unions: The Canadian Experience*. Victoria, New Zealand 1977

Maybee, Carlton. *The Seaway Story*. New York 1961

Minifie, James, M. *Open at the Top*. Toronto 1979

Montero, Gloria. *We Stood Together*. Toronto 1979

Musk, George. *Canadian Pacific: The Story of the Famous Shipping Line*. Toronto 1981

Nielsen, Richard. 'Hal Banks and His High Class Friends.' *Globe and Mail Magazine*, 5 Dec. 1970, 7–11

Pearson, Lester B. *Mike*, III: *1957–1968*. Toronto 1975

Porter, Alan, A. 'The Maritime Unions Trusteeship Act – A Departure in Canadian Labour Law.' *The Conference Board Record* (March 1964): 24–8

Raskin, Bernard. *On a True Course: The Story of the National Maritime Union.* Washington, DC 1967

Review of the British Dock Strike, 1949. London 1949

Scott, Jack. *Canadian Workers, American Unions.* Vancouver 1978

Seafarers' International Union. *Statement of the Seafarers' International Union Relative to the Report of the Industrial Inquiry Commission on the Disruption of Shipping.* Sept. 1963

'Sentence Banks.' *Canadian Labour* 9 (1964): 28

Shea, R.A. 'The Norris Report: Review and Reflection.' *Faculty of Law Review* 22 (1964): 41–59

'SIU Re-elects McLaughlin.' *Canadian Labour* 14 (1969): 38

Stanton, John. *Life and Death of the Canadian Seamen's Union.* Toronto 1978

Stursberg, Peter, *Lester Pearson and the Dream of Unity.* Toronto 1978

Sullivan, J.A. (Pat). *Red Sails on the Great Lakes.* Toronto 1955

Taft, Phillip. *The Structure and Government of Labour Unions.* Cambridge, Mass. 1954

'Testimony of Violence in Great Lakes Probe.' *Canadian Labour* 7 (1962), 43

'Trustees Fire Banks.' *Canadian Labour* 9 (1964): 41

'Trusteeship and the Maritime Unions.' *Canadian Labour* 8 (1963), 5–7

Urquhart, M.C., and K.A.H. Buckley, eds. *Historical Statistics of Canada.* 2nd ed. Ottawa 1983

Weisbord, Merrily. *The Strangest Dream.* Toronto 1983

'Where Is the Seamen's Strike?' *TLC Journal* 28 (1949): 7

Whitaker, Reginald. 'Origins of the Canadian Internal Security System, 1946–1953.' *Canadian Historical Review* 65 (1984): 154–83

Williams, Jack. *The Story of Unions in Canada.* Toronto 1975

Woods, H.D., and S. Ostry. *Labour Policy and Labour Economics in Canda.* Toronto 1962

Wright, Maurice. *Extract from Hearing of Industrial Commission as to Shipping in the Great Lakes and St Lawrence River System.* Ottawa 1963

Zwelling, Marc. *The Strikebreakers.* Toronto 1977

Theses

Miko, Joanne, H. 'The Rise and Fall of the Canadian Seamen's Union, 1963–1951. MA thesis, University of Guelph, 1974

Reaver, Kathleen, M. 'The Demise of the Canadian Seamen's Union.' Senior year thesis, Carleton University, 1978

Swartz, Gerald S. 'Hal Banks: The Rise and Fall of the Maritime Union Leader in Canada.' MA thesis, University of Illinois, 1969

Unpublished Manuscripts

Hunter, David. 'The History of the CSU and the SIU.' Osgoode Hall Law School, 1976

Lester, Fraser. Draft History of the Department of Labour. Department of Labour Library, undated.

MacDonald, Charles. 'Betrayal: The History of the Canadian Seamen's Union.'
Department of Labour Library, 1980

Government Documents

Annual Reports of the Canadian Maritime Commission
Annual Reports of the Maritime Board of Trustees
Annual Reports of the Royal Canadian Mounted Police
Annual Reports of the St Lawrence Seaway Authority
Communiqués of the Maritime Board of Trustees
Department of Labour. *Survey of Hours Worked in Great Lakes Shipping.*
Ottawa 1967
House of Commons, *Debates*
Labour Gazette
Legislative Assembly of Ontario, *Debates*
Norris, T.G. *Report of an Industrial Inquiry Commission Concerning Matters
Relating to the Disruption of Shipping on the Great Lakes, the St Lawrence
River System and Connecting Waters.* Ottawa 1963
Spence, J.W.F. *Report of the Royal Commission on the Coasting Trade.*
Ottawa 1957

Private Papers

Eric Brand Papers, Department of National Defence, furnished to author
courtesy of Eric Brand
British Columbia Shipping Federation Papers, Vancouver Archives
Canadian Brotherhood of Railway Transport and General Workers Union, PAC
Canadian Labour Congress Papers, PAC
J.L. Cohen Papers, PAC
Harry Crowe Papers, York University Archives
Department of Justice Papers, Federal Bureau of Investigation
Department of Labour Papers, PAC, Department of Labour Library
Department of State Papers, furnished to author courtesy of the Department of
State
Victor Dryer Papers, furnished to author courtesy of Victor Dryer and John
Howard
Richard Greaves Papers, furnished to author courtesy of Richard Greaves
George Haythorne Papers, furnished to author courtesy of George Haythorne
Thomas Houtman Papers, furnished to author courtesy of Tom Houtman
John Howard Papers, furnished to author courtesy of John Howard
Lyndon B. Johnson Papers, furnished to author courtesy of LBJ Library,
Austin, Texas
John F. Kennedy Papers, furnished to author courtesy of JFK Library, Boston,
Mass.
Richard Kuh Papers, furnished to author courtesy of Richard Kuh
Richard Nielsen Papers, furnished to author courtesy of Richard Nielsen
Royal Canadian Mounted Police Papers, furnished to author courtesy of the
RCMP

Michael Sheehan Papers, furnished to author courtesy of David Moore
Margot Thompson Papers, PAC
Bernard Wilson Papers, PAC

Interviews (selected)

Willis Armstrong, 6 May 1985
Eric Brand, 27 May 1982
Lionel Chevrier, 30 October 1981
Luc Couture, 17 December 1981
William Dodge, 14 June 1982
Bud Doucette, 7 July 1982
Victor Dryer, 15 December 1983
Charles Dubin, 25 February 1982
E. Davie Fulton, 8 January 1982
John Geller, 12 November 1981
H. Carl Goldenberg, 13 February 1982
Richard Greaves, 31 January 1982
James Hartford, 28 December 1981
George Haythorne, 27 May 1982
John Howard, 6 June 1982
Tom Houtman, 19 April 1982, 3 June 1982, 29 June 1982
Marc Lalonde, 16 December 1981
Patrick Lavelle, 5 April 1982
J.D. Leitch, 23 December 1981
René Lippe, 20 July 1982
Charles MacDonald, 6 January 1982
Donald MacDonald, 15 June 1982
Joseph Mackenzie, 26 March 1985
J.J. Mahoney, 14 June 1982
David Moore, 20 January, 1982, 15 March 1982
Richard Nielsen, 2 April 1982, 3 June 1982
Joseph Nuss, 17 June 1982
P.B.C. Pepper, 4 February 1982
J.J. Robinette, 14 January 1982
Elroy Robson, 2 June 1982, 7 July 1983
Joe Salsberg, 17 February 1985
Michael Sheehan
William Smith, 26 May 1982
Michael Starr, 4 February 1982
Gerald Swartz, 25 February 1982
James Todd, 4 May 1982
Alan Watson, 26 November 1981
John Wood, 9 July 1983
Bernard Wilson, 14 December 1981
Maurice Wright, 15 December 1981

Index

Abruzzo, Salvatore 177–80, 186

ACCL, *see* All Canadian Congress of Labour

AFL, *see* American Federation of Labour

AFL-CIO, *see* American Federation of Labour – Committee for Industrial Organization

AFL Select Committee 57

Ahern, John 114, 117, 119

All Canadian Congress of Labour 16, 17, 18, 26, 92–3

American Federation of Labor 15, 16, 18, 19, 24, 25, 39, 40, 55, 56, 57, 58, 69, 83, 127, 139, 190

American Federation of Labour – Committee for Industrial Organization 93, 107, 111, 135, 136, 140, 141, 142, 143, 147, 150, 168, 181, 185, 193, 194

Angus, Bruce 69

arbitration and conciliation 13–14, 24, 25, 30–1, 42, 44, 45, 47, 49, 50, 51, 52, 61, 62, 69, 87, 106, 109

Association of Lake Carriers 85, 86, 87, 88, 97, 98, 99, 100, 109, 170, 171

Banks, Harold Chamberlain ix, 62, 67–168, 189–96, passim; attempt to extradite 154, 174–88 passim;

citizenship application and 94, 126; criminal charges and bail application 149–50, 151–2, 152–6, 183; relationship with federal government ix, 66–7, 72–3, 74, 76, 82, 83, 102–4, 133, 143, 154, 188; retirement and date of death 189; *see also* Norris Commission

Bengough, Percy 36, 39, 40, 53, 54, 55, 56, 57, 58, 63, 65, 68, 71, 83, 84, 127, 190, 192

Bennett, W.A.C. 96

Black Ball Ferry Line 95

Blacklist, *see* Do Not Ship List

Board of Trustees, *see* Trusteeship

Borsa, J. 176

Boulanger, Bernard 119–20

Boycotts, *see* Secondary Picketing

Branch Lines Limited 70

Brand, Eric S. 44, 45, 46, 47, 48

British Docker's Strike 64–5

British North America Act 142

British Yukon Navigation Company 95

Brockington, Leonard 50, 52

Brodsky, Abraham, H. 177–81

Brydson, Jack 79

Building Trades Union 117

Cabinet Emergencies Committee (UK) 64

Canada, *see* federal government